MW00980564

Mac OS® X
Snow Leopard™
Digital
Classroom™

Mac OS® X
Snow Leopard™
Digital
Classroom™

Chad Chelius & the AGI Training Team

Wiley Publishing, Inc.

Mac OS® X Snow Leopard™ Digital Classroom™

Published by
Wiley Publishing, Inc.
10475 Crosspoint Boulevard
Indianapolis, IN 46256

Copyright © 2009 by Wiley Publishing, Inc., Indianapolis, Indiana
Published by Wiley Publishing, Inc., Indianapolis, Indiana
Published simultaneously in Canada
ISBN: 978-0-470-52568-5
Manufactured in the United States of America
10 9 8 7 6 5 4 3 2 1

No part of this publication may be reproduced, stored in a retrieval system or transmitted in any form or by any means, electronic, mechanical, photocopying, recording, scanning or otherwise, except as permitted under Sections 107 or 108 of the 1976 United States Copyright Act, without either the prior written permission of the Publisher, or authorization through payment of the appropriate per-copy fee to the Copyright Clearance Center, 222 Rosewood Drive, Danvers, MA 01923, (978) 750-8400, fax (978) 646-8600. Requests to the Publisher for permission should be addressed to the Legal Department, Wiley Publishing, Inc., 10475 Crosspoint Blvd., Indianapolis, IN 46256, (317) 572-3447, fax (317) 572-4355, or online at http://www.wiley.com/go/permissions.

Limit of Liability/Disclaimer of Warranty: The publisher and the author make no representations or warranties with respect to the accuracy or completeness of the contents of this work and specifically disclaim all warranties, including without limitation warranties of fitness for a particular purpose. No warranty may be created or extended by sales or promotional materials. The advice and strategies contained herein may not be suitable for every situation. This work is sold with the understanding that the publisher is not engaged in rendering legal, accounting, or other professional services. If professional assistance is required, the services of a competent professional person should be sought. Neither the publisher nor the author shall be liable for damages arising herefrom. The fact that an organization or Website is referred to in this work as a citation and/or a potential source of further information does not mean that the author or the publisher endorses the information the organization or Website may provide or recommendations it may make. Further, readers should be aware that Internet Websites listed in this work may have changed or disappeared between when this work was written and when it is read.

For general information on our other products and services or to obtain technical support, please contact our Customer Care Department within the U.S. at (800) 762-2974, outside the U.S. at (317) 572-3993 or fax (317) 572-4002.

Please report any errors by sending a message to errata@agitraining.com

Library of Congress Control Number: 2009928168

Trademarks: Wiley and related trade dress are registered trademarks of Wiley Publishing, Inc., in the United States and other countries, and may not be used without written permission. The AGI logos are trademarks of American Graphics Institute, LLC in the United States and other countries, and may not be used without written permission. All other trademarks are the property of their respective owners. Wiley Publishing, Inc. is not associated with any product or vendor mentioned in this book.

Wiley also publishes its books in a variety of electronic formats. Some content that appears in print may not be available in electronic books.

About the Authors

Chad Chelius is an instructor with AGI Training. His formal education is in publishing technology, but it is his trial-by-fire production experience working with the Mac OS and many creative software programs that makes him such a valuable contributor to every project on which he works. He has served as the lead consultant for major publishing technology migrations at leading book and magazine publishers. In his work with AGI Training, he has assisted such clients such as Rodale Press (publishers of Prevention Magazine, Runner's World, and multiple other magazine titles), and the publishing group of the National Geographic Society. Chad holds professional certifications from both Adobe and Apple.

Chad is joined in writing this book by his fellow instructors from the AGI Training Team—the expert instructors and consultants from AGI Training. They work collaboratively, combining their dozens of years of training and professional development experience with expert technical skills to create useful, practical training materials. AGI has authored official training guides, books, and videos for many major technology companies, and the AGI Training Team works with many of the world's most prominent companies. The AGI Training Team works with marketing, creative, and communications organizations around the world, and teach regularly scheduled classes at AGI's locations. More information at agitraining.com.

Acknowledgements

To my wife Rebecca, my son Gabriel, and my daughter Claire. To all of my friends at AGI past and present who have provided me with great feedback and expertise. You guys are a great crew.

Credits

Additional Writing
Greg Heald, Jeremy Osborn

Series Editor
Christopher Smith

Executive Editor
Jody Lefevere

Technical Editors
Cynthia Greene, Steve Koldenda

Editor
Marylouise Wiack

Editorial Director
Robyn Siesky

Editorial Manager
Cricket Krengel

Business Manager
Amy Knies

Senior Marketing Manager
Sandy Smith

Vice President and Executive Group Publisher
Richard Swadley

Vice President and Executive Publisher
Barry Pruett

Senior Project Coordinator
Lynsey Stanford

Graphics and Production Specialist
Lauren Mickol

Media Development Project Supervisor
Chris Leavey

Proofreading
Barn Owl Publishing

Indexing
Broccoli Information Management

Contents

Starting Up

Lesson 1: Navigating and Organizing in Snow Leopard

Lesson 2: Customizing the OS X Interface to Suit Your Needs

Lesson 5: Backing Up and Protecting Your Data

Lesson 6: Connecting to the Internet and using Safari

Lesson 7: Creating and Using Your Own Network

Lesson 8: Printing

Lesson 9: System Preferences

Lesson 10: Using Applications in Snow Leopard

Lesson 11: Using the Terminal

Lesson 12: Installing Snow Leopard and Applications

Starting up

About Mac OS X Snow Leopard Digital Classroom

This release of Mac OS X incorporates numerous improvements to the performance, quality, and efficiency of the operating system that will make your computing experience even more enjoyable than before. The improvements made to Snow Leopard will allow applications installed on your computer to run faster by allowing those applications to take advantage of your Mac's hardware like never before. Snow Leopard, version 10.6, marks the sixth major release of what Apple refers to as the world's most advanced operating system.

The *Mac OS X Snow Leopard Digital Classroom* helps you to understand these capabilities, and how to get the most out of your Mac, so that you can get up-and-running right away. You can work through all the lessons in this book, or complete only specific lessons. Each lesson includes detailed, step-by-step instructions, along with lesson files, useful background information, and video tutorials.

Mac OS X Snow Leopard Digital Classroom is like having your own expert instructor guiding you through each lesson while you work at your own pace. This book includes 12 self-paced lessons that let you discover essential skills, explore new features, and understand capabilities that will save you time. You'll be productive right away with real-world exercises and simple explanations. Each lesson includes step-by-step instructions and lesson files available on the DVD that is included with the book.

Prerequisites

Before you start the *Mac OS X Snow Leopard Digital Classroom* lessons, you should have your computer unpacked and, if necessary, assembled. The lessons in the book will help you connect to a network, the Internet, and to a printer—so these can wait if you don't have them set-up yet.

Before starting the lesson files in the *Mac OS X Snow Leopard Digital Classroom*, make sure that you have a copy of the Mac OS X Snow Leopard operating system. The software is sold separately, and not included with this book. If you have purchased a computer that includes Snow Leopard, start with the first lesson. If you are upgrading to Snow Leopard and have not yet installed the software, you should start with Lesson 12, "Installing Snow Leopard and Applications," which covers the process of installing the operating system.

System requirements

Before starting the lessons in the *Mac OS X Snow Leopard Digital Classroom*, make sure that your computer is equipped for running Snow Leopard, which you must purchase separately. The minimum system requirements for your computer to effectively use the software are listed below.

• Mac computer with an Intel processor
• 1GB of memory
• 5GB of available disk space
• DVD drive
• Internet connection

Loading lesson files

The *Mac OS X Snow Leopard Digital Classroom* DVD includes files that accompany the exercises for many of the lessons. You may copy the entire lessons folder from the supplied DVD to your hard drive, or copy only the lesson folders for the individual lessons you wish to complete. Because some of the lessons include discussions on copying files, we suggest copying the lesson files as instructed with each lesson rather than copying them all at the start of the book. Each lesson includes information about what files are needed from the DVD.

For each lesson in the book, the files are referenced by the file name of each file. The exact location of each file on your computer is not always used, as you may have placed the files in a unique location on your hard drive.

Copying the lesson files to your hard drive:

1   Insert the *Mac OS X Snow Leopard Digital Classroom* DVD supplied with this book.

2   On your computer desktop, navigate to the DVD and locate the folder named sllessons.

3   You can install all the files, or just specific lesson files. Do one of the following:

   • Install all lesson files by dragging the sllessons folder to your hard drive.

   • Install only some of the files by creating a new folder on your hard drive named sllessons. Open the sllessons folder on the supplied DVD, select the lesson you wish to complete, and drag the folder(s) to the sllessons folder you created on your hard drive.

   • We suggest waiting to copy the lesson files until you start each lesson.

Menus and commands are identified throughout the book by using the greater-than symbol (>). For example, the command to print a document appears as File > Print.

Because you cannot write additional files onto the DVD that came with the book, it is considered locked. Some Mac OS computers view the files transferred from a DVD as being locked, even after they are copied off the DVD. While this is rare, it can easily be addressed if you are working in the lessons and receive a message that any of the files copied from the disc are locked. You only need to perform these steps if you encounter a warning message while working in the lessons. After copying the files to your computer, select the sllessons folder, then choose File > Get Info. In the sllessons info window, click the drop-down 'Sharing and Permissions' section of this window. Click the arrow to the left of Details, then click the Apply to enclosed items... button at the bottom of the window. You may need to click the padlock icon to change these permissions. After making these changes, close the window. A detailed discussion on changing permissions is covered in the 'Changing Permissions' section in Lesson 7, on page 181.

Working with the video tutorials

Your *Mac OS X Snow Leopard Digital Classroom* DVD comes with video tutorials developed by the authors to help you understand the concepts explored in each lesson. Each tutorial is approximately five minutes long, and demonstrates and explains the concepts and features covered in the lesson.

The videos are designed to supplement your understanding of the material in the chapter. We have selected exercises and examples that we feel will be most useful to you. You may want to view the entire video for each lesson before you begin that lesson. A DVD video icon reminds you to view the video content associated with each lesson.

DVD video icon.

Setting up for viewing the video tutorials

The DVD included with this book includes video tutorials for each lesson. You can view the lessons on your computer directly from the DVD, or the folder labeled *Videos* from the *Mac OS X Snow Leopard Digital Classroom* DVD to your hard drive.

Copying the video tutorials to your hard drive:

1   Insert the *Mac OS X Snow Leopard Digital Classroom* DVD supplied with this book.

2   On your computer desktop, navigate to the DVD and locate the folder named Videos.

3   Drag the Videos folder to a location onto your desktop or hard drive.

Viewing the video tutorials with the Adobe Flash Player

The videos on the *Mac OS X Snow Leopard Digital Classroom* DVD are saved in the Flash projector format. A Flash projector file wraps the Digital Classroom video player and the Adobe Flash Player in an .app executable file. While the extension may not be visible, projector files allow the Flash content to be deployed on your system without the need for a browser or any other video player.

Playing the video tutorials:

1   On your computer, navigate to the Videos folder you copied to your hard drive from the DVD. Playing the videos directly from the DVD may result in poor quality playback.

2   Open the Videos folder and double-click SLvideos to view the video tutorial.

3   Press the Play button to view the videos.

The Flash Player has a simple user interface that allows you to control the viewing experience, including stopping, pausing, playing, and restarting the video. You can also rewind or fast-forward, and adjust the playback volume.

*A. Go to beginning. **B**. Play/Pause. **C**. Fast-forward/rewind. **D**. Stop. **E**. Volume Off/On. **F**. Volume control.*

Playback volume is also affected by the settings in your operating system. Be certain to adjust the sound volume for your computer, in addition to the sound controls in the Player window.

Is this book for you?

The *Mac OS X Snow Leopard Digital Classroom* book is designed for the beginner to intermediate user who wants to become more proficient working on their Mac computer, using Snow Leopard. Throughout the book, you will be guided through lessons that show you how to use the different components, applications, and options within Snow Leopard and how to take advantage of the new features found in this latest release of Mac OS X. You'll also be introduced to some amazing applications that are included in Snow Leopard, such as Mail, Safari, iCal, and many more. This book will show you how to set up your computer so that everyone in your family or workgroup will have their own personal account on your Mac so you don't accidentally modify another person's files or change each other's settings. If you're looking to feel more comfortable working on your Mac and want to make the most of your investment, this book is for you.

This book does not discuss applications that do not ship with Snow Leopard, such as the iLife suite of applications, as there are entire books dedicated to those topics. If you are an advanced-to-expert user, looking for a book that covers advanced networking concepts or detailed specifics of how to configure your operating system or OS X server, this book probably isn't the right choice. You may be surprised, however, to discover some nice tricks that even the most experienced users may not know, but this book is designed to primarily focus on the needs of Mac OS X users and not IT professionals.

What is an operating system?

An operating system is the software that provides the user interface that you use to interact with your computer. It is the direct link between your computer's hardware and the software applications that you install onto the computer. Some common operating systems in use today include Windows, Linux, UNIX, Solaris, and, of course, Mac OS. The operating system is what gives your computer the common personality—from locating files to the appearance of icons on your desktop.

The Mac operating system

In the case of Mac OS X, the integration between the operating system and the hardware is unparalleled. This is because Mac OS X runs using hardware from Apple. So your operating system and hardware come from the same place. Other PCs have hardware from one vendor, like HP or Dell, and an operating system from another vendor, typically Microsoft. By controlling both the hardware and software, Apple maintains the integrity and stability of its computers. Because Mac OS X is designed to run on specific computer hardware, it can take full advantage of the computer.

Whether you are purchasing a brand-new Mac computer or are upgrading your existing Mac to Snow Leopard, you can rest assured that all of the hardware built into your Mac computer will have the proper drivers installed to ensure optimum functionality and performance. As an added benefit, Snow Leopard also ships with many printer drivers, so installing your printer is easy because Snow Leopard already has the drivers required for your printer.

Under the hood, Snow Leopard is a UNIX operating system. To be more specific, it is based on the FreeBSD distribution of UNIX, which dates its origins back to the mid-1970s. This means that the Snow Leopard system has more than 30 years of development behind it. Snow Leopard builds upon this solid foundation. Add the stability of UNIX to the modern, elegant Mac interface and you have an amazing operating system at your fingertips: Snow Leopard.

Ease of use

Snow Leopard provides a very intuitive and friendly environment where you can enjoy your computing experience. All technical jargon aside, using Snow Leopard allows you to enjoy working on your computer without having to dig too deep to find what you need. Right out of the box, Snow Leopard includes basic applications to help you work more efficiently in your daily computing life. Applications such as Address Book, Mail, and iCal help you stay organized and on track throughout your day. Pre-installed printer drivers help you to quickly print your documents, and basic applications, such as TextEdit for typing letters and Stickies for creating virtual sticky notes on your computer screen, to ensure that you don't forget anything important.

Running Snow Leopard for the first time

The Snow Leopard welcome screen greets you when you boot your Mac for the first time after installing Snow Leopard.

Whether you have just unpacked your brand-new Mac computer, or you just finished installing Snow Leopard, when you boot your Mac for the first time, Snow Leopard presents you with a brief animated movie prior to displaying a welcome screen. Depending upon whether you are upgrading from an earlier version of Mac OS X or starting your computer for the first time, you will be guided through the process of registering your computer or getting to work with Snow Leopard. For more information about installing Snow Leopard, refer to Lesson 12, "Installing Snow Leopard and Applications."

Additional resources

The Digital Classroom series goes beyond the training books. You can continue your learning online, with training videos, at seminars and conferences, and in-person training events from the authors. Contact AGI Training for more information at *info@agitraining.com*.

Book series web site

Expand your knowledge of creative software applications, operating systems, and office productivity tools with the Digital Classroom training series. You can also find updates and a list of errata for existing books. Learn more at *digitalclassroombooks.com*.

Seminars and conferences

The authors of the Digital Classroom seminar series frequently conduct in-person seminars and speak at conferences, including the annual CRE8 Conference. Learn more at *agitraining.com*.

Resources for educators

Contact your Wiley educational representative to access resources for educators for incorporating Digital Classroom into your curriculum. Visit *wiley.com* for more information.

Private Training

The authors are available for corporate training and speaking engagements. Contact AGI Training for more information at *info@agitraining.com*.

What you'll learn in this lesson:

- Navigating the file and folder structure
- Multiple ways to view files
- Searching for files and folders on your computer
- The purpose of the Home folder

Navigating and Organizing in Snow Leopard

This lesson will guide you through the different components of the Mac OS X interface while explaining how to customize the interface to make it your own.

Starting up

Because this lesson is about copying and moving files, you'll perform this step later in the chapter as part of the lesson. Make sure you have the Digital Classroom DVD that came with this book near by to use when needed. If you are upgrading to Snow Leopard and do not have it installed on your Mac, jump ahead to Lesson 12, "Installing Snow Leopard and Applications," and then return to this lesson once the installation is complete.

See Lesson 1 in action!

Use the accompanying video to gain a better understanding of how to use some of the features shown in this lesson. The video tutorial for this lesson can be found on the included DVD.

The Finder

The core user interface component of Mac OS X is the Finder. The Finder is the visual connection between you and the computer. Without the Finder, you'd be relegated to a cryptic, code-based method of interacting with your computer—entering commands and instructions by typing instead of using your mouse.

The Finder provides windows for navigating files on your hard drive, looking at the files, and a number of ways for interacting with your Mac. It also displays any hard drives, CDs, DVDs, and external drives you have connected to your computer. Let's take a closer look at the Finder.

A. Hard drive. *B*. Finder. *C*. Dashboard. *D*. Mail. *E*. Safari. *F*. iChat. *G*. Address Book. *H*. iCal. *I*. Preview. *J*. iTunes.
K. Time Machine. *L*. System Preferences. *M*. Dictionary. *N*. Applications. *O*. Documents. *P*. Downloads. *Q*. Trash.

Finder windows

The primary way of navigating and working with files and folders on your Mac is through Finder windows. As the name implies, a Finder window allows you to see all the files and folders that are stored on your computer. Let's take a look at how Finder windows work.

1   Open a new Finder window by double-clicking the hard drive icon in the upper-right corner of your desktop screen. A new Finder window appears on your screen. When you open a Finder window in this manner, it shows you the contents of the hard drive that you double-clicked to create the Finder window.

   Think of your hard drive as a filing cabinet. Within your hard drive (or filing cabinet) are files and folders containing things like photos, songs, and word processing documents. Think of a folder as an organizational component where you can store files of varying types. Everything that you see on the hard drive is either a file or a folder. In the Finder window that you just opened, you should see four folders: Applications, Library, System, and Users. These are the four main folders that are used by Snow Leopard. You will rarely work with the System and Library folders, as they are reserved for the operating system. Now let's look a little deeper into the folder structure of your hard drive.

2   Press the Column view button (⊞) at the top of the Finder window and select the Applications folder in the first column of folders that are displayed in the Finder window. In the second column of the Finder window, all the application files are displayed. The Applications folder is the main folder where all your application files are stored in Snow Leopard.

The Finder window displaying the Applications folder and all the application files within that folder.

3 Scroll down to the bottom of the second column and click Utilities. Again, the Finder window displays a new column with the contents of the Utilities folder. You can also tell what folder you are currently viewing by looking at the name of the Finder window at the top of the window. For example, after clicking the Utilities folder, you see that folder's name displayed at the top of the window.

4 Click the lower right corner of the Finder window where there are three small diagonal lines, and drag to the left. This allows you to resize the Finder window, and controls how much content is displayed. If you make your Finder window too small, a scroll bar appears at the bottom of the window that allows you to scroll from one column to the other.

Resizing a Finder window that is too small to display all the content generates a scroll bar at the bottom of the Finder window to make navigating your files and folders easier.

5 There are three buttons in the upper left corner of each Finder window: the Close button (⬤), the Minimize button (⬤), and the Zoom button (+).

Press the green Zoom button to resize the Finder window to fit all its content. Sometimes, if you are very deep into your folder structure, the Finder can only zoom your window as big as your screen. In these cases, you still have a scroll bar at the bottom of the Finder window to assist with navigating your folders and files.

6 Press the green Zoom button again, and your window returns to its previous size.

7   Press the yellow Minimize button (⊖). Your Finder window does a fun genie effect that minimizes the Finder window to a small icon in the Dock at the bottom of your screen. You'll learn more about the Dock in the next lesson.

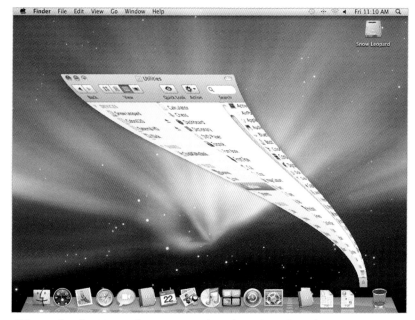

Clicking on the yellow Minimize button minimizes the Finder window to the Dock using Mac OS X's genie effect.

To get a really good look at the effect that Mac OS X uses to minimize windows, hold down the Shift key on your keyboard while you click on the yellow Minimize button.

8   Move your cursor to the right side of the Dock. As you hover over each icon, it displays the icon's name. When you see the Utilities window, click that icon and the window is maximized on the screen.

9   Press the red Close button (⊗) to close the Utilities window.

The toolbar

Every Finder window that you open contains a toolbar at the top of the window that is, by default, divided into five areas. Let's explore the toolbar in more detail.

Navigating files and folders

1   Double-click the hard drive icon to open a new Finder window. Select the Library folder in the first column, then the Preferences folder in the second column, then the Audio folder in the third column.

From this point forward in this book, to direct you to a specific folder, the following path annotation will be used /Library/Preferences/Audio. The first forward slash indicates the main or root level of your hard drive. You navigate to the Library folder, then the Preferences folder inside the Library folder, then the Audio folder inside of the Preferences folder. You'll often see this type of annotation used when describing a folder path in Mac OS X.

2   The first area of the toolbar you'll work with includes the navigation buttons, indicated by a left (◄) and right arrow (►). Click the left arrow, and you are taken to your previous view; now the focus is on the Preferences folder.

The toolbar contains buttons that assist in navigation, viewing files, previewing files, and searching files.

3   Click the left arrow again to move back one more level in your viewing order. The current folder that you should be working in is the folder that is currently highlighted.

4   From the menu bar at the top of your screen, choose View > Show Path Bar. This displays the path bar at the bottom of each Finder window, which assists you when navigating files and folders, and allows you to easily identify your current folder path.

5   Click the right arrow button in the toolbar to move forward in your view history. This button is only available when you've already used the back button because the Finder already knows the last folder that was viewed. Otherwise, the Finder doesn't know where you want to go.

6   Click the right arrow button again. You are now back to your original location of /Library/Preferences/Audio. This is easily identifiable in the path bar at the bottom of the Finder window. Think of this as a trail that allows you to find your way back to where you started.

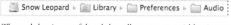

The path bar is a useful tool that allows you to quickly view your current path structure.

7   Press the red Close button (●) to close this window.

Changing how files and folders are displayed

Snow Leopard's default view is the column view. It is the view that you've been working with, so far throughout this lesson. Let's explore other viewing methods that Snow Leopard offers.

1   Double-click the hard drive icon to open a new Finder window.

2   Press the first button (⊞) in the view section of the toolbar to display the files as icons. This view is a simpler method of viewing files and folders, and is useful for viewing files that have a preview; such as photos.

3   Navigate to /Library/Application Support/Apple/iChat Icons/Planets. A folder of photos exemplifies the benefit of the icon view because you get a nice preview of each icon and of what the file looks like.

4   In icon view, you see a slider in the lower right corner of the Finder window. Click and drag the slider to the right to make the file icons larger; click and drag the slider to the left to make the file icons smaller. Another benefit of the icon view is that whatever size you set these icons to using the slider becomes the default size whenever you choose this view in Snow Leopard.

In icon view, you can adjust the size of the icons by dragging the slider.

5   Press the second button (⊟) in the view section of the toolbar to change the view of the files to list view. This view displays the icons at a much smaller size than icon view but reveals pertinent information about each file, such as the date that the file was last modified and the file's size and kind.

By default, files are sorted alphabetically when viewing them in list view. You can easily change this order by clicking any of the categories above the list of files in the Finder window.

6   Click the Name category, and the arrow to the right of Name changes direction, indicating that the sort order has been changed from ascending to descending.

7   Click the Name category again to switch back to ascending order. You can also sort by Date Modified, Size, and Kind by clicking any of the header categories.

8   In the path bar at the bottom of the Finder window, double-click the hard drive icon to navigate to that location, then open the Applications folder.

9 Press the fourth button (▣) in the view section of the toolbar to change the view of the files to Cover Flow view. Cover Flow view is a very dynamic way of viewing files, allowing you to quickly browse through a folder to see the contents of each file. This is a very useful view when working with a folder full of images.

Cover Flow view provides a dynamic method for browsing files within a folder.

Click the right arrow (▸) in the main area of the Cover Flow view to browse the various files within the Applications folder.

For a quicker method, click the slider in the main area of the Cover Flow view to browse the files.

10 Scroll through the list of files below the main area of the Cover Flow view and click a file to select it. The file is displayed in the main area of the Cover Flow view.

Moving and copying files

The Finder is the primary location where you will be moving and copying (organizing) files on your computer. What is the difference between moving and copying? Well, moving a file relocates that file to a different area on your computer, and the file no longer exists in its original source location. Copying, on the other hand, duplicates the file to a different area on your computer, and the file exists in both the source and destination locations. How the Finder determines whether a file is copied or moved depends on a couple of factors. To further understand copying and moving files, you'll copy files from the enclosed DVD.

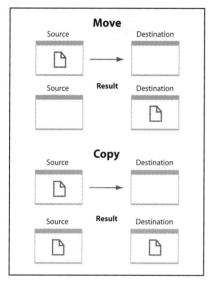

Moving a file causes the original file to be removed from the source location.
Copying a file leaves the file in both the source and destination locations.

Copying files

In this section, you will copy files from the DVD supplied with this book to understand the process of copying files.

1   Insert the included DVD into your computer's DVD drive.

2   When the DVD disc icon appears on your desktop (the main viewing area), double-click it to view the contents of the DVD.

3   Press the third button (▥) of the view section of the toolbar to display the files using column view; then select the sllessons folder to display its contents.

4 Drag the sl01lessons folder from the Finder window to the desktop. You'll notice a cursor that displays a green circle with a plus sign (🜋), indicating that the folder you are dragging will be copied.

Dragging a file or folder from one volume to another makes a copy of that file or folder.

At this point, it's important to understand that the sl01lessons folder was copied, not moved. The reason for this is that the sl01lessons folder was copied from a volume that is separate from your hard drive, a volume being defined as a single, accessible storage area. In this case, the DVD is that separate storage volume. Whenever a file or folder is dragged from one volume to another, the file or folder is automatically copied, not moved. Notice that the sl01lessons folder still resides on the DVD from which it was dragged.

5 Close all open Finder windows by pressing the Close button (🔴) in each Finder window.

You can also close Finder windows using the keyboard shortcut Command+W.

What is a shortcut?

As you are beginning to see, there are many ways to do the same thing within Snow Leopard. Shortcut keys are a way of performing repetitive tasks more efficiently. You perform shortcut keys by holding down a modifier key, then pressing other keys on the keyboard. For example, to close an open Finder window using a shortcut key, hold down the Command key on your keyboard with one finger (preferably your thumb), then press the W key. The combination of these two keys tells Mac OS X to close the active Finder window.

Click the File drop-down menu in the menu bar at the top of your screen. If you chose the item Close Window, you'll notice a shortcut key listed to the right of the menu item. This is that command's shortcut key. You'll notice a multitude of shortcut keys listed next to each menu command, and you'll notice even more of those shortcuts as you continue working with Snow Leopard and with other applications. Does that mean you need to know all of these shortcut keys? Absolutely not! If you find that you are continually going to the menu bar to perform the same action over and over again, learn the keyboard shortcut. You'll find yourself becoming a much more efficient user by doing so.

Double-click the sl01lessons folder on your desktop to open it. You see a number of pictures inside the sl01lessons folder. If you look at the very bottom of the Finder window, you can see more detailed information about the sl01lessons folder. Specifically, you see that there are eight items within the folder and the amount of space remaining on the volume where this folder resides.

The bottom of the Finder window displays valuable information about the contents of a folder and the amount of space left on the volume.

Moving files

Files are moved whenever they are dragged to a different location within the same volume or disk. During a move, the file is relocated and no longer exists in its original location.

1   Close any Finder windows that are currently open on your screen.

2   Double-click the hard drive icon on your desktop to open a new Finder window.

3   Make sure that your view is set to column, and navigate to /Users/Home folder/ Pictures, where Home folder is the icon within the Users folder that has a house icon (⌂) next to it. The Home folder will be discussed in more detail later in this lesson.

4　Select the sl01lessons folder on your desktop with your mouse, then drag and drop it onto the Pictures folder in the Finder window. This time, you'll notice that the sl01lessons folder is moved to the Pictures folder and is no longer available on the desktop. This is because the Pictures folder and the desktop are on the same volume. When a file or folder is moved from one location to another on the same volume, the file or folder no longer resides in the source location.

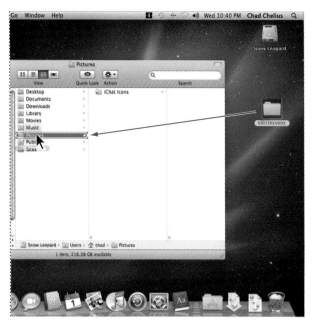

Dragging the sl01lessons folder from the desktop to the Pictures folder moves the folder because both the source and destination locations reside on the same volume.

If you need to copy a file from one location to the other within the same volume, you can do so by clicking on the file or folder in the source location and choosing Edit > Copy from the menu bar. Then click the destination folder and choose Edit > Paste. For an even faster method, simply hold down the Option key on your keyboard while your drag a file or folder from one location to the other; instead of moving the file or folder, the system copies it.

Organizing files and folders

As you work with files and folders in Snow Leopard, you'll want to stay organized by grouping files into folders that represent a category where files will be stored.

1 Make sure you are still viewing the Pictures folder within your Home folder and are in Column view.

2 Click the Pictures folder to highlight it, then choose File > New Folder. The folder name defaults to *untitled folder* and is highlighted, meaning that you can change the name of the folder by simply typing. Type **Nature** and press Return on your keyboard. Pressing Return commits the name change.

3 Click the Pictures folder again to highlight it and choose File > New Folder. Name this folder **Creative**.

4 Repeat step 3 to create a **New York** folder.

5 Click the sl01lessons folder within the Pictures folder. Drag the Boat.jpg file and drop it onto the Creative folder. Repeat this for the Bridge.jpg file.

6 With the sl01lessons folder still selected, hold down the Command key and click the Apple.jpg, Clouds.jpg, Ice.jpg, and Sweet Gum.jpg files. Drag any of the highlighted files to the Nature folder.

Holding down the Command key when selecting files allows you to non-contiguously select more than one file at a time.

7 With the sl01lessons folder still selected, hold down the Shift key and click Liberty.jpg and NYC.jpg. Drag any of the highlighted files to the New York folder. The sl01lessons folder is now empty.

Holding down the Shift key when selecting files allows you to select a range of contiguous files.

8 Click each of the folders that you created earlier in this exercise to see the files that you have moved. Each folder now contains files related to each category.

9 The sl01lessons folder is now empty and is no longer needed. Click the sl01lessons folder, drag it to the bottom of your screen, and drop it on the Trash icon at the right side of the Dock. The Trash icon now appears full, meaning that it contains a file.

When you drag files to the Trash icon, the icon changes to a full trash can.

10 Dragging a file to the Trash icon moves it from its current location but doesn't actually delete the file. If you double-click the Trash icon in the Dock, you can see the sl01lessons folder within the Trash folder.

11 Close the Trash folder.

12 In the menu bar at the top of the screen, choose Finder > Empty Trash.

13 You'll receive a dialog box asking if you are sure you want to permanently erase the items in the Trash. Press the Empty Trash Button. This permanently removes the contents of the Trash folder.

Quick Look

So far in this lesson, you've seen how easy it is to change the different viewing options within a Finder window, which allows you to see your files and folders in different ways. There will be times, however, when you have a folder that contains pictures where you'd like to see those files in more detail without opening them with another program. That's where Quick Look comes in. Although Quick Look is not new in Snow Leopard, it is a welcome tool that allows you to preview files on your computer quickly and easily.

1 Open a new Finder window, if there isn't one already open, and navigate to the Nature folder within the Pictures folder that you created in the previous exercise.

2 Select the file called Apple.jpg and press the Quick Look button (⊙) in the toolbar. The Finder displays a full-sized preview of the file for you to examine.

Quick Look allows you to quickly see a preview of a file without opening it in a separate application.

3 When you are finished, press the Close button (⊗) in the upper left corner of the Quick Look window.

4 Select the Clouds.jpg file and this time, press the spacebar on your keyboard. Pressing the spacebar is the shortcut to quickly open a file using Quick Look.

5 Press the double-arrow button (⇱) at the bottom of the Quick Look window to view the file at full screen.

6 Let go of your mouse for a few seconds; all navigation tools temporarily disappear, giving you an unobstructed view of the image.

7 Move your cursor on screen; a navigation bar appears, giving you two options, Exit Full Screen and Close. Choose Exit Full Screen, then press the Close button to close the Quick Look window.

Moving your cursor back onto the Full Screen view displays the navigation bar, allowing you to Exit Full Screen, or Close the window.

8 Close any open Finder windows.

When you are in Full Screen mode in Quick Look, you can also exit Full Screen mode by pressing the Esc key on your keyboard.

As you can see, Quick Look can be an extremely useful tool when browsing visually relevant files such as photos and other graphics. Experiment on your own with Quick Look by viewing some of your own images that you've copied to your hard drive.

The sidebar

In addition to the toolbar, every Finder window also has a sidebar. The sidebar is an area that contains available resource locations on your computer, including hard drives, shared network drives, frequently visited locations, and popular searches. Let's examine how the sidebar can make easy work of navigating your computer.

1 Double-click the hard drive icon on your desktop to open a new Finder window.

2   Notice that the hard drive of your computer is selected in the sidebar and its contents
    are displayed in the main area of the Finder window. This is what the Devices section is
    for. You can see in the following figure that any external hard drives that you plug into
    your computer also show up in this category. Clicking any of these drives in the sidebar
    displays that drive's contents.

The sidebar displays available resource locations, as
well as commonly accessed areas of your computer.

The Shared section of the sidebar displays any computers on the same network as yours
that have File Sharing enabled. If you don't see this section on your screen, it's because
there are no shared computers on your network to display.

3   Click the Applications entry under the Places section of the sidebar. You are immediately
    taken to the Applications folder on your computer, the same location that you've been
    manually navigating to thus far in this lesson. The Places section of the sidebar displays
    commonly accessed areas of your computer for quick navigation.

4   Select the Today entry in the Search For section of the sidebar. This displays all files that were opened today, including applications. This can be useful when trying to locate files that you just opened and need to quickly access again. The files listed on your computer will most likely be different than the following example.

The Search For section allows you to quickly see files that have been opened within a specific time frame or within a certain category.

5   Click the All Images entry in the Search For section of the sidebar. This displays all the images on your computer. Although not particularly useful in itself, it does demonstrate the power of Smart Folders, which you'll learn about later on in this lesson. Smart Folders can be customized to suit your particular needs.

The Home folder

Probably the most important folder to you as a Snow Leopard user is the Home folder. The Home folder is a central storage location for all your files and is designated by a house icon (🏠); it protects your information from other users of your computer, and organizes your information for quick access. The Home folder is also what allows each user on a computer to have a customized working environment that complements the way they like to work. Every user account created on your computer has its own Home folder where that user can store his or her information. Let's explore the Home folder in more detail.

1 Choose File > New Finder Window or press Command+N on your keyboard. When you create a new Finder window in this manner, your Home folder is displayed automatically by default.

2 Set the view method to List view. There are nine folders created inside of your Home folder automatically, although you are certainly not limited to those nine. You can add as many as you like, but you'll find that most categories that you need are covered within the default folders that are provided.

Desktop

The Desktop of your computer—the area where your hard drives are displayed and the large space image is visible by default— can also be accessed as a folder. There are actually two desktop folders, let's take a look at how you access them.

1 Navigate to the Applications folder on your computer.

2 Find the application called TextEdit and double-click it to launch the application. TextEdit is a basic text-editing application provided with Snow Leopard, in which you can type documents.

3 In the Untitled window that appears, type **This is my first file**.

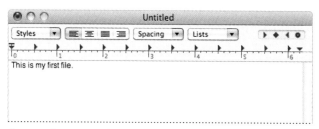

Creating a file using TextEdit.

When an application is opened in Snow Leopard, the name of the application appears in the menu bar in the upper left corner of your screen. This tells you that the application is currently active. If, by chance, you click on the desktop of your computer, *Finder* appears in the upper left corner of your screen, indicating that the Finder is now the active application. If you've done this, be sure to click the TextEdit window to make TextEdit the active application.

4   Choose File > Save. Because this file has never been saved, Mac OS X automatically opens the Save As dialog box, which asks for a name for the file. Type **My File** in the Save As text field.

5   Choose Desktop from the Where drop-down menu.

6   Click the arrow to the right of the Save As text field to display the standard Save As dialog box, which provides more options than the ones available in the Where drop-down menu.

7   Press Save. The file is saved to your Desktop folder.

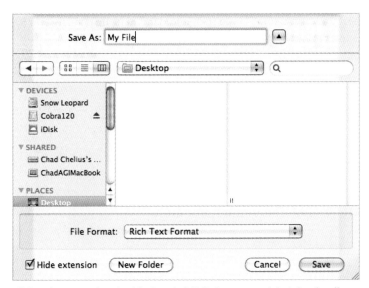

Clicking the arrow to the right of the Save As field displays an expanded window that allows you to save your file in a specific location.

8 Quit TextEdit by choosing TextEdit > Quit TextEdit.

This is where the concept of the Desktop folder becomes more evident. If you look on your computer's desktop, you see the file that you just saved, My File. However, if you navigate to the Desktop folder using a Finder window, you see that My File also resides there. It's important to understand that these are not two separate locations; they are one and the same. Anything that you copy to the main desktop of your computer always appears in the Desktop folder of your Home folder as well.

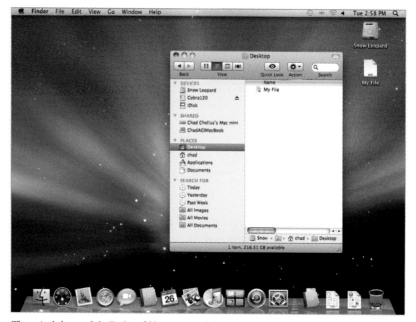

The main desktop and the Desktop folder are one and the same.

Documents

The Documents folder is a catchall for the majority of documents that you create on your computer. Word documents, TextEdit documents, and any other application files that you create can be stored here. Some programs even automatically use your Documents folder to store the support files required by the application.

Downloads

This folder can be used to store files that you have downloaded from the Internet and other locations. Safari, the Web browser supplied with Snow Leopard, uses this folder any time you download a file from the Internet.

Library

This folder is reserved for system files that are specific to your user account. You will spend the least amount of time in this folder, and it's actually recommended that unless you are directed to modify this folder by a support professional, or you are an advanced user, you should leave this folder alone.

Movies

Simply stated, this folder is an area to store movies. Applications such as iMovie, which is a movie-editing program created by Apple as part of the iLife suite of applications, uses this folder to store imported movie files and editing information about your movies.

Music

This folder can be used to store all the digital music that you've downloaded to your computer. You probably won't spend too much time directly in this folder. The free iTunes music player uses this folder to store all music imported using iTunes or downloaded from the iTunes Music Store. If you're already using iTunes, you'll notice that an iTunes folder already exists in this location. Another application that uses this folder is GarageBand, which is also an application that Apple provides as part of the iLife suite of applications.

Pictures

Earlier in this lesson, you moved a folder of images into the Pictures folder as an organizational step. The Pictures folder is a central repository where you can store all the images that you copy to your computer. The iPhoto application, which is an application created by Apple as part of the iLife suite of applications, uses your Pictures folder to store your photos as well as information about them. If you're already using iPhoto, you'll notice that there is an iPhoto Library located within your Pictures folder. The Photo Booth application, which ships with Snow Leopard, also stores files within the Pictures folder for easy organization.

Public

The Public folder allows you to share files with other users, and vice versa. File Sharing is discussed in Lesson 3, "Using Snow Leopard with a Group."

Sites

Every copy of Snow Leopard ships with powerful, fully functional web server software, allowing you to create and share web pages with anyone on your network and potentially anywhere in the world! Although sharing web pages beyond the boundaries of your network is beyond the scope of this book, Lesson 7, " Creating and Using Your Own Network," discusses how to enable the web server software on your computer and how to share a basic web page.

When writing out a folder path for files in your Home folder, you often see it written like this: ~/Pictures/Christmas Vacation. The tilde (~) indicates your Home folder. So to access the folder, you would open your Home folder, the Pictures folder, then the Christmas Vacation folder.

Now that you understand the concept behind the Home folder and what each folder is used for, you can begin storing files in their appropriate locations. Don't forget that within each folder, you can create subfolders to further organize your files. For instance, in the Documents folder, you may create a subfolder called recipes where you store all the recipes that you've typed out on your computer for later retrieval.

Finding your files

No matter how careful or experienced you are as a computer user, you're bound to move, copy, or save a file in a location that you hadn't intended to. Or maybe you do know where you saved the file, but there are so many files displayed that it's difficult to find the file you're looking for. Regardless of the reason for your frustration, Snow Leopard offers a number of useful methods that make finding your files easier and faster than looking for them manually. Let's explore some of the different methods that can be used to find your files.

Smart Folders

Smart Folders in Snow Leopard are, well, smart! They are different from the standard folders that you created earlier in this lesson, which are basically storage locations where you can organize your files. Smart Folders add a level of intelligence that allows you to work more efficiently and find files with ease by establishing criteria by which the folder automatically displays those files.

So far, in the Pictures folder of your Home folder, you've organized some photos into logical categories. This will make it easier to find a photo in the future. Let's say, however, that you can't remember what category you filed your photo in and you want to just look at all the images in your Pictures folder. That would be rather difficult to do, as everything is filed inside one of several folders within the Pictures folder. In the following steps, you'll create your own Smart Folder to find all the images in your Pictures folder.

1   Open a new Finder window and navigate to the ~/Pictures folder.

2   Choose File > Find. This changes your Finder window into a Search window.

3   In the Search bar below the toolbar, click Pictures to limit the search to only the Pictures folder.

4   In the criteria bar below the Search bar, choose Kind from the first drop-down menu, Image from the second drop-down menu, and JPEG from the third drop-down menu. You are now finding all images that are in the JPEG format inside of the Pictures folder.

Smart Folders allow you to define search criteria for each folder.

5   At the far right of the Search bar, press the Save button. A dialog box appears, asking where you would like to save your Smart Folder.

6   Type **Images** in the Save As text field.

7   You can save this Smart Folder anywhere you'd like. In this example, leave it set to the Saved Searches folder and leave the *Add To Sidebar* checkbox selected.

Specify a name and location for your Smart Folder

Save As: Images

Where: Saved Searches

☑ Add To Sidebar

Cancel   Save

Selecting the Add To Sidebar check box causes the Smart Folder to appear in the sidebar of every Finder window for easy access.

8   Press Save. If you look at the sidebar of any Finder window, you now see your Smart Folder called Images. If you click this Smart Folder in the sidebar, you see all the JPEG files that exist in the Pictures folder.

9   Click the Apple.jpg file to select it. Note the path in the path bar at the bottom of the Finder window.

It's important to understand that none of the files that appear within a Smart Folder actually reside in that Smart Folder. It simply displays images that match the criteria that are defined by the Smart Folder. You'll notice that this image actually resides in the ~/Pictures/Nature folder. The exact same file can appear in multiple Smart Folders if it meets the criteria of all those Smart Folders, but the actual file only resides in one location.

What makes Smart Folders so powerful is that they are dynamic. This means that as you add pictures to the different categories of your Pictures folder or even add new categories, Smart Folders that you have created display those new images automatically because the images match the search criteria defined within the Smart Folders.

Let's create another Smart Folder to see how more than one criterion can be used to find applications that have been opened within the last two days.

11   Open a new Finder window and navigate to the Applications folder.

12   Press Command+F on your keyboard to display the search window.

13   Click Applications in the Search bar.

14   In the criteria bar, choose Kind from the first drop-down menu, and Application from the second drop-down menu. This displays all applications in the Applications folder.

15 Click the plus sign (+) to the right of the criteria bar to add another criterion by which to filter the applications. Choose Last opened date from the first drop-down menu, within last from the second drop-down menu, type **2** in the text field, and choose days from the last drop-down menu.

Defining multiple search criteria in a Smart Folder refines what the Smart Folder displays.

16 Press the Save button to the right of the Search bar to save these settings as a Smart Folder.

17 Name this folder **Recent Applications**, save it in the Saved Searches folder, and leave the *Add To Sidebar* checkbox selected.

18 Press Save.

Now that you've seen the capabilities of Smart Folders, your only limit is your imagination. Smart Folders can simplify your computing experience and save you a lot of time by displaying what you want to see in one folder.

Burn Folders

Burn folders are another special type of folder that allow you to prepare files to be burned to a CD or DVD disk. Depending on which computer you own, your ability to write CDs and DVDs will depend on which model Mac you purchased. All recent Macs have the ability to write to or *burn* a CD but not all models can write to or burn a DVD.

1 Make sure there are no Finder Windows open on your screen. Choose File > New Burn Folder. A folder is created on your Desktop. You can name this folder whatever you like but for this exercise, you'll leave the name as Burn Folder.

A burn folder allows you to copy files to this folder and later be written to a CD/DVD.

2 Choose File > New Finder Window and open the Pictures folder in the Home folder.

3 Drag the Nature, Creative, and New York folders onto the Burn Folder on the Desktop.

4 Double-click the Burn Folder to display its contents. Note that each folder has an arrow in the lower left corner of each folder's icon. This indicates that each folder is an alias, which is a pointer to the original folders. The original folders still reside in the Pictures folder. Aliases are covered in more detail in Lesson 2, "Customizing the OS X Interface to Suit Your Needs."

5 With the current Finder Window displaying the contents of the Burn Folder, you'll notice a Burn button in the upper right corner of the Finder Window. Press the Burn button to initiate writing to a CD or DVD. Don't worry, you won't actually burn a disk here, you'll just walk through the steps.

The burn button in the upper right corner of the Finder Window
initiates the writing of files to a CD or DVD disk.

6 A Burn Disc dialog box is displayed indicating that it is ready to burn the files to a disc. If you insert a blank disc at this point, the files will be written to that disc. Press the Cancel button to abort the process.

The Burn disc dialog box asks for a blank disc to begin burning the files to a CD or DVD.

7 Close any open Finder windows and drag the Burn Folder to the Trash.

Spotlight

Spotlight is a search tool built into Snow Leopard that allows you to search and find files on your computer or other computers on your network with unbelievable ease. You're bound to encounter a situation where you've saved a file somewhere on your computer, but simply can't recall where you saved it. But unless you remember what you named the file, the process of finding that file can be lengthy.

Spotlight solves that problem by providing an extremely powerful tool for finding files on your computer. It is to your computer what Google is to the World Wide Web. Although Spotlight is not new in Snow Leopard, its functionality has been enhanced to provide you, the user, with a simple and elegant method for finding files on your computer. You already used Spotlight in the previous exercise when you created a Smart Folder. Although Spotlight can be accessed using the Search field in any Finder window, you'll access Spotlight directly in the following steps. Let's see how easy it is to find files using Spotlight.

1   Click the Spotlight icon (Q) in the upper right corner of your screen, or use the keyboard shortcut, Command+spacebar, to launch Spotlight.

Let's say that you remember saving a file called Clouds.jpg (you did this in a previous exercise) somewhere on your computer, but can't remember where.

2   In the Spotlight search text field, type **clouds**. Immediately, under the Top Hit section of the search results, you see that the Clouds.jpg file is listed.

Notice that you didn't even have to type the entire name of the file; Spotlight automatically searched your computer for files that contained the word Clouds in the name and displayed the results.

3   Hover your cursor over the Clouds.jpg entry in the search results, and notice that the file path is displayed, showing you exactly where the file is stored.

Hover your cursor on an item in the search results list and the file path is displayed.

4   Click the item in the search results, and Spotlight opens the image using the Preview application.

5   Choose Preview > Quit Preview to close the application.

Beyond filenames

You've just seen how quickly you can find a file on your computer by using Spotlight, and typing in the name of the file in Spotlight's search field. However, what happens if you can't remember the filename? This is where Spotlight's power reveals itself. You see, whenever you copy, save, update, or delete a file on your computer, the Spotlight Store goes to work. The Spotlight Store is a database stored on your computer that keeps track of a file's content and metadata. What's metadata? Let's ask Spotlight.

1   Click the Spotlight icon (Q) in the upper right corner of your screen and type **metadata** in the search text field.

2   In the search results, click the Definition entry for a description of metadata. The Dictionary application on your computer is launched and the definition of Metadata is displayed in a new window.

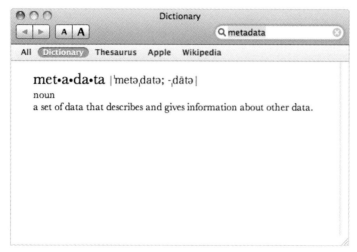

Spotlight also displays word definitions.

As you can see, Spotlight searches much more than just a file's name. As a matter of fact, it searches more than files; it also searches definitions and even web pages. As the Dictionary reveals, metadata is data that describes other data. For example, images often contain metadata describing what type of camera was used to capture an image, as well as keywords about the image that may have been entered by the photographer. In the following steps, you'll search for photos on your computer that were taken using a Canon camera.

3   Press Command+spacebar on your keyboard and type **Canon** in the search text field. A number of files are displayed in the search results, all categorized neatly in a list.

4   Look under the Images category. You see all the images that you copied to the Pictures folder.

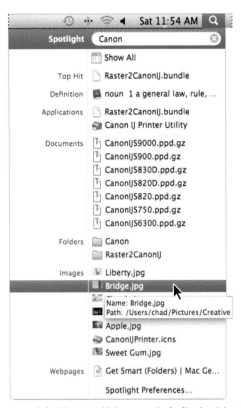

A search for "Canon" yielded many results for files that did not contain the word in the filename but did contain the word within the metadata.

How did Spotlight know that these files should be listed when a search for Canon was performed? Metadata. Metadata is embedded within each file by the digital camera that took the picture, and Spotlight recognized that *Canon* was contained within that metadata.

5   Click the Bridge.jpg file to open it with the Preview application.

6   Choose Tools > Show Inspector to display information about the file.

7   Click the More info button (❶), then click the TIFF button to display the Metadata information for that category; you can see the make and model of the camera that was used to capture this image.

8   Choose Preview > Quit Preview to exit the application.

In addition to metadata, Spotlight also indexes the contents of each file automatically. Remember the file called My File that you created earlier in this lesson? Let's say that you can't remember what you named the file, but you remember maybe a sentence or two from the content that was typed within that file. Spotlight can search for that information as well.

9   Press Command+spacebar on your keyboard and type **this is my** in the search text field. The first file listed under the Documents category is My File, the file that you created earlier.

Now you can begin to understand how powerful Spotlight's search capabilities are and how you can put them to use in your daily computing experiences. Spotlight also searches your e-mail messages, contacts, calendar events, and much more, which enhances your ability to find what you need.

Self study

Practice what you've learned in this lesson by copying your own files to your computer. Use the relevant categories within your Home folder to make finding your files easier. Then use Spotlight's search capabilities to find specific files based on their content or metadata. Practice navigating the folder structure of your hard drive. Try to become more comfortable with the Finder windows and the different views that allow you to browse your files in different ways.

Review

Questions

1   How do you force a file to be copied when moving that file within the same volume?

2   What is the purpose of the Home folder?

3   What type of folder can filter files on your computer based on specific search criteria?

Answers

1   Hold down the Option key on your keyboard while moving the file.

2   The Home folder provides a location for you to store your files where they are not accessible to other users on the computer. It also allows each user on a computer to have his or her own personalized working environment separate from everyone else.

3   A Smart Folder.

What you'll learn in this lesson:

- Customizing the desktop and Finder windows
- Setting a screen saver
- Working with the Dock
- How to work smarter using Exposé & Spaces
- Labeling files and folders

Customizing the OS X Interface to Suit Your Needs

In this lesson, you will be guided through the process of customizing Snow Leopard. You'll learn what options can be customized and how you can change the appearance of Snow Leopard to suit your needs.

Starting up

You will work with several files from the sl02lessons folder in this lesson. Make sure that you have copied the contents of the sl02lessons folder into the Pictures folder of your Home folder from the *Snow Leopard Digital Classroom* DVD. There are three folders to copy; New York, Creative, and Nature. This lesson may be easier to follow if those folders are in your Pictures folder. If you completed the previous lesson, these files may already exist in this folder and do not need to be copied.

See Lesson 2 in action!

Use the accompanying video to gain a better understanding of how to use some of the features shown in this lesson. The video tutorial for this lesson can be found on the included DVD.

The desktop

As described in the previous lesson, the desktop is a folder within each person's Home folder where files can be stored; however, the desktop is also what you see on your screen when you are working in Snow Leopard with the Finder active. Because this is the area that you see first when you start up your Mac, it's where you will also begin customizing the Mac OS X interface.

The desktop background

The image that appears on your screen behind any files or hard drives that are displayed on your desktop is called the desktop background. Because this is the first area that you see on your Mac and because much of your computing time is spent here managing files, it stands to reason that you'd want to customize its appearance with images that reflect your personality or mood.

The default desktop background.

1 Press the Apple menu button (⌘) in the upper left corner of your screen and choose System Preferences. System Preferences are where you can customize different aspects of your system, and are covered in more detail in Lesson 9, "System Preferences."

2 Click the Desktop & Screen Saver icon under the Personal section of the System Preferences pane to display the Desktop & Screen Saver preference pane.

3   Make sure that the Desktop button is selected at the top of the pane; you see various options for setting your desktop background. At the top of the pane, you see that the current desktop background is Aurora.

The Desktop & Screen Saver preference pane allows you to customize the appearance of your desktop.

4   Select the Nature category in the sidebar, then click the Ladybug image to the right. Your desktop background changes to that image. You may need to move the Desktop & Screen Saver preference pane out of the way to see your new desktop background. Choose some other images to see what they look like as desktop backgrounds.

5   Select the Plants category in the sidebar, then click the Dandelion image to set that image as your desktop background. Whenever you choose a new image, that image is displayed at the top of the preference pane, indicating that it is the active desktop background.

6   Continue experimenting with the other categories in the sidebar, which include Black & White, Abstract, and Solid Colors.

Some beautiful images have been provided for you in the categories within the sidebar that are sure to provide inspiration when you are working. However, you are not limited by the default choices provided, you can also use your own images as desktop backgrounds.

7 At the bottom of the sidebar in the Desktop & Screen Saver preference pane, you see an item called Folders. Click the disclosure triangle to the left of the word Folders to expand the Folders category. Within the Folders category there is a folder called Pictures. Select the Pictures folder to display the contents of your Pictures folder. If you have any images in the root of the Pictures folder, they are displayed in the area to the right of the sidebar. Because your images are filed in subfolders of the Pictures folder, they are not displayed. In order to see the images within those subfolders, you need to add those subfolders to the sidebar to make them accessible.

8 Click the plus sign (+) at the bottom of the preference pane.

9 In the sidebar, select your Home folder, click the Pictures folder, then click the Creative folder; press Choose. The Creative folder is now displayed in the sidebar, and the images within that folder are displayed to the right.

10 Select the boat image to make it the active desktop background.

The desktop background can be customized using your own images.

The bottom of the Desktop & Screen Saver preference pane provides additional options for customizing your desktop background.

There are several options available for controlling the behavior of your desktop background.

- **Change picture** automatically changes the picture of your desktop background within the category that you have selected. You can also choose how often the picture is changed from the list to the right.

- **Random** is only available when the Change picture check box is enabled. It randomly chooses the next image within the category that is selected.

- **Translucent menu bar** reduces the opacity of the menu bar at the top of your screen so that the image can be seen through the menu bar.

11 Set the desktop background back to the default by clicking the Nature category and choosing the Aurora image.

12 Close the Desktop & Screen Saver preference pane by pressing the Close button (●) in the upper left corner.

The screen saver

Screen savers were initially developed because if an image remained in the same position on a screen for long periods of time, it could actually burn into the computer screen and leave a ghosted version of that image on the screen at all times. Fortunately for you, that problem is no longer a factor on modern CRT and LCD displays. Currently, screen savers serve one of two purposes: to provide security so that nobody can access your computer when you have stepped away from your desk and to simply provide an attractive image or animation to look at after your computer experiences a period of inactivity. Let's examine the screen saver options provided by Snow Leopard.

1 From the Apple menu (●) in the upper left corner of your screen, choose System Preferences.

2 Click the Desktop & Screen Saver icon under the Personal section of the System Preferences pane to display the Desktop & Screen Saver preference pane.

3 Press the Screen Saver button at the top of the pane, and you see two main categories, Screen Savers and Preview. The Screen Savers section allows you to choose which screen saver is active, and the Preview window displays a preview of what the screen saver will look like. By default, a Screen Saver is selected at random when needed. Let's see how to specify a Screen Saver.

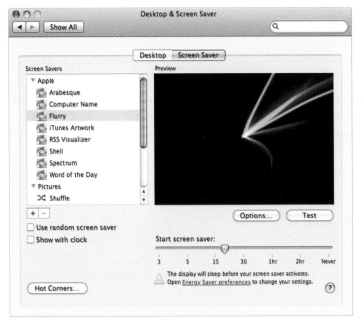

The Screen Saver section of the Desktop & Screen Saver preference pane allows you to customize the appearance and behavior of the screen saver on your computer.

4 Select the Arabesque screen saver to see what it looks like in the Preview window.

5 Press the Test button in the lower-right corner of the preference pane. This manually initiates the active screen saver on your computer.

6 Move your mouse or press any key on your keyboard to exit out of the screen saver.

7 Select the Word of the Day screen saver, and you're introduced each day to a new word to expand your vocabulary!

You're not at all limited to the default screen savers that ship with Snow Leopard. You can use the images found in your Pictures folder or any other folder, just like you can with your desktop backgrounds. You can even download custom screen savers from the Apple web site, *apple.com*.

8 Click the plus sign (+) in the lower left corner of the preference pane, and you see additional options available for customizing your screen saver.

• **Add Folder of Pictures** uses a specific folder of images as the active screen saver.

• **Add MobileMe Gallery** uses galleries of images created and stored using the Apple MobileMe service.

• **Add RSS Feed** allows you to enter a Web URL that displays the latest news and updates of that URL as a screen saver.

• **Browse Screen Savers** takes you to the Apple web site, *apple.com,* where you can download hundreds of free screen savers to your computer.

9 Choose the Browse Screen Savers option. Safari launches and displays the Apple web site of downloadable screen savers that you can browse, search, download, and install onto your computer.

If you don't have an Internet connection, you cannot perform step 9.

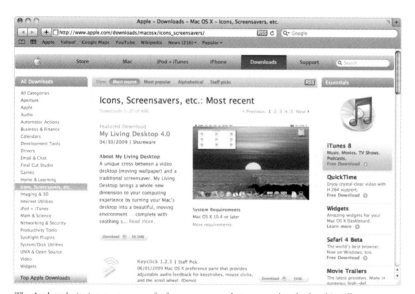

The Apple web site is a great resource for free screen savers that you can download and install on your computer.

10 Quit Safari by choosing Safari > Quit.

11 Select Flurry to set the screen saver back to the default.

The options at the bottom of the preference pane allow you to control the behavior of the screen savers.

- **Use random screen saver** simply chooses a screen saver at random when the screen saver is activated.

- **Show with clock** simply displays the current screen saver with the current time.

- **Options** provides controls for the active screen saver. This may be grayed out if the active screen saver doesn't provide any options.

- **Test** allows you to test how the screen saver appears when it is active.

- **Start screen saver** sets the length of inactivity required before the screen saver activates.

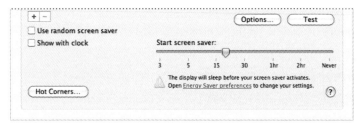

The options at the bottom of the Desktop & Screen Saver preference pane allow you to control the behavior of each screen saver.

12 Press the Options button to display the options for the Flurry screen saver. Experiment with these controls by adjusting the options. Press OK.

13 The Flurry screen saver displays in the Preview window using the new controls set in step 12.

In the Start screen saver section of the Preference pane, you see a warning icon (⚠) indicating that the computer's display is set to go to sleep before the screen saver has time to activate. You will learn about the Energy Saver preferences later in this book, but you'll solve this problem now by reducing the period of inactivity that is required before the screen saver activates.

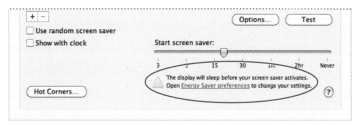

A warning sign displays because the screen saver will not have time to activate before the display is put to sleep by the Energy Saver preferences.

14 Drag the slider in the Start screen saver section to the left until the warning icon disappears. The screen saver will now activate properly.

15 Press the Close button (⊗) to close the Desktop & Screen Saver preference pane.

The Dock

The Dock provides users with a convenient place to quickly access commonly used applications and documents. Without the Dock, you'd need to delve into folders and subfolders to access applications and files that you want to work with.

Positioning the Dock

By default, the Dock appears at the bottom of your screen; however, it can be moved to different areas of your screen and it can be highly customized to meet your needs. Basic Dock features can be accessed directly from the Apple menu (⌘).

The default location of the Dock at the bottom of the screen.

1 From the Apple menu, choose Dock > Position on Left. The Dock switches to a vertical orientation and is *docked* to the left side of your screen.

2 From the Apple menu, choose Dock > Position on Right. The Dock remains in its vertical orientation but is moved to the other side of your screen.

3 Choose Apple menu > Dock > Position on Bottom to return the Dock to the bottom of your screen, its default location.

Only you can decide which positioning of the Dock will best benefit you, and you may not know until you try the different options.

Hiding the Dock

As helpful as the Dock is, it does occupy valuable screen real estate that could be utilized when viewing web pages or reading long documents. Fortunately, Snow Leopard provides some options that allow you to make better use of the space that the Dock occupies.

1 Choose Apple menu > Dock > Turn Hiding On. The Dock disappears.

2 Move your cursor all the way to the bottom of your screen. The Dock appears, making itself visible while your cursor is in the Dock area.

3 Move your cursor up and out of the area that the Dock occupies. The Dock disappears, hiding once again.

The Dock hidden (top) and visible (bottom).

Hiding the Dock is incredibly efficient because the Dock only appears when you need it. At any other time, the Dock is hidden and out of the way so that you have extra space in which to work.

4 Choose Apple menu > Dock > Turn Hiding Off. This will keep the Dock visible while working throughout this book.

The appearance of the Dock

In the following steps, you'll learn how to change the appearance of the Dock and its behavior. Earlier, you adjusted the Dock by using the commands in the Apple menu. Additional options are available by accessing the preference pane for the Dock.

1 Choose Apple menu > System Preferences and click the Dock icon in the Personal category of the System Preferences pane.

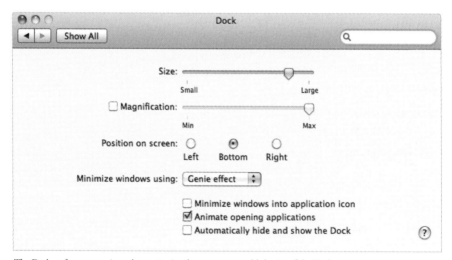

The Dock preference pane is used to customize the appearance and behavior of the Dock.

2 Click and drag the Size slider to the left and right to see the size of the Dock change on your screen. As you'll see later in this lesson, you can add additional items to the Dock for easy access. As you do, the Dock will fill more of your screen. Adjusting the Size slider allows you to compensate for these additional items when you add them.

3 Click the *Magnification* checkbox.

4 Move your cursor into the Dock area and move it to the left and right in the Dock. As you move your cursor, the icons magnify, displaying at a larger size. This is helpful when you have several items in your Dock and you've made the Dock fairly small. The icons magnify, giving you a better view of each.

5 Drag the Magnification slider to the left and move your cursor back into the Dock area. The icons magnify less now because of that adjustment.

6 Drag the Magnification slider all the way to the right to magnify the icons to the maximum amount.

7 Uncheck the *Magnification* checkbox to turn off magnification of the icons.

The Minimize windows using drop-down menu controls how Finder windows are minimized to the Dock. The Genie effect is the default behavior.

8 Press the yellow Minimize button (●) to minimize the Dock preference pane to the Dock. The animated behavior that you see is called the Genie effect.

9 Click the Dock preference pane icon at the right side of the Dock to maximize the window.

10 From the Minimize windows using drop-down menu, choose Scale effect and press the yellow Minimize button to minimize the Dock preference pane again. The effect that you see now is a simpler animation effect.

11 Click the Dock preference pane icon at the right side of the Dock to maximize the window.

12 Choose Genie effect from the Minimize windows using drop-down menu to reset the behavior to the default setting.

The *Animate opening applications* checkbox determines how an application's icon appears in the Dock when you launch the application.

13 With the *Animate opening applications* checkbox selected, click the Safari icon in the Dock and watch the icon as the application launches. Depending on the speed of your computer, the icon *bounces* once or twice to indicate that the application is launching. Quit Safari.

14 Uncheck the *Animate opening application* checkbox and click the Safari icon once again to launch the application. Notice that the icon no longer *bounces*, but instead retains its normal display. Quit Safari.

15 Check the *Animate opening applications* checkbox to return to the default setting.

16 Click the Minimize windows into application icon then minimize the Dock preference pane. Instead of the window minimizing to the right side of the Dock, it minimizes to the System Preferences icon in the Dock.

17 Click the System Preferences icon to maximize the Dock preference pane.

18 Uncheck the Minimize windows into application checkbox for now to return the setting to its default.

19 Close the Dock preference pane.

Adding contents to the Dock

Now that you understand how to change the appearance of the Dock, you can personalize it by adding your own applications to the Dock as well as frequently accessed folders. Let's say that you regularly use the Dictionary to look up words, but you're tired of manually navigating to your Applications folder to launch the Dictionary application.

Adding Applications

1 In the menu bar of the Finder, choose Go > Applications. Your Applications folder is displayed in a new Finder window on your screen.

You can use the keyboard shortcut Shift+Command+A to open your Applications folder.

2 Click the Dictionary icon in the Finder window and drag it down to the Dock. As you are dragging the icon toward the Dock, notice that the Dock is divided vertically into two sections; you want to drag the Dictionary icon into the left section.

3 Still holding down the mouse button, move your cursor left and right within the Dock. Notice that as you move your cursor, the existing icons in the Dock move out of the way, creating space for you to drop the icon that you are moving.

4   Release the mouse button at the location where you would like the Dictionary icon to appear.

As you drag an icon to the Dock, the other icons make room for the new one.

5   Add the DVD Player icon to the Dock.

It's important to understand that you're not actually moving the applications into the Dock. You're simply creating an alias, or shortcut, to that application or file. Note that when you added the Dictionary and DVD Player to the Dock, they remained in the Applications folder.

6   Utilizing these icons in the Dock couldn't be easier. Click the Dictionary icon to launch the Dictionary application.

7   Quit the Dictionary application by choosing Dictionary > Quit.

Adding folders

Just like applications, folders can also be added to the Dock. Folders, however, can only be added to the right side of the Dock. In the following steps, you'll add your Pictures folder to the Dock for easy access of that folder.

1 The Finder window from the previous exercise should still be open on your screen; if not, then open a new Finder window.

2 Select your Home folder in the sidebar of the Finder window to display its contents.

3 Drag the Pictures folder from the Finder window to the right side of the Dock. The other icons move out of the way, creating space for you to place the Pictures folder.

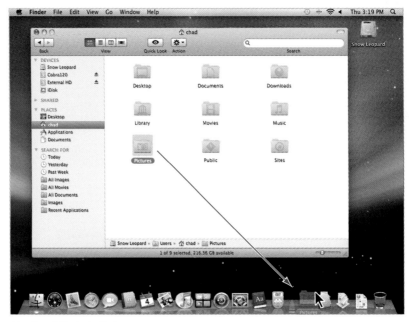

Dragging a folder to the Dock.

4 Close the Finder window.

5 Double-click the hard drive icon on your desktop to open a new Finder window.

6 Drag the Applications folder to the Dock, and then close any open Finder windows.

Stacks

When you drag a folder to the Dock, it becomes a stack. A stack serves the same purpose as a folder but behaves differently.

1 Click the Pictures folder in the Dock, which is now a stack. The stack springs from the Dock in a fan to display the contents of the stack.

When you click on a stack, it springs from the Dock in a fan to display its contents.

2 Click the Nature folder within the fan. A new Finder window of the Nature folder displays.

3 Close the Finder window.

4 Click the Applications folder in the Dock. This is a stack just like the Pictures stack; however, it displays the contents in a grid. Stacks display their contents in a fan or a grid, based on the number of items in the stack.

Snow Leopard includes two premade stacks for your Documents and for Downloads, both of which are folders that reside in the Home folder. Stacks can be customized to change how they appear and how they display their contents.

5 Position your cursor over the Applications stack icon, right-click or Ctrl+click to display a menu. This menu allows you to customize the behavior of the stack.

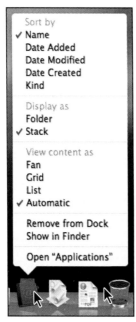

The stack menu controls how the stack and its contents are displayed.

- **Sort by** allows you to specify how the contents of the stack are sorted when viewed.

- **Display as** determines how the stack icon is displayed in the Dock—as a folder or as a stack. When displayed as a stack, the icon appears as the first item in the contents of the stack, based on the current sort order.

- **View content as** determines whether the contents of the stack are displayed as a Fan, Grid, List, or Automatic. Automatic picks the best option, depending on how many items are inside the stack.

- **Remove from Dock** removes the stack from the Dock.

- **Show in Finder** displays the actual folder in a Finder window. Remember, the stack is just an alias, or shortcut, to the actual folder.

- **Open** opens the stack in a Finder window.

6   Choose Folder under the Display as section of the stack menu. This changes the icon of the stack to look like a folder.

The stack icon displayed as a stack (left) and as an icon (right).

7   Display the stack menu again, and choose Fan from the View content as section of the menu.

8   Click the Applications stack icon to display the contents. Now the contents of the Applications folder are displayed as a fan.

9   Display the stack menu again, and choose List from the View content as section of the menu.

10 Click the Applications stack icon to display the contents. Now the contents of the Applications folder are displayed as a list.

Removing contents from the Dock

As you perform different tasks on your computer, your needs, as well as your habits, will change. So, too, will the items in the Dock. Fortunately, Snow Leopard makes it just as easy to remove items from the Dock as it does to add them. The DVD Player launches automatically when you insert a DVD into the DVD drive of your Mac, and so there's really no need for it to take up space in the Dock.

1   Position your cursor over the DVD Player icon in the Dock, then click and hold the mouse button until a menu appears.

2   Choose Remove from Dock from the Options submenu. A cloud of smoke appears, indicating that the item has been removed from the Dock.

3   Remove the Pictures folder from the Dock as well, using a different technique this time. Using your mouse, click the Pictures folder in the Dock and drag upwards away from the Dock; then release the mouse button.

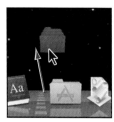 

Dragging an icon from the Dock (left). Releasing the mouse creates a puff of smoke, indicating that the icon has been removed from the Dock (right).

Customizing Finder windows

Now that you've learned how to customize the general appearance of your desktop and the Dock, you'll dive in a bit deeper and learn how to customize the appearance of the Finder windows, making it even easier for you to access files quickly.

Customizing the sidebar

1   Press Command+N on your keyboard to open a new Finder window.

2   Choose Finder > Preferences from the menu bar to display the Finder Preferences.

3 Press the Sidebar button at the top of the Finder Preferences window.

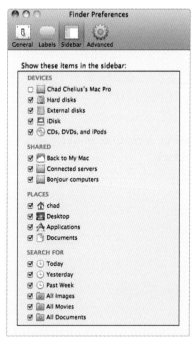

The sidebar section of the Finder Preferences window allows you to control what is displayed in the sidebar of each Finder window.

The Sidebar section of the Finder Preferences window allows you to control what components are displayed in the sidebar of each Finder window that you open. There are four categories that contain options to be displayed in each Finder window. They are:

- **Devices:** Internal and external attached hard drives, optical disks such as CDs and DVDs, iPods, and your iDisk, if applicable.

- **Shared:** Any visible computers that appear on your network.

- **Places:** Common folders in your Home folder.

- **Search For:** Built-in searches that display files opened within a given time period, as well as categories such as All Images, All Movies, and All Documents on your computer.

Simply enable or disable the options that you would like to see in each Finder window.

4   Close the Finder Preferences window.

There are several options listed in the Sidebar section of the Finder Preferences window that allow you to customize the appearance of the sidebar. You will find, however, that there may be items you'd like to appear in the sidebar that aren't available in the Finder Preferences window. That's OK, because you can further customize the sidebar to your liking without having to do so within the Finder Preferences window.

5   Press Command+N on your keyboard to open a new Finder window.

6   Select the Home folder in the sidebar to display the contents of your Home folder.

7   Click the Movies folder and drag it onto the sidebar. A bar appears, indicating the location where the Movies folder will be placed. When the bar appears under the Applications folder in the sidebar, release the mouse button. The Movies folder now appears in the sidebar.

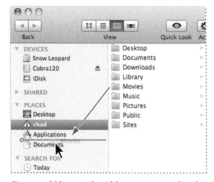

Drag any folder onto the sidebar to create an alias that will appear in every Finder window.

Just as when you added items to the Dock, you're not actually moving any of the folders to the sidebar. You're simply creating an alias to that folder so that when you click on that entry in the sidebar, you're taken directly to that folder. In addition to folders, applications can also be added to the sidebar for easy access.

8   Drag the Pictures and Downloads folder to the sidebar so that they can also be easily accessed from any Finder window.

9   Choose File > New Finder Window. Notice that every Finder window contains the custom sidebar that you created earlier.

10 Regardless of whether you added items to the sidebar manually or they were added using the Finder Preferences, you can remove them just as easily. Simply select the Downloads in the sidebar and drag it off the sidebar to remove it.

Removing an item from the sidebar is also easy. Simply click and drag the icon off of the sidebar and it's instantly removed.

11 Close all open Finder windows.

As you can see, it's very easy to customize the sidebar in Snow Leopard to your liking. Utilizing the customization features of the sidebar makes working in Snow Leopard even easier.

Customizing the toolbar

In Lesson 1, "Navigating and Organizing in Snow Leopard," you discovered how to navigate through files and folders using the toolbar, and you also realized how easy it is to change the view of those files. In this exercise, you will discover ways that the toolbar can be customized to fit your specific needs.

1 Choose File > New Finder Window to display a new Finder window on your screen.

2 Choose View > Customize Toolbar to display the Customize Toolbar pane.

If you find that Customize Toolbar is not available under the View menu, it's because a Finder window is not displayed on your screen. The Customize Toolbar pane allows you to drag different icons from the pane directly to the toolbar. In addition, if you find that there are items in the toolbar that you simply don't use, you can also remove them when this pane is displayed.

3 To make it easier to identify the icons in the Toolbar, choose Icon and Text from the Show menu in the lower left corner of the Customize Toolbar pane.

4   Click the New Folder icon (📄) in the Customize Toolbar pane, drag it up to the toolbar, and drop it directly to the left of the Quick Look icon (◉). This adds the Add Folder icon to the toolbar of every Finder window.

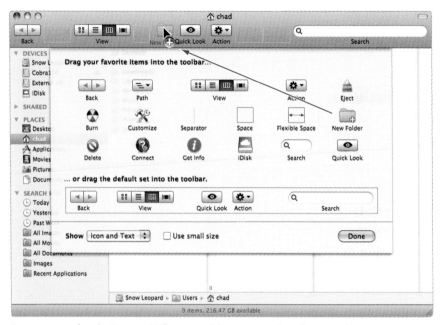

Dragging an icon from the Customize Toolbar pane and dropping it into the toolbar makes that icon available in every Finder window that you open in Snow Leopard.

5   Click the Path button in the Customize Toolbar pane, drag it up to the toolbar, and drop it directly to the left of the Quick Look icon.

6   The light-gray squares in the toolbar indicate spaces used to separate icons into categories. Click the Space icon in the Customize Toolbar pane, drag it up to the toolbar, and drop it directly to the left of the Quick Look icon. This adds a space between the icons that you just added and the Quick Look icon.

The bottom of the Customize Toolbar pane contains a Show drop-down menu that allows you to choose how the icons are displayed in the toolbar. In addition, there is a *Use small size* checkbox that reduces the size of the icons in the toolbar. If you find that you are running out of room to place icons in the toolbar, this checkbox gives you a little more room in the toolbar in which to place new icons.

7 Click one of the squares to the right of the toolbar, drag straight up, and release the mouse button when you are out of the Finder window. A puff of smoke appears, indicating that the space has been removed.

Dragging an icon off the toolbar, when the Customize Toolbar pane is open, removes an icon from the toolbar.

8 Right-click or Ctrl+click the Quick Look icon in the toolbar, and choose Remove item. The Quick Look icon is removed from the toolbar.

9 Press Done to close the Customize Toolbar pane.

There's a little-known secret to customizing the toolbar that isn't found in the Customize Toolbar pane. Any file or application can also be added to the toolbar for easy access in any Finder window.

10 Click the Applications icon in the sidebar of the Finder window to display the contents of the Applications folder.

11 Click the Stickies icon in the Applications folder, drag it up to the toolbar, and drop it to the left of the New Folder icon. The Stickies application icon is added to the toolbar.

12 Click the Calculator icon in the Applications folder, drag it up to the toolbar, and drop it to the left of the Stickies icon. The Calculator application icon is added to the toolbar.

The customized toolbar.

Removing items from the toolbar

Removing items from the toolbar couldn't be easier. Any item can be removed from the toolbar without having to go back into the Customize Toolbar pane.

1 Ctrl+click or right-click the Calculator icon in the toolbar, and choose Remove Item.

2 Ctrl+click or right-click the Action icon in the toolbar, and choose Remove Item.

Resetting the toolbar to the defaults

After experimenting with the toolbar and customizing its contents, you may decide that you'd like to start fresh using Snow Leopard's default icons.

1 With a Finder window displayed on the screen, choose View > Customize Toolbar.

2 Click the default icon set at the bottom of the Customize Toolbar pane, and drag it and drop it onto the toolbar. All the icons in the toolbar are reset to the defaults.

3 Press Done.

4 Close any open Finder windows.

Aliases

An alias is a special copy of a file or folder on your computer. An alias is not a byte-for-byte duplicate of a file or folder, but a pointer to the original file. It takes up virtually no storage space, and so you can create as many as you like without significantly affecting storage limitations. An alias is useful when you want to organize items but you don't want to physically move them, or when you want quick access to files in a particular location or more than one location. Let's take a look at how aliases work.

1 With no Finder windows open on your computer, choose File > New Folder or press Shift+Command+N on your keyboard. A new folder is created on your desktop, called untitled folder.

2 Type **My Favorite Pictures** as the folder name, and press Return on your keyboard or click anywhere on your desktop to commit the folder name change.

3   Choose File > New Finder Window and click Pictures in the sidebar to display
    the contents of the Pictures folder. Select the New York folder, and then select the
    NYC.jpg file.

4   Choose File > Make Alias or press Command+L on your keyboard. A new alias file is
    created called NYC.jpg alias.

5   Rename the NYC.jpg alias file to **Nighttime NYC**, then press Return on your
    keyboard to commit the name change.

6   Drag the Nighttime NYC file to the My Favorite Pictures folder that you created on
    the desktop.

7   Click the Creative folder within the Pictures folder and select the Boat.jpg file. If you
    can not see the Creative folder, you will need to click the Pictures folder first.

8   Press Command+L on your keyboard to create an alias of this image.

9   Rename the Boat.jpg alias file to **Ocean City Boat**. Drag the alias to the My Favorite
    Pictures folder on your desktop.

10 Double-click the My Favorite Pictures folder to display its contents.

11 Change the view of the Finder window to icon view so that you can see the icons.

    The arrow in the lower left corner of each icon indicates that the file is an alias of
    another file. Double-clicking these files to open them actually opens the original file,
    even though the names of the aliases have been changed. Alias names can be whatever
    you like, because they always point to the original file or folder from which they were
    made. In addition, deleting an alias never deletes the original file; it only deletes the alias
    that is pointing to that original file.

The arrow in the lower-left corner of the icon
indicates that the file is an alias to another file.

12 Double-click the Nighttime NYC alias. The original image, NYC.jpg, opens with the
    Preview application. Even though you changed the name of the alias, it still points to the
    original file.

13 Choose Preview > Quit to quit the Preview application.

14 Right-click or Ctrl+click the Nighttime NYC alias and choose Show Original. The original file from which the alias was made is displayed in the Finder window.

15 Close any open Finder windows and drag the My Favorite Pictures folder to the Trash, as you will no longer need it.

Aliases can be very powerful and useful. In this exercise, you discovered how aliases could be used to store your favorite pictures in a common location without having to move the original file from its current location. Aliases are also great for applications that you use frequently and want to access from a specific location. As you work with Snow Leopard, you may find specific uses for aliases that help you to perform tasks faster and more easily.

Labels

Labels are a way to color files and folders to identify them more easily when viewing them. Let's say, for instance, that you need to review several documents in a folder; labels allow you to color them as you complete each document or to identify the files that need to be completed. Let's label some files.

Labeling files

1 Press Command+N to create a new Finder window, and navigate to ~/Pictures/Nature.

2 Change the current view to list view by clicking on the List view button (▤) in the toolbar.

3 Select the Apple.jpg file. From the File menu, choose the green button under the Label section. The Apple.jpg file is now colored green. You may use this color to identify photos that need to be worked on.

4 Select the Ice.jpg file, right-click or Ctrl+click on the file, and choose blue under the Label section. The Ice.jpg file is now colored blue. You could use this color to indicate that the file is completed.

5 Label the Clouds.jpg file as red, and label the Sweet Gum.jpg file as purple using the same process as in step 3.

Labels allow you to identify files easily in a Finder window.

Customizing label names

Snow Leopard provides default names for the labels using basic color names. If you are using labels for a more specific task, you may want to customize the label names to more accurately represent how the labels are used. Let's look at how label names can be customized in Snow Leopard.

1 Choose Finder > Preferences to display the Finder Preferences window.

2 Click the Labels button in the toolbar to display label name options.

3 In the Red field, type **Needs Updating**; in the Green field, type **Completed**; in the Blue field, type **Print**.

4 Close the Finder Preferences window.

5 Right-click or Ctrl+click the Clouds.jpg file and hover your cursor over the red label in the Label section of the menu. You can see that the new label names that were assigned in step 3 are now reflected when applying labels to files.

The new label names are reflected when applying labels to a file.

6 Press Esc on your keyboard to exit out of the active menu.

7 Close any open Finder windows.

You can name these labels using any naming convention that you like. This exercise should give you some ideas as to how you can use this labeling system to better organize your files and folders.

Dashboard

Dashboard is an application that provides you with quick access to useful utilities that provide information in a quick and efficient way. Dashboard is completely customizable, allowing you to add tools called Widgets that provide information to you.

Many of the Widgets used by Dashboard obtain their information from the Internet, and therefore require an Internet connection to work properly. However, most of this lesson can be completed without an Internet connection. See Lesson 7, "Creating and Using Your Own Network," for information about setting up Internet access in Snow Leopard.

1 Press F12 on your keyboard. Depending on the type of keyboard you are using, you may need to hold down the fn key while pressing F12. This displays Dashboard on your screen.

The Dashboard screen.

2 By default, Dashboard displays four useful Widgets: Calculator, Weather, World Clock, and iCal. Weather and World Clock are the only two Widgets that currently require Internet access.

3 Click the large plus sign in the lower-left corner of the Dashboard screen. A new pane is displayed at the bottom of the Dashboard screen with additional Widgets that can be added to Dashboard.

4 If necessary, click the arrows at the left or right of the pane to scroll through the available Widgets. Select Unit Converter in the pane to add it to Dashboard.

5 Click the newly added Unit Converter Widget and drag it to a new location within Dashboard. Any Widget can be removed at this point by clicking on the X in the upper left corner of the Widget.

6 Click the large X in the lower left corner of the Dashboard screen to close the Dashboard pane and commit your change.

7 In the Currency Widget, choose Currency from the Convert drop-down menu. Choose US Dollar from the left drop-down menu and type **20** in the text field below it. Choose Euro from the right drop-down menu to see the Euro equivalent for $20.

8 Press F12 again, or click anywhere on the desktop, to exit Dashboard.

The Currency Widget is one example of the information that is provided by Widgets.

This is the type of information that Widgets provide, and you can see how easy it is to add them to Dashboard. Now you'll add a Widget that is not included with Snow Leopard but that can be easily accessed from the Dashboard Widgets web site.

 You need an active Internet connection to follow along in the next section.

Adding additional Widgets

1 Click the Dashboard icon in the Dock to display Dashboard.

You can access Dashboard by clicking on the icon in the Dock.

2 Click the large plus sign in the lower left corner of the Dashboard screen. A new pane is displayed at the bottom of the Dashboard screen with additional Widgets that can be added to Dashboard.

3 Press the Manage Widgets button above the Widgets pane. The Manage Widgets Widget is displayed on the Dashboard screen.

4 Press the More Widgets button at the bottom of the Manage Widgets Widget. Safari launches and displays the Dashboard Widgets web page.

5 In the Search text field at the upper-right corner of the web page, type **Radar In Motion**. The search results are displayed on a new web page.

6 Click the entry that displays Apple – Downloads – Dashboard Widgets – Radar In Motion. The Radar In Motion web page is displayed.

7 Press the Download button at the upper right corner of the page to download the Widget to your computer.

8 After a brief period of time, a window displays, asking if you'd like to install the Widget. Press the Install button.

Installing a Widget from the Apple web site is quick and easy.

9 Dashboard launches automatically with the new Widget active. Press the Keep button, and then reposition the new Widget within the Dashboard screen. You may need to reposition several Widgets to make room for them, depending on your monitor size.

10 Click anywhere on your desktop to close Dashboard.

The new Widget installed on the Dashboard screen.

11 Close Safari and Downloads window.

Exposé

As you work in Snow Leopard, you'll find that occasionally things get cluttered. You may end up with multiple files open in an application, as well as multiple Finder windows. Exposé provides a way to temporarily organize those windows to make it easier to find what you're looking for. It's like having the ability to take a pile of papers on your desk and quickly display them all in a neat, organized manner to see the contents of each paper more clearly. Although the last option probably won't happen anytime soon, at least you can have that type of organization on your computer.

Exposé has three modes:

- Application Windows
- All Windows
- Show Desktop

Let's examine each of these modes to see how they can be used to make order out of chaos.

Application Windows

1 Press Command+N to open a new Finder window, and navigate to ~/Pictures/Nature.

2 Change the view to list view, and double-click each file in the Nature folder to open each file in Preview. If the files open in an application other than Preview, you may need to right-click or Ctrl+click each file and choose Open With > Preview.

3 Preview should be the active application and there should be four files open, each in a separate window. With all the windows stacked on top of one another, it's difficult to see each image, much less select it.

4 Press F10 or fn+F10 on the keyboard to activate Exposé in the Application Windows mode. All windows of the current application are organized into a neat grid, allowing you to see the contents of each window.

You may need to hold down the fn key while pressing F10 to activate the Application Windows mode.

5 As you hover your cursor over each window, the file's name is displayed and the image's intensity is reduced. Select the Apple.jpg image to bring it in front of the other windows.

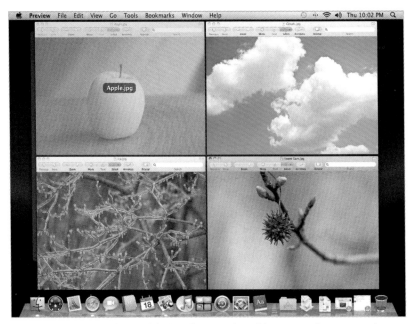

In Application Windows mode, Exposé displays all open windows of the current application in a grid.

6 Click the Finder icon in the Dock to make the Finder the active application. The Finder window containing the Nature folder is displayed.

7 Press Command+N on your keyboard to display a new Finder window.

8 Press F10 on your keyboard, and only the Finder windows are displayed because the Finder is the active application.

9 Press F10 on your keyboard to close Exposé.

10 New in Snow Leopard is a feature called Dock Exposé. Click and hold the Finder icon in the Dock and it will activate Exposé for all windows of that application. This works for any application!

11 Select any window in Exposé to make that window active in the Finder.

All Windows

Things are beginning to get a bit cluttered on the screen, as there are now a total of six windows open in two different applications.

1   Press F9 or fn+F9 on your keyboard to activate Exposé in All Windows mode. Every window of every open application is displayed on the screen in a nice, organized grid.

2   Select the Clouds.jpg image to make it active in the Preview application.

Show Desktop

Regardless of how many windows are open, there will be times when you need to access files on your desktop quickly. That's where the Show Desktop mode of Exposé is very useful.

1   Press F11 or fn+F11 on your keyboard. All windows in all applications slide off the edge of the screen to display the entire desktop. This makes it easy to copy files from a CD or to move or open files from the desktop. Very convenient.

2   Press F11 again to return the windows to their original positions.

Customizing Exposé

1   From the Apple menu (), choose System Preferences.

2   Under the Personal category, choose Exposé & Spaces.

3   Make sure the Exposé button is selected at the top of the Exposé & Spaces preference pane.

4   In the Active Screen Corners section of the preference pane, you can choose Exposé modes from any of the drop-down menus. In the upper left drop-down menu, choose All Windows.

5   Drag your cursor to the upper left corner of the screen. Notice that Exposé is activated when your cursor reaches the corner.

6   Click the Exposé & Spaces preference pane to make it active.

7   Choose the dash (–) from the upper left drop-down menu to remove the feature applied in step 4.

8   In the Exposé section of the preference pane, you can also reassign shortcuts if the defaults don't suit your needs. Simply choose a different shortcut from the list to reassign the shortcuts.

9   Quit System Preferences. Leave the windows open for the next exercise.

Spaces

Spaces is all about organizing windows on your computer into more than one *Virtual Desktop*. So far in this book, you've been working with windows and have learned how to navigate through them. Oftentimes, though, you need to work on more than one project at a time, and each project resides in a different window. Before long, you find you have windows on top of windows and it's hard to stay organized. Spaces gives you multiple desktops in which to organize windows.

1   To make Spaces easy to access, you'll add it to the Dock. Open /Applications/Utilities in a new Finder window.

2   Drag the Spaces icon from the Utilities folder to the Dock. Now spaces can be easily accessed from the Dock.

3   Close any open Finder windows.

4   Click the Spaces icon in the Dock to activate Spaces.

The Spaces icon.

5   A window appears, indicating that Spaces is not set up. Press Set Up Spaces button.

6   The Exposé & Spaces system preference pane is displayed. Click the *Enable Spaces* checkbox to make Spaces active on your computer, then click the *Show Spaces in menu bar* checkbox to display an icon providing quick access to Spaces.

7   Close the Exposé & Spaces system preference pane.

8   Click the Spaces icon in the Dock again to activate Spaces. Four squares are displayed, showing you the four different desktops that are available.

9   Click in the upper-right square. All of the previously open windows disappear. They're not really gone; they just reside on another virtual desktop.

10   Press Command+N on your keyboard to open a new Finder window, and navigate to ~/Pictures/New York.

11   Click the Spaces icon again. You can now see your original desktop in the upper left corner and the new desktop with the new Finder window in the upper-right corner.

12   Click the square in the upper left corner to make it active again.

13   Select the Clouds.jpg window to make it active.

14 Click the Spaces icon again. Drag the Clouds.jpg window from the desktop in the upper left corner to the desktop in the lower-left corner to move it to a new desktop or *Space*.

12 Select the Clouds.jpg window in the lower-left corner to make that the active desktop.

13 You can also activate different Spaces from the Spaces button (⚏) in the menu bar . Simply click the icon and choose Space 1, 2, 3, or 4 to make each one active.

14 Quit Preview and close any open Finder windows in each of the Spaces used in this exercise.

Self study

Go back to Dashboard and explore the different Widgets that can be added to Dashboard to provide important and interesting information to you quickly. Think of information that you need to look up regularly and then search for Widgets that might help you find that information faster. Practice using Exposé to help you sift through the multiple windows to find the files and folders that you're looking for. Create aliases of frequently accessed areas of your hard drive and put those aliases in a convenient location so that you can access them quickly.

Review

Questions

1 What Snow Leopard feature allows you to quickly organize several open windows so you can find the one that you're looking for?

2 How can you add an application or file icon to a Finder window so that it's easy to access from any window?

3 How would you move the Dock from its default location at the bottom of the screen to the left or right side of the screen?

Answers

1 Exposé.

2 Select the application icon and either drag it to the sidebar or to the toolbar.

3 Go to the Dock pane in System Preferences and choose left or right from the Position on screen section. You can also access this feature by choosing Apple menu > Dock, and choosing the position from the submenu.

What you'll learn in this lesson:

- Setting up accounts
- Logging in and Switching users
- Sharing files with other users
- Setting Parental Controls to limit access to content

Using Snow Leopard with a Group

In this lesson, you will learn how to set up and use Snow Leopard in a group environment where multiple people use the same computer.

Starting up

You will work with several files from the sl03lessons folder in this lesson. Make sure that you have copied the contents of the sl03lessons folder into the Pictures folder of your Home folder from the Digital Classroom DVD. There are three folders to copy: New York, Creative, and Nature. This lesson may be easier to follow if those folders are in your Pictures folder.

See Lesson 3 in action!

Use the accompanying video to gain a better understanding of how to use some of the features shown in this lesson. The video tutorial for this lesson can be found on the included DVD.

Multiple users

Snow Leopard is a multi-user operating system, which means that it is designed to be used on a computer that has one or more users. Although a multi-user operating system is not new to Snow Leopard, it is one of the key features of OS X, making it ideal for use in a family, small group, or large group environment.

In the good old days of computing, operating systems were not designed with multiple users in mind, which created some problems when multiple people used the same computer. This is because not all people use a computer in the same way. For example, maybe one person likes to view files in column view while another likes to view files in icon view. Without a multi-user operating system, there is a constant struggle back and forth because you have to change the computer environment to suit your needs each time you work on the computer. This is where a multi-user operating system really shines. Each person on the computer is given their own account, which allows them to customize their computing environment exactly the way they like to work. So when settings are changed, those settings only apply to their own personal account, leaving all other accounts untouched.

User accounts

Snow Leopard makes the distinction between multiple users on a computer through user accounts. Each person using the computer needs to create an account, or have one created for them, in which to log on to the computer. Without an account, a person cannot gain access to the computer. This serves three purposes:

1 It protects the content of each user on the computer from unwanted access to their files.

2 It prevents legitimate users of the computer from accessing files of other users of the computer.

3 It allows each user to customize the appearance and settings of the computing environment.

There are five different types of user accounts that can be created in Snow Leopard:

- Administrator
- Standard
- Managed with Parental Controls
- Sharing Only
- Guest

Administrator

An Administrator account is the most powerful type of account that can be created in Snow Leopard. An Administrator has complete control over settings and configuration on the computer. When you set up your computer for the first time after unpacking your computer or after installing Snow Leopard, an Administrator account is created. Every computer must have an Administrator account that provides access for setting up new accounts and other tasks related to the management of the computer. It is important to remember the password of the initial account that is set up on the computer, as it will be needed to add user accounts and make changes to the operating system in the future.

Standard

A Standard account is a little more limited than an Administrator account. This type of account is for a typical user who will be using software, copying files, checking e-mail, and accessing the Internet, but will not be in charge of making modifications to the computer and doing things such as adding user accounts and running software updates. Most accounts created for adults on a computer fall under this category.

Managed with Parental Controls

This type of account is designed for children of all ages who will be accessing the computer. Managed with Parental Controls allows you to set a designated time frame when the user is allowed to log on to the computer. It also provides tools for limiting Internet content and applications that can be accessed using this account, and even allows you to create a list of Web sites that can be viewed or e-mail addresses that can be used on the computer.

Sharing Only

A Sharing Only account doesn't allow the user to log onto the computer. It does, however, provide low-level file sharing access via the file sharing or FTP option in the Sharing preferences pane.

Guest

A Guest account allows a guest to temporarily log on to your computer in order to perform basic tasks such as checking e-mail, browsing the Internet, and printing files. A Guest account is created automatically in Snow Leopard, but is disabled by default. Once enabled, the Guest account, which does not require a password, can be used for the time that the person is logged in using that account. Once the person logs out of the Guest account, all the information and files in the Guest account's Home folder are deleted, making it easy for several guests to access this account. It always stays organized and will not accumulate unnecessary or unwanted files.

Creating user accounts

In the next exercise, you'll begin by creating a new Standard account on your computer to allow another user to access the computer. Standard accounts are useful for coworkers, spouses, or friends who also need to use your computer.

If you follow the steps to create a new user account, the account can be easily deleted at the end of the lesson. You can also replace the names used in the following steps with the actual name of another person who needs access to your computer. The account you'll be creating in the following steps is an actual working account.

Creating a Standard account

1   From the Apple menu (), choose System Preferences to display the System Preferences pane. Click Accounts under the System category to display the Accounts preferences pane. Before you can make any changes in the Accounts preference pane, you need to authenticate using an Administrator account on this computer.

2   Click the Lock icon () in the lower-left corner of the Accounts preference pane. Type the username and password of an Administrator account on this computer. This should be the account you are currently using or the account that you initially used when you configured Snow Leopard.

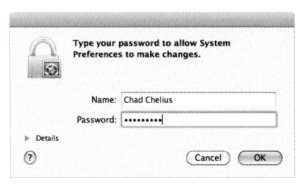

To make any changes to the Accounts preference pane, you must authenticate using an Administrator's account.

3   Click the plus sign (+) in the lower-left corner of the Accounts preference pane to add a new account to the computer.

4   In the New Account drop-down menu, choose Standard. In the Full Name text field, type **John Doe** or type the full name of the actual person who will be using this account. Press the Tab key to enter the next text field.

5   In the Account name text field, you can use the suggestion johndoe that is created when you tabbed into the text field, or you can enter your own name. This is commonly referred to as the short name. Keep the suggested value of johndoe. Press the Tab key on the keyboard.

6   Type a password that you'd like to use for this account. It's common practice to provide an initial basic password to provide to the user, then allow them to change the password once they've logged into their account. Type the word **password** in the Password text field and also in the Verify text field. This simply verifies that both text fields contain the same value. Press the Tab key on your keyboard.

For added security, use upper- and lowercase characters as well as numbers when creating a password. This makes the password harder for someone to guess. If you want help creating a password, you can click the Password Assistant icon (?) to the right of the password text field to generate a password for you.

7   In the Password hint text field, type a hint that will help the user remember their password if they happen to forget it. Type **your name** in the Password hint text field, then press the Create Account button. A window appears asking if you would like to keep automatic login. Click the Turn Off Automatic Login button. If automatic logon remains on, any user can gain access to your information when the computer is restarted because your account will automatically logon without requiring a password. The new account appears in the account list on the left side of the Accounts preference pane.

If a standard user forgets his or her password, any user with an Administrator account can reset the password for that account. If an Administrator forgets his or her account, another user with administrative access can reset the password.

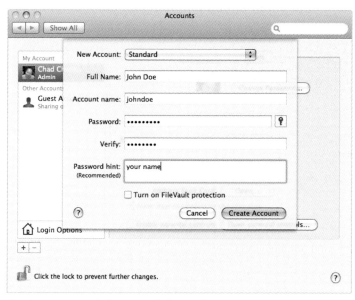

Creating a new account in Snow Leopard allows another user to access your computer.

Congratulations! You've created a new account that another user can use to log on to your computer.

FileVault

When creating a new user account in Snow Leopard, there's a checkbox to *Turn on FileVault protection*. This feature encrypts the Home folder of the user of the account, providing secure protection in the event that someone steals your computer and tries to access the information in your Home folder. FileVault is a very intelligent feature that decrypts your Home folder when you log into your account but re-encrypts it when you log out of your account. This feature is useful if you store sensitive data on your computer that you wouldn't want to be accessed by anyone else. For more information on FileVault, go to the Apple web site at *apple.com*.

Creating a Managed with Parental Controls account

A Managed with Parental Controls account is useful for children in your family that will be accessing your computer. This type of account allows an Administrator to limit a child's access to certain applications and content on the computer.

1 With the Accounts preference pane still open on your screen, click the plus sign (+) in the lower left corner of the Accounts preference pane.

2 In the New Account drop-down menu, choose Managed with Parental Controls.

3 In the Full Name text field, type **Jane Doe**. Press the Tab key on your keyboard.

4 In the Account name text field, accept the default value of janedoe. Press the Tab key on your keyboard.

5 In the Password and Verify text fields, type **password**.

6 In the Password hint text field, type **your name**. Press the Create Account button.

7 Choose System Preferences > Quit System Preferences to exit the System Preferences pane.

Now that you've created an account that is controlled with Parental Controls, read the next section to see how you can configure Parental Controls to limit a user's access on the computer.

Configuring Parental Controls

As the name implies, Parental Controls allows a parent or guardian to control what type of access is allowed for a user account created for a child or minor. With Parental Controls, you can limit which applications can be accessed using the account, as well as what Internet sites can be accessed, thereby protecting a user from viewing inappropriate material.

System

1   From the Apple menu (⚫), choose System Preferences to display the System Preferences pane.

2   Press the Parental Controls button under the System category to display the Parental Controls preference pane.

3   To make any changes, you need to authenticate as an Administrator by clicking the Lock icon (🔒) in the lower-left corner of the Parental Controls preference pane. Type the username and password of an Administrator of this computer. Again, this is probably the user that you initially set up when configuring Snow Leopard.

4   Select the Jane Doe account in the accounts list on the left side of the Parental Controls preference pane.

5   Make sure that the System button is highlighted at the top of the preference pane.

6   The *Use Simple Finder* checkbox at the top of the screen provides a simplified user interface for inexperienced users. This setting can be useful for young children or even users who are not adept at using a computer. You'll leave this option unchecked.

7   The *Only allow selected applications* checkbox allows you to limit the applications that can be used by the selected user. Turn this checkbox on. Upon doing so, the *Select the applications to allow* section becomes active, allowing you to specify which applications the user can or cannot access with this account.

8   Click the disclosure triangle next to the Internet category to display the Internet applications that can be controlled. Click the checkbox next to *Safari* to disable access to the Safari web browser. Leave the rest of the settings at their defaults.

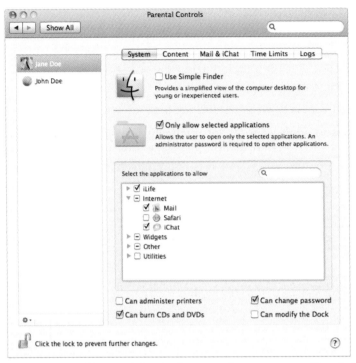

The System section of the Parental Control preference pane allows you to access specific applications and features.

There are four checkboxes at the bottom of the System category of the Parental Controls preference pane:

- **Can administer printers** allows the user to add, remove, and configure printers on your computer.

- **Can burn CDs and DVDs** allows the user to write data to CDs and DVDs using the CD/DVD drive of the computer.

- **Can change password** allows the user to change his or her password. If this is not checked, the user will have to use the password that you or another Administrator assigns to them.

- **Can modify the Dock** allows the user to add and remove items from the Dock.

9   Leave these four checkboxes at their defaults.

Content

1   Press the Content button. The Content category allows you to limit the types of content available to a managed account.

2   The *Hide profanity in Dictionary* checkbox is enabled by default. This prevents the user of a managed account from accessing inappropriate words in the Dictionary application in Snow Leopard. Keep this checkbox enabled.

The Website Restrictions section pertains to Internet access to inappropriate web sites. This section is divided into three categories:

- **Allow unrestricted access to websites** does not limit access in any way.

- **Try to limit access to adult websites automatically** uses a predefined list of known adult web sites to restrict access to those sites. Pressing the Customize button allows you to add or remove web sites from the list of web sites that would otherwise be filtered.

- **Allow access to only these websites** implicitly limits access to only sites that you add to the list of approved sites. This is the most restrictive setting and therefore provides the highest level of control.

3   Leave all these settings at their defaults.

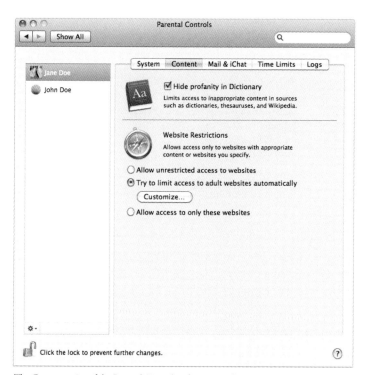

The Content section of the Parental Control preference pane limits access to inappropriate content.

Mail & iChat

1 Press the Mail & iChat button. This section allows you to limit e-mail and iChat exchanges for the user of this account. Enabling either of these checkboxes or both will activate the Only allow emailing and instant messaging with section. Click the *Limit Mail* and *Limit iChat* checkboxes to activate them.

2 Click the plus sign (+) at the bottom left of the Only allow emailing and instant messaging section to add a new address to the accepted list. In the First name text field, type **Mac**, and in the Last name text field, type **User**.

3 In the Allowed accounts section, type **muser@example.com** in the text field and choose Email from the drop-down menu. This adds the accepted e-mail address to the list.

4 Click the plus sign to the right of the Allowed accounts section to add another accepted account for Mac User. Type **muser@aimexample.com** in the field and choose AIM from the drop-down menu.

5 Press the Add button. You have now permitted the user of the account *Jane Doe* to send and receive e-mail and iChat messages to and from Mac User.

Adding an entry to the list of accepted e-mail and iChat addresses permits the user of this account to send and receive e-mail and iChat messages with that address.

At the bottom of the Mail & iChat section of the Parental Controls preference pane is a checkbox and a text field to enter an e-mail address. Enabling this checkbox and providing an e-mail address will send a request to the provided e-mail address whenever the user of the managed account attempts to exchange e-mail with a contact that is not in the approved list. An Administrator of the computer can then decide whether to add the e-mail address to the list of approved addresses.

6 Keep this window open for the next exercise.

Time Limits

Time Limits allow you to control when a user is permitted to log onto the computer using the managed account.

1 Press the Time Limits button.

2 The Weekday time limits and the Weekend time limits enable you to choose a duration of time that the user is allowed access to the computer. Simply enable the *Limit computer use to* checkbox in each section and specify a time duration for each section. For this exercise, leave these checkboxes unchecked.

3 The Bedtime section limits the time frame that the user is allowed to access the computer. Simply enable the *School nights* and *Weekend* checkboxes, then specify a time range that the user is *not* permitted to log onto the computer. Leave these settings unchecked for this exercise.

Time Limits allows you to restrict when a user can use the computer, as well as the duration of time that they can use the computer.

4 Keep this window open for the next exercise.

Logs

The Logs category of the Parental Controls preference pane provides a record of web sites that have been visited, web sites that have been blocked, applications that have been opened, and iChat users that have been contacted. This allows you to keep track of activity that is performed by the user of this managed account.

1   Press the Logs button.

2   The Show activity for drop-down menu allows you to choose a period of time from which to display activity for the selected account. Leave this set to One week.

3   Select the Websites Visited entry under the Log Collections window to display all web sites that have been visited by the user of this account in the past week.

4   Under the Log Collections window, you can also display web sites that have been blocked, applications that have been used, and iChat messages that have taken place. There are currently no entries in the Logs section because nobody has logged in using this account yet.

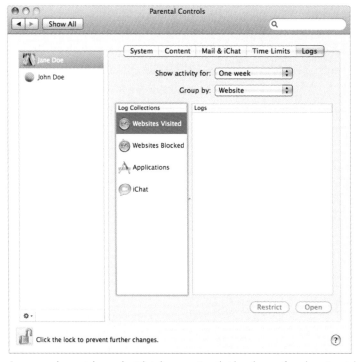

In a managed account, logs are kept that show operations that have been performed or attempted.

5   Choose System Preferences > Quit System Preferences.

Logging in and out of accounts

Now that you've created several accounts on your computer, it's time to understand how to use them for the different users who have accounts on the computer. When multiple accounts exist on the same computer, you need to log in to the computer using the username and password of the account belonging to each user. In addition, when you are finished using the computer, you will log out of your account so that nobody can access your information.

Disabling Automatic Login

When you set up the very first account on your computer (typically done when you initially boot a brand-new computer or immediately after you install Snow Leopard on your computer), Automatic Login is enabled. This means that when a computer is initially booted or restarted, Snow Leopard automatically logs in using the first account that was set up on the computer. This is fine if you are the only one using the computer, but in a multi-user environment, it defeats the purpose of having multiple accounts, because any user can access your account as it is automatically logged in. In the following steps, you'll disable Automatic Login so that a password is required to access all accounts on the computer.

1   Click the System Preferences icon in the Dock to display the System Preferences pane.

2   Press the Accounts button, then press the Login Options button in the lower left corner of the Accounts preference pane. All the options are grayed out by default because you need to authenticate as an Administrator before you can make any changes.

3   Click the Lock icon (🔒) in the lower-left corner of the Accounts preference pane, and type the name and password of an Administrator's account on this computer. Press OK.

After clicking on the Login Options button, you must click on the Lock icon and authenticate as an Administrator in order to make changes to the Login options.

4   In the Automatic login drop-down menu, choose Off to disable Automatic Login at startup.

5   In the Display login window as section, you have the choice to display a list of users who have accounts on your computer, or simply a text field to enter both the username and password of an account on the computer. Leave this setting set to List of users.

6   Choose System Preferences > Quit System Preferences.

Now that you've disabled Automatic Login, it's time to test the accounts that you've created. Continue to the next exercise to learn how to do this.

Testing the accounts

In order to log into another account, you first need to log out of the current account that you're using.

Testing the John Doe account

1   From the Apple menu (), choose Log Out your username where your username is the name of the account that is currently logged in.

2   A window displays, asking if you are sure that you want to quit all applications and log out now. Press the Log Out button.

3   A window with a list of accounts on your computer is displayed. This window is displayed when nobody is logged into the computer. Click the John Doe account icon. When asked for the password for this account, type **password**.

4   You are now logged into the John Doe account.

5   Click the System Preferences icon and in the Personal section of the System Preferences pane, click Desktop & Screen Saver.

6   Make sure that the Desktop button is selected; then click the Nature folder and select the Ladybug screen saver to make it active. Close the Desktop & Screen Saver preference pane.

Changing the Desktop background of each account is a useful way to quickly identify which user is currently logged on to the computer.

7   From the Apple menu, choose Log Out John Doe. When the Log Out dialog box is displayed, press the Log Out button.

Everything seems to be working just fine for this account; now you'll test the managed account for Jane Doe that was created in a previous lesson.

Testing the Jane Doe account

1   Click the Jane Doe icon in the Accounts list and type **password** at the prompt.

2   Once you are logged into the account, click the Safari icon in the Dock to launch the application.

3   Due to the restrictions imposed on this account when you set it up, a dialog box is displayed, indicating that you don't have permission to use the application.

At this point, the user has two options:

- Press OK and work without access to the application.

- Press the Always Allow or the Allow Once button. This option requires the username and password of an Administrator account on this computer.

Due to the restrictions imposed on the Jane Doe account, they can't open the Safari application.

4   Press the Always Allow button and type the name and password of the Administrator account on your computer. Safari launches and displays the default web site. From here on, Jane Doe now has access to the Safari application.

5   Choose Safari > Quit Safari to exit the Web browser.

6   From the Apple menu (), choose Log Out Jane Doe.

You've now seen how to test accounts that you've added to your computer, as well as how to grant access to a managed account when access is not initially allowed.

Fast User Switching

Logging in and out of each account any time another user wants to use the computer takes time and can be inconvenient when several users regularly need to access the computer. Snow Leopard provides a useful tool called Fast User Switching that allows multiple users to be logged on to the computer at the same time. When Fast User Switching is enabled, logging in to a different account is quicker but still requires the password of the account being logged into.

1   Select the Administrator account in the account list and type the password for that account. Press the Login button.

2   From the Apple menu (), choose System Preferences and press the Accounts button.

3 Press the Login Options button and click the Lock icon (🔒) at the bottom left corner of the Accounts preference pane. Type the username and password of the Administrator of the computer.

4 Click the *Show fast user switching menu as* checkbox and choose Name from the drop-down menu. This enables Fast User Switching on this computer.

5 Choose System Preferences > Quit System Preferences.

6 You should now see the short name of the currently logged-in account in the upper-right corner of your screen. Click that name and select John Doe.

7 Type **password** in the Password text field and press the Log In button.

8 A cube effect revolves, switches over to, and logs in to the John Doe account. The John Doe and your Administrator account are both now logged into the computer.

9 Select the name John Doe in the upper right corner of the screen. All of the accounts on this computer are listed, and the accounts that are currently logged in appear with a checkmark to the left of their name.

All accounts that are currently logged in appear with a check mark to the left of their name.

10 Select Jane Doe to log in using that account.

11 Type **password** in the Password text field and press the Log In button.

All three accounts are currently logged in to the computer at the same time. Switching back and forth between the different accounts is now very fast and easy. You're finished testing the accounts, and so you can log out of the Jane Doe and John Doe accounts.

13 With the Jane Doe account active, choose Log Out Jane Doe from the Apple menu (🍎). Press the Log Out button when prompted.

The Accounts list also displays a check mark next to accounts that are currently logged in.

14 Select the John Doe account and type **password** in the Password text field to log into the account.

15 Choose Log Out John Doe from the Apple menu. Press the Log Out button when prompted.

Sharing files with other users

When multiple accounts are created on the same computer, each person's information is kept separate from users of other accounts on the computer. For the most part, this is a good thing; however, there may be times when you want to share a photo or document with another user on the same computer. Fortunately, Snow Leopard provides a means for doing this. Let's take a look at how files can be shared with other users of the same computer.

The Public folder

The Public folder is a folder created automatically for each user that provides a way to share files with other users. The Public folder has permissions of read-only assigned to it. This means that other users can see the contents of each user's Public folder but can't write to it.

1   Log into the computer using the Administrator account by clicking the Administrator's icon in the Accounts list and typing the password for that account. Press Log In.

2   Press Command+N on your keyboard to open a new Finder window, and set the view to list view by clicking the List View button in the toolbar.

3   Navigate to your Home folder. Click the disclosure triangle to the left of the Pictures folder, and also click the disclosure triangle to the left of the Public folder.

Let's say you want to share the New York photos that are in your Pictures folder with other users on your computer.

4   Click the New York folder in your Pictures folder and, while holding down the Option key on your keyboard, drag the New York folder on top of the Public folder; then release your mouse button. The New York folder is copied to the Public folder and is now visible to other users.

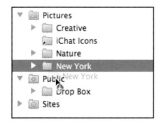

Copying files into your Public folder makes them visible to other users on your computer.

The Drop Box

There will be times when, instead of sharing files with all of the users who have an account on your computer, you want to share a file with only a specific person or persons. This is where the Drop Box comes into play. Each user is automatically given a Drop Box within the Public folder. This Drop Box folder has write-only permissions that allow users to copy files to that folder, but not to see what's inside. This is perfect when you don't want other users to see the files you are sharing with another user. Let's see how to share a file with only John Doe.

1 Press Command+N on your keyboard to open a new Finder window, and press the Icon View button (⬛) in the toolbar.

2 Navigate to ~/Pictures/Creative. This is the Creative folder inside the Pictures folder in your Home folder.

3 Double-click the hard drive icon on your Desktop to open a second Finder window, and position it to the right of the first Finder window.

4 Open the Users folder, then the johndoe folder, and then the Public folder. This file path is /Users/johndoe/Public.

5 Drag the Bridge.jpg file from the window on the left onto the Drop Box folder in the window to the right.

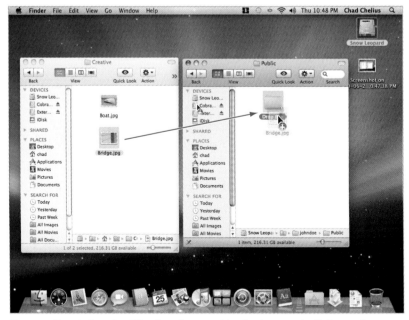

Dragging a file to the Drop Box folder allows the owner of that drop box to see the file, but no other users are able to.

6 A dialog box appears, indicating that you can put files into the Drop Box folder, but you won't be able to see the files. Press OK.

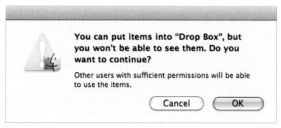

The Drop Box folder can be written to, but you will be unable to see the files in that folder.

Permissions

Permissions refer to the access that is granted to a file, folder, or volume. Sometimes referred to as *privileges*, permissions control who can read, write, or execute a file. Think of a filing cabinet in your home or office that only certain people have a key for. Those people who have a key to the filing cabinet can open and look at or *read* the contents within.

Permissions take this concept one step further by allowing only certain people to write to some folders, meaning they can put contents into a folder but can't see the contents of the folder. It would be difficult to enforce this concept using the filing cabinet analogy. In this lesson, you're simply using the permissions that have already been configured for the Public and Drop Box folders, but it is possible to customize these permissions to meet different needs.

Viewing the results

Now that you've made files available to other users, you'll log into those other accounts to see how other users will access those files.

1 From the Apple menu (), choose Log Out *Your User*, where *Your User* is the name of the Administrator's account that is currently logged in.

2 Press the Log Out button.

3 Choose Jane Doe from the Accounts list and type **password** in the Password text field.

4 Double-click the hard drive icon on the Desktop to open a new Finder window.

5 Open the Users folder, then the folder that contains the name of the Administrator's account on your computer. Open the Public folder, then the New York folder. In this example, the user's name is Chad.

The files are accessible to you because the files are in the Administrator's Public folder. Keep in mind that you don't have to have an Administrator's account to put files in your Public folder. Any user can do this.

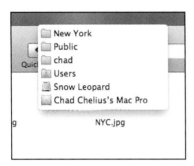

The files are visible in the Administrator's Public folder.

6 From the Apple menu (), choose Log Out Jane Doe. Press the Log Out button.

7 Click the John Doe icon in the accounts list and type **password** in the Password text field.

8 Double-click the hard drive icon on the Desktop to open a new Finder window.

9 Open the Users folder, then the folder that contains the name of the Administrator's account on your computer. Open the Public folder, then the New York folder. Even when you are logged in as a different user, the files are still available from that Administrator's Public folder.

10 Navigate to John Doe's Home folder. Open the Public folder, then the Drop Box folder. The Bridge.jpg file is in the Drop Box folder from when the Administrator copied it there. Only John Doe can see this file.

Because the Bridge.jpg file was copied to John Doe's Drop Box folder, only he can see the file.

11 From the Apple menu, choose Log Out John Doe. Press the Log Out button.

Cleanup

You've created several *test* accounts in this lesson that you probably don't want to remain on your computer. If you created legitimate accounts on your computer using this lesson and want to keep those accounts, you can skip these steps. Otherwise, follow along to remove the John Doe and Jane Doe accounts from your computer.

1 Log into your computer using the Administrator's account.

2 From the Apple menu (), choose System Preferences.

3 Press the Accounts button under the System section of the System Preferences pane.

4 Authenticate with an Administrator's username and password by clicking the Lock icon () in the lower-left corner of the Accounts preference pane.

5 Select the Jane Doe account from the list of accounts on the left side of the Accounts preference pane.

6 Click the minus sign (-) below the accounts list.

At this point, a window appears asking if you are sure that you want to delete this account. You have three options:

- **Save the Home folder as a disk image** saves the contents of this user's Home folder as a disk image so that the contents can still be accessed at a later date if necessary.

- **Don't change the Home folder** leaves the entire Home folder intact within the Users folder, even though the account itself no longer exists.

- **Delete the Home folder** deletes this user's Home folder along with the account.

7 Choose the *Delete the Home folder* radio button and press OK.

8 Repeat steps 5 to 7 for the John Doe account.

9 Choose System Preferences > Quit System Preferences.

Congratulations! You've completed the lesson. You should now have a better understanding of how accounts work, as well as the purpose of the different types of accounts.

Self study

Practice what you've learned in this lesson by setting up real working accounts for other people who need access to your computer. If your computer is in your house and you have children, set up managed accounts for each of them and set limits to when they can log on to their accounts and for how long they can use the computer each day. Once accounts are set up, explain the Public folder and the Drop Box folder to the other users and begin sharing files with one another.

Review

Questions

1 Why is it important to create a user account for each user of a computer?

2 What feature allows you to limit access to Internet content and set daily limits on when the computer can be used for an account?

3 How can you easily share a file with a specific user of a computer without allowing any other users to see that file?

Answers

1 User accounts allow each user to have their own personal working environment that can be customized to their preferences. In addition, user accounts provide privacy to each user, as the files within that user's Home folder are protected from other users.

2 Parental Controls allows you to limit access to Internet content and set daily computer limits.

3 Copy the file to that specific user's Drop Box folder. The Drop Box folder is write-only, meaning that files can be copied to it, but only the owner of that user account can actually see the files.

What you'll learn in this lesson:

- Editing and exporting video with QuickTime X
- Managing media in iTunes
- Working with Front Row

Your Mac as a Media Center

In this lesson, you'll learn how to work with the applications in Snow Leopard that help you organize and access digital media, including music, movies, and photos.

Starting up

You will work with several files from the sl04lessons folder in this lesson. Make sure that you have copied the contents of the sl04lessons folder onto your desktop. This lesson may be easier to follow if those folders are on your desktop.

See Lesson 4 in action!

Use the accompanying video to gain a better understanding of how to use some of the features shown in this lesson. The video tutorial for this lesson can be found on the included DVD.

The Mac as media center

Apple operating systems have always been very conducive to working with digital media; whether music, images, or video, there is a long history between these media and the Apple operating systems. In fact, the management of music, video, podcasts, and iPhone applications is really the job of iTunes. An application such as iPhoto is also designed to help you organize the mountains of digital images you may be creating. What you are beginning to see is the line blurring between the creation of content and the management of this content. In Snow Leopard, there is no better example of this than the updated QuickTime X Player.

QuickTime X

QuickTime technology has been around for quite a while, and with the newly named QuickTime X Player, you have the most fully featured and useful version ever. In the past, upgrading to QuickTime Pro gave you access to very basic editing capabilities such as trimming your video, adding or removing video and audio tracks, and the ability to export to various formats such as MPEG-4.

In addition to the playback features you would expect in a media player, the new version of QuickTime Player has much more powerful features, including the ability to create movie and screen recordings as well as export video to iTunes, MobileMe and YouTube.

QuickTime X Player has undergone a fairly significant visual overhaul. In addition to the new icon for the application, the brushed steel console from previous versions of QuickTime has been replaced with a minimal black user interface. In fact, the entire console for the player has technically disappeared. Player controls are now embedded into the movie, and placing your cursor outside of the player hides the entire interface.

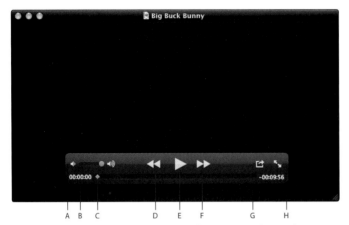

A. *Volume control.* *B*. *Time counter.* *C*. *Seek controller.* *D*. *Reverse Play.* *E*. *Play.*
F. *2x Fast Forward.* *G*. *Trim.* *H*. *Toggle Full Screen.*

QuickTime X Player controls

The controls in the QuickTime X Player are similar to those found in most CD and DVD players and should therefore be familiar to you. However, there are a few extra features that you may also find useful.

1   Locate your sl04lessons folder. Double-click the BigBuckBunny_640x360.mov file to open it in QuickTime X Player. When the movie opens, the controls appear inside your movie. Click and drag the controller bar to the top of the player. You can move this controller anywhere you like, however, it is always inside the player frame.

This lesson makes use of the movie BigBuckBunny, a short movie made as part of the Peach open movie project and licensed under the Creative Commons Attribution 3.0 license. The copyright belongs to the Blender Foundation. For more information, visit www.bigbuckbunny.org.

2   Press the Play button. The controls remain onscreen. Place your cursor outside the player, and both the controls and the QuickTime X Player title bar disappear.

3   Press the spacebar to pause the movie, and the controller reappears. Press the right arrow key on your keyboard to advance the movie one frame at a time. Press and hold the right arrow key down to advance through the frames continuously. This also works with the left arrow key, only in reverse.

4   Press the Fast Forward button, and the movie begins to play at twice the speed. Press the Fast Forward button again to play at 4x speed. Press the Fast Forward button one more time to play at 8x speed.

Press the Fast Forward button to play the movie at twice the speed.

Press the spacebar to stop playback.

Press and hold the Option key and click either the Fast Forward or Rewind button to advance speed by 1/10 at a time.

5 Click and drag the playhead beneath the player controls to locate a specific point in the movie. Notice that to the left of the controls, the time counter displays how much time has passed, and to the right there is a display of how much time is left.

KEYBOARD SHORTCUTS	VIEW
Command+F	Enter full screen
Command+1	View actual size
Command ı 3	Fit to screen
Command+4	Fill screen (only available while in Full Screen mode)
Command+5	Panoramic mode (only available in Full Screen mode)

QuickTime X Player recording capabilities

New to QuickTime X Player is the ability to record movie, audio, and screen recordings. These features transform QuickTime X Player into an application that creates content rather than just playing it back.

Creating movie recordings

This exercise relies on access to a built-in iSight camera or external webcam. You can quickly and easily create videos using QuickTime X Player if you have a web or video camera connected to your system. This is made even easier if you have a laptop or iMac model that has a web camera pre-installed. If you have used the Photo Booth or iChat applications in previous versions of OS X, you may be familiar with the concept of built-in video recording.

1   With QuickTime X Player open, choose File > New Movie Recording. If you have one of the iSight-enabled systems or have connected a webcam or video camera, you see a preview of your image in the Movie Recording window. In this case, you are using the built-in camera in your MacBook.

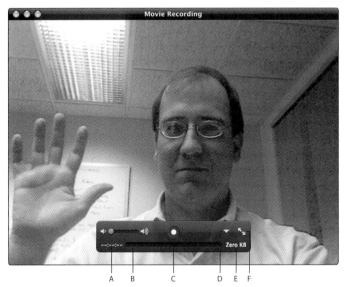

A. Time elapsed. B. Audio play through slider. C. Record. D. Recording options menu.
E. File size F. Full Screen.

2   Click on the Recording options menu in the controller bar. Here you have options to choose which device to use for video and audio input; for example, this would be relevant if you had a built-in iSight camera and a webcam connected. For audio input, you could use either your system's built-in microphone or another input source such as a USB microphone.

3   Select the Maximum quality option. You have three options for the quality of your videos; changing these values affects the size of your final video file.

QUALITY	CODEC	RESOLUTION
Medium	H.264 (video) AAC (audio)	320x240
H.264 (video) AAC (audio)	H.264 (video) AAC (audio)	640x480
Maximum	Y'CbCr (video) 24-bit integer	640x480

4 By default, new movies are saved in the current user's Movies folder.

You may designate another folder to save movies to by selecting the Choose option, navigating to the folder, and pressing Choose again.

5 Below the Record button are your recording levels. Clap your hands loudly or speak loudly; if your microphone is picking up a signal, you see the levels respond. In the top left corner of the controller is the playthrough slider. Click and drag this slider carefully to about the middle of the control to determine the volume of the external playback.

In general, you do *not* want playthrough on if you are using a microphone, as it will likely cause audio feedback. However, because you have the option of connecting the line-in from a musical instrument, for example, this control would allow you to hear the instrument as you play.

6 Press the Record button, and QuickTime X Player begins to capture video. Note that the counter on the left tallies the time, and on the right, the file size begins to increase as the recording continues.

Press the Record button.

7 Press the Stop button. After a few moments, the completed movie appears in QuickTime X Player, ready for playback.

Audio recording works the exact same way as video recording: both result in a Quicktime.mov file. In the case of an audio recording, you simply have no video track.

8 Double-click the hard drive icon on your desktop, then navigate to the current user's Movies folder. The first movie recording you make is given the generic filename Movie Recording.mov. Additional movie recordings will add successive numbers to the filename: Movie Recording 2.mov, Movie Recording 3.mov, and so on.

9 Double-click the file Movie Recording.mov to view your movie. When you are done, close the file.

Creating a screen recording

In addition to creating original video and audio recordings, QuickTime X Player allows you to make a screen recording of your desktop. Creating a still screenshot has been a feature of the Mac OS X operating system for a while, however, creating a screen recording in Mac OS X always required a third-party application. Now, you can create screen recordings for tutorial or other purposes using the built-in capabilities of QuickTime X Player.

1 In QuickTime X Player, choose File > New Screen Recording. The simple Screen Recording controller appears.

2 Click the small menu in the bottom-right corner to view options for screen recording. For the Microphone settings, you have three options: None, Built-in Input, and Built-in Microphone. If you choose None, you will have no audio track, just video. Built-in Input allows you to connect an external microphone or other audio source, and Built-in Microphone uses your Mac's internal microphone (if available).

If you have an internal microphone, choose the Built-in Microphone option; otherwise, choose None.

Choose a Microphone option.

To see if a sound input is active, check to see if the audio meter is activated by clapping. You should see levels appear if the audio input is functioning.

If you still do not see audio levels, you may need to check the sound input on your system. Open System Preferences, click the Sound icon, then select the Input tab. Here you can set the input volume for the microphone; make sure it is not set to mute. A sound level of about half way is a good place to start.

3 In the Sound Recording menu for Quality, choose High. You only have two choices here: Medium and High. Both record the entire screen; the main difference is the codec used. Medium quality uses Photo-JPEG compression, and High quality uses H.264. Creating files using the High quality setting can result in smaller file sizes than Medium quality, however older systems may not have the processing power necessary for this option.

If you have used third-party screen-capturing software in the past, you may be used to setting the frame rate and resolution for your recordings. QuickTime X Player automatically sets the frame rate based on the characteristics of your system and always records full screen. Before recording any important screen recordings, you should always do some tests using any sample applications you want to record. Also, close any non-relevant applications that you have open in order to maximize your system resources.

4   Ensure that the Save to section in the menu is set to Movies. Like the video recording from the last exercise, this places the screen recording into the Movies folder.

5   Press the Record button. A warning appears, letting you know that the window will be hidden during the recording. This is necessary to allow a clear view of your desktop during the recording. Press the Start Recording button.

6   To record a brief sample of video, click the Safari icon in the dock. If you want to test your audio, say a few words as the recording is taking place. After 10 or 15 seconds, close Safari, then stop the recording by pressing the Stop Recording button in the top-right corner of your screen. (You could also use the keyboard shortcut Command+Ctrl+Esc.)

Press the Stop Recording button.

7   When you are done recording, the final movie appears on your screen. Press the spacebar to play the screen recording. After a few seconds, press the spacebar again to pause.

By default, QuickTime X Player scales the size of the movie to fit on your desktop; however, the movie is actually the same size as your screen.

8   Choose Window > Full Screen, and your movie expands to full screen. Although this is when the recording looks the best (because there is a 1:1 ratio between the monitor resolution and the movie), it may be impractical for the user to view, as they will not have access to their desktop. In certain cases, exporting this movie at a smaller width and height may provide a more usable experience for the user, although, as you will see in later exercises, iTunes provides a convenient interface for viewing high-resolution movies.

9   Press the Esc key to exit the full screen view.

Editing video with QuickTime X Player

QuickTime X Player allows you to make simple edits to your movie files. For example, if you edit the recording from the previous exercise, you might want to remove the first 5 seconds or so in order to go immediately to the important section. It's important to note that the editing features of QuickTime X Player are very convenient for making quick and easy edits; however, if you want to do more substantial editing, you should consider a dedicated editing application such as iMovie.

1 Navigate to the Movies folder on your hard drive and double-click the file Screen Recording.mov that you created in the last exercise. You can find a short screen recording with the same name in the sl04lessons folder if you want to use this one instead.

2 Choose Edit > Trim, and the player controls change into the Trim controls; your movie displays as a timeline with a series of thumbnail images.

3 Place your cursor over the yellow handle on the far-left side of the timeline, and click and drag to the right. As you drag, you see the current frame displayed in the player; this frame will end up being the first frame of your movie. If you completed the previous exercise, locate the point at which Safari first opens. If using the file from the sl04lessons folder, locate the 6-second mark (approximately).

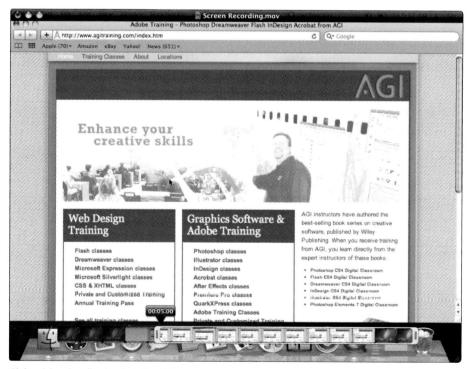

Click and drag the yellow handle to the right.

4 Place your cursor over the yellow handle on the far-right side of the timeline, and click and drag to the left. This frame represents the last frame of your trimmed movie. Locate the point directly after you closed Safari. If using the sl04lessons file, drag to approximately the 16-second mark.

5 Press the yellow Trim button on the lower-right corner of the controller, and you have a new shortened movie. Press the spacebar to begin playing your newly trimmed movie.

6 Choose File > Save As and navigate to your sl04lessons folder. Note that you do not technically have a Save command available because if you were to save right now, all the original video you trimmed would be lost. Saving as a new file gives you a new trimmed version while leaving the original as a backup. Rename your file **ScreenRecording_trimmed** and press Save.

Exporting video with QuickTime X Player

Using QuickTime X Player, you can export video in file formats targeted for different scenarios. The important thing to remember is that QuickTime X Player presents you with a number of different presets to export your movie and that these presets are based on the original resolution of your video. There are a few different ways to export your video in QuickTime X Player: you can always export using the standard Save as commands, but there is also the new Share command in the menu that allows you to export video optimized for iTunes, MobileMe, or YouTube. You'll first take a look at the standard exporting options.

Exporting video for the desktop

QuickTime X Player dynamically presents you with various presets to choose from when it comes time to export your video. These presets are based on the original size of your movie: Apple's goal here is to remove options that result in poor-quality video. You'll see how this works by first looking at the options for a high-resolution screen recording and then looking at the options for a low-resolution file.

1 Open Screen_recording_1280x800t.mov. Choose Window > Show Movie Inspector. The Movie Inspector window shows you the settings for this movie; this video is 1280x800 pixels and is exported from a screen recording. Press the Close button in the top-left corner to close the Movie Inspector window.

2   Choose File > Save As. Click the drop-down menu labeled Format.

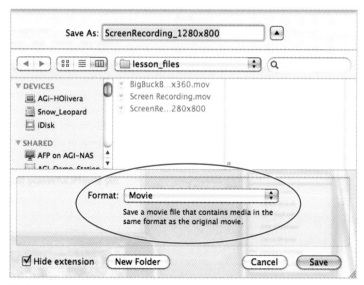

The Save As dialog box.

This table contains all the available formats for export.

FORMAT	DESCRIPTION	RESOLUTION	FILE EXTENSION
iPhone (Cellular)	Optimizes a movie for viewing on an iPhone (or other mobile device) on a cellular network	176x110	.3gp
iPhone	Optimizes a movie for viewing on an iPhone	640x400	.m4v
iPod	Optimizes a movie for viewing on an iPod	1152x720	.m4v
Apple TV	Optimizes a movie for viewing on Apple TV	640x480	.m4v
Computer	Optimizes a movie for viewing on a computer	Same size (1280x800)	.m4v

As you can see, with the exception of the iPhone (Cellular) version, all of the formats are exported in the MPEG-4 standard, .m4v; however, they all have different widths and heights based on the standard for their respective platforms.

What about those HD formats?

There are three presets in this dialog for HD. Although it's a bit beyond the scope of this lesson to fully explain what's happening here, the concept is fairly straightforward: The QuickTime X Player always presents you with as many options as possible when exporting. *High Definition* video is just a term that represents the number of pixels in a video file.

There are different types of HD video, however. In the case of the screen recording in this example, you have a file that has sufficient pixel information (1280x800) so that it can be downsampled to the common HD sizes: HD 1080p, HD 720p, and HD 480p.

Note that this does not mean you convert existing *standard video* to HD using QuickTime. If you do not have a video file of sufficient quality to begin with, QuickTime X Player does not give you these options.

Press Cancel, then press the Close button (⊗); you won't be exporting this file. Choose File > Open File, select the BigBuckBunny_640x360.mov file from your sl04lessons folder, and choose File > Save As. Make sure you are saving into the same sl04lessons folder. Click the Format drop-down menu. Notice that you now have fewer presets to choose from because this movie is only 640x360. QuickTime does not let you export to sizes significantly larger than your original.

The format options change based on the file you are trying to save.

3   Press Cancel, then press the Close button (⊗). If you want to test exporting on your system, choose the iPhone option; however, the source movie is 10 minutes long, and even on relatively speedy systems, this will take a few minutes to export. In this next step, you will be opening an exported version to save time.

4   In QuickTime X, choose File > Open File, choose the BigBuckBunny_iPhone.m4v file located in your sl04lessons folder, and press Open. This would be the resulting file if you had saved the file using the iPhone setting. The original file was approximately 121MB, and this file, optimized for the iPhone, is 71MB.

5   Choose File > Close to close the video file.

Exporting video for the Web

QuickTime X Player has excellent options for saving your videos for the Web. In this exercise, you will learn how to export your screen recording file in formats optimized for online viewing.

1   In QuickTime X Player, choose File > Open File, select the Screen Recording.mov file, and choose Open.

2   Choose File > Save for Web. From the Where drop-down menu, choose Other, and navigate to your sl04lessons folder. Locate the folder export_video_for_web (which is currently empty) and press Choose.

Make sure all the checkboxes for the three export types (iPhone, iPhone [Cellular], and Computer) are checked. This exports three files at a time.

Set the options in the Save for Web dialog box.

3   In the Save as field, type **my_movie** and press Save. Three different versions of your movie are created. (Even though this is a short clip, the exporting process takes a few moments.)

4   In the Export Progress window, you can keep track of the progress of the three files. When finished, navigate to your sl04lessons folder on the desktop, then the export_ video_for_web folder that you designated. Double-click to open it, then double-click the my_movie folder to view the exported files, as well as additional files that were generated by QuickTime X Player.

View the files created by the QuickTime X Player.

Double-click the my_movie.html file to open it in Safari. This page contains automatically generated instructions on how to work with the exported movie files. Helpful tips on how to upload your files and work with the movie controllers are listed here for your benefit.

5   Click the large thumbnail to see a preview of how your movie would appear in the browser. When you are finished, close your browser.

Sharing movies for iTunes, MobileMe, and YouTube

Although the Save for Web feature demonstrated in the last exercise is very useful, it also assumes that you have access to a web server and are responsible for the last step of putting the files online. QuickTime X Player's sharing feature simplifies this step by exporting your video directly to specific locations locally and on the Web.

This exercise refers to two services: Apple MobileMe and the YouTube web site. Both these services require user accounts. If you do not have an account, feel free to read through these steps; however, you will not be able to export to the Web.

1   Click File > Open File, navigate to your sl04lessons folder if necessary, and choose the ScreenRecording_1280x800.mov file. Choose Share > iTunes, and a window appears with three options for your movie: iPhone&iPod, Apple TV, and Computer.

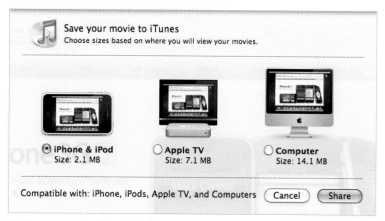

The Save your movie to iTunes dialog box.

These three settings are virtually identical to the settings you saw in the earlier *Exporting video for the desktop* exercise. The main difference here is that exporting using this command *always* puts your exported movie into the user's Movies folder. iTunes links to this folder by default, and all movies found here are picked up and available to iTunes.

2   Press Share. An Export Progress dialog box appears. The file is exported and triggers the opening of iTunes when complete.

Exporting to your MobileMe Gallery on the Web

MobileMe is a service provided by Apple that helps you synchronize your local data to the Internet. One component of the service is the Gallery space, which allows you to post images and videos to share on the Web. If you have an active MobileMe account and are currently online, you may follow these steps to publish your movies to the Web.

1   Choose Share > MobileMe Gallery. If you are currently connected to the MobileMe service, you are presented with a Publish window and asked to provide a title and description for your movie. (If you are not connected, you need to provide login information.)

2   Click Share, and your movie is published to your iDisk storage space. After processing, your movie is saved to a gallery page and you are provided with a URL in the Export Progress window when the export is complete.

3   Clicking the generated link in the Export Progress window brings up your MobileMe gallery page in the browser. You can now share this URL with others, and anyone with an Internet connection can now view your movie.

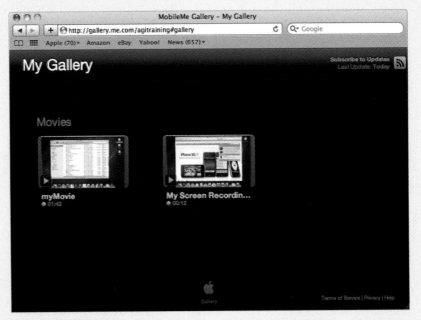

The MobileMe gallery with two movies

Exporting to YouTube on the Web

If you have a YouTube account, you may publish your movies using the QuickTime X Player.

1 Choose Share > YouTube. You need to enter your YouTube name and password. (You must be online for this to work.)

2 After successful login, you should choose an appropriate category for your video, as well as a title, description, and any tags you would like to be associated with your video. By default, videos are publicly accessible, however, you can check the *Make this movie personal* checkbox to make the video private.

Choose a category and add any tags to your video.

3 Press Next when all the information is complete, and your video is exported to YouTube. Based on the size of this file, it may take a while to process. When the process is complete, you are provided with a URL in the Export Progress window. Clicking this URL sends you to your YouTube page.

Managing Media with iTunes 8

Although iTunes was once just an application for organizing and playing your music, over the years it has expanded and now can be seen as the media center for your Mac. In addition to music, you can also view movies and TV shows, listen to audio and podcasts, and, using the Bonjour networking technology, share this music over a local network. Additionally, if your Mac has support for Apple Remote, you can leverage iTunes and Front Row for an interactive experience with your digital media. You'll get a chance to work with Front Row in the next exercise, but first you'll learn how to access, organize, and share your media with iTunes.

Working with the iTunes library and media views

iTunes is used to store, organize, and play your digital media. Much of the process of working with media is handled automatically in Snow Leopard. For example, iTunes uses the current user's Music folder to store music files purchased from the iTunes Store or when you synchronize an iPod or iPhone to your computer.

1   Open the sl04lessons folder and double-click the BigBuckBunny_iphone.m4v file. This launches iTunes and simultaneously copies this file to a subfolder named Movies in the iTunes Music folder. The extension .m4v indicates an MPEG-4 file, and double-clicking these files automatically opens them in iTunes. The movie begins to play. Press the spacebar to stop it, then press the Close button (●) in the upper-left corner.

2   Keep iTunes open, open the sl04lessons folder on the desktop, then drag and drop the two files, Screen_Recording.mov and ScreenRecording_1280x800.mov, into the iTunes interface. Whether music or movie files, it is important to note that when a media file is added to iTunes, a copy is made and placed into the iTunes library. So technically, you now have two copies of each of these files: one in the sl04lessons folder and one in the iTunes library.

3 The left-hand column of the iTunes interface divides functionality into three categories: Library, Store, and Playlists. The Library organizes your media by type, in this case, you have Music, Movies, TV Shows, Podcasts, and Radio. The Store and Playlists categories also have their own sections. Select the Movies category in the Library section.

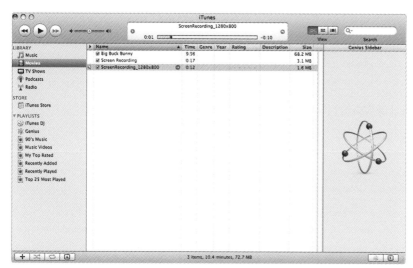

The iTunes application.

 You can customize which categories appear in the Library by choosing iTunes > Preferences and selecting or deselecting the categories as desired.

4 There are three ways to view media in iTunes: the list view, the grid view, or Cover Flow. If it is not already selected, press the list view button (▦) in the View section located in the upper right corner. In list view, all your media are listed, along with additional information about your media.

5   Choose View > View Options. This list represents the additional columns you can add (or remove) to your views. Select the *Size* checkbox to add this column.

Select additional columns to add to the Movies section.

 You can also Ctrl+click or Right-click the columns in the list view to add or remove categories.

A size column has now been added, and you can view the file sizes of your media. Columns that you add are specific to the type of media selected. The Music columns, for example, are independent from the Movie columns.

6   Double-click the Big Buck Bunny movie in the list view, and the movie begins to play in the iTunes window. The movie scales to the current size of the application. The same controller found in QuickTime X Player is also here in iTunes.

After a few moments of playing, place your cursor in the top left corner of the movie, and a Close button appears. Click it once to close the movie and return to the list view.

7   Press the grid view button (▦). When viewing movies, this view displays a frame of the movie. When viewing music, it displays the album cover if available.

8   Press the Cover Flow button (▤). This view splits your iTunes application into two screens. The top half presents the thumbnail images of your movies (or in the case of music, the album covers) in a perspective view. You also have the benefit of the list view in the bottom half of the screen.

The Cover Flow view.

You have two forms of navigation: clicking on the title in the list view advances the *cover* images; using the slider in Cover Flow view allows you to visually reverse or advance through the images.

9   With the Big Buck Bunny movie still selected, press Command+F to enter Full Screen mode. Your Cover Flow view is now in full screen and the controls are below. Press the Play button, and the movie plays in full screen. (In the case of music, when you press Play in the full-screen Cover Flow view, the song plays and the title of the song appears beneath the album cover.)

10 Press the Esc key to exit full screen, and Esc again to return to the Cover Flow view.

11 Press the Close buttton (⊗) in the upper left corner to close iTunes.

Sharing your iTunes library over a network

If you have more than one Mac on the same network, you can enable iTunes for sharing. Once the sharing feature is turned on, that system then becomes discoverable on the network and other people can play the media you have stored in your iTunes library.

1   In iTunes, choose iTunes > Preferences and then click on the Sharing icon. To share your entire library, select the checkbox labeled Share my library on my local network. You may also choose to share only certain playlists and categories by choosing Share selected playlists and checking only the categories you want to share. You may also set a password to prevent unauthorized users from accessing your iTunes library.

2   The Look for shared libraries option should be on by default. When checked, this feature browses the local network and locates any systems currently sharing their libraries.

Using Front Row to manage your media

Front Row is an application that you can think of as an extension of iTunes. As the role of the personal computer continues to evolve, the desire to have the sort of full-screen experience of television has merged with the instant-access nature of the iTunes library to form Front Row.

Combined with an Apple Remote, you can remotely navigate through your digital library using Apple's distinctive user interface, and play music, movies, and more. Although some of the larger Apple hardware comes close to duplicating the experience of a small- or medium-sized television, with widescreen televisions becoming more popular, there is still a long way to go. However, if you are technically savvy and have the proper cables and ports on your television, you can theoretically bring the Front Row experience to your living room.

 Although the full potential of Front Row is enabled with an Apple Remote, it is still possible to walk through this lesson without one.

1   Navigate to your Applications folder, locate Front Row, and double-click it to launch the application. By design, the Front Row interface is full screen and you do not have access to your Mac OS X desktop.

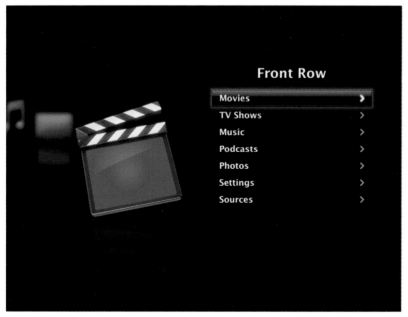

Launch the Front Row application.

You see a number of different categories onscreen. Any media you have added to iTunes are available here. In a similar fashion, any images in your Pictures folder (imported using iPhoto, for example) are available.

2   If you have your Apple Remote, press the - (minus) button to navigate down the list. Alternatively, you may use the down arrow key on your keyboard. Navigate down to the Settings category and press the Play button on the Apple Remote (or press the Return key on your keyboard).

3   In the settings screen, you can turn the Screen Saver and Sound Effects option on or off. Don't make any changes. To return to the main menu, press the Menu button on the Apple Remote (or press the Esc key on your keyboard).

Using the Apple Remote or your keyboard arrows, navigate up to the Movies category and press the Play button (or press the Return key on your keyboard).

Navigate to the Movies Folder category and press Play or press Return. Movies that you have added to the Movies folder are visible and can also be played.

Add the Movies folder to Front Row.

If you are connected to the Internet, you can view trailers for movies and television shows that are available for purchase or rent on iTunes, and also view theatrical trailers that are being hosted on the apple.com/trailers *web page.*

4   Navigate back to the Movies category by pressing the Menu button on the Apple Remote or pressing the Return key on the keyboard. Press the minus button (–) on your remote to highlight the Big Buck Bunny movie. Press the Play button to select it. Press the Play button again, or press Return key on your keyboard, to begin playing the movie.

5   On the Apple Remote, once a movie (or music file) is playing, the controls you used to navigate the list are now controlling the movie. Press the minus button (–), and the volume decreases. Press the Forward button once to jump ahead 30 seconds at a time. Press and hold the Forward button to fast-forward through the movie.

When using the keyboard, the up and down arrow keys control the volume, and the right and left arrow keys control the fast forward and rewind. The spacebar pauses and plays.

6   Continue to press the Menu button on the Apple Remote to return to the Movies menu. Press the Menu button a few times, and you eventually exit out of Front Row. On the keyboard, pressing the Esc key achieves the same goal.

Playing media through Apple TV or a compatible television

If using Front Row interests you and you want to create a true media center that integrates your Mac with your television or entertainment center, there are a few options. The number of variables involved makes it difficult to provide a single solution, but two options are Apple TV and connecting directly to your computer.

Apple TV

Apple TV is Apple's official hardware solution that allows you to watch movies from your computer on your TV. On its own, Apple TV allows you to buy and rent movies and view them through a standard wired connection (an HDMI cable, for example). It is a standalone system that does not need a computer, but there are benefits to connecting your Mac system to Apple TV, including the ability to synchronize your iTunes music and even play movies and view photos located on your computer. For up-to-date information, visit *apple.com/appletv*.

Connecting directly from your system

It is also possible to connect your computer to a TV to playback directly, however, this option can be tricky if you are not familiar with the various ports, cables, and adapters that might come into play on both your computer and your TV. Here is a relatively basic configuration:

*   A Mac system with a DVI port (traditionally used to connect to a computer monitor)

*   An HDTV television with a connection for an HDMI cable

*   An HDMI cable

*   A DVI-to-HDMI converter

*   A 1/8-inch to RCA cable for the audio

This configuration allows you to connect your DVI Mac system to an HDMI-enabled TV. However, it does not necessarily solve other dilemmas such as connecting to a larger home theater system.

Self study

Create a new video or screen recording for at least one minute. Experiment with exporting different sizes in the Format menu. If you have your own web server, try saving to the Web and then following the generated instructions for putting the files online. In iTunes, create playlists and experiment with accessing them in Front Row. If you have photos on your current system, try viewing them through Front Row.

Review

Questions

1 When exporting a movie from QuickTime X Player, how are the presets in the format determined and why is that important?

2 When you drag and drop a media file such as music or a movie onto the iTunes Player, what happens to this file?

3 When using Front Row, do you need to be connected to the Internet?

Answers

1 The Preset movie sizes in the Format menu are determined by the original resolution of the movie file. This is important because you can only export a movie down to the same or smaller resolution. Exporting a movie at a larger width and height than the original would result in a poor-quality video, and QuickTime X Player prevents you from doing this.

2 Dragging and dropping a media file onto the iTunes Player creates a copy of the file in the iTunes music library located in the user's Music folder.

3 No, although being connected to the Internet would allow you to view iTunes trailers online and access any Shared iTunes libraries that you may be connected to.

Lesson 5

What you'll learn
in this lesson:

- Burning CDs and DVDs
- Using Time Machine
- Using MobileMe
- Using Disk Utility
- Using Software Update

Backing Up and
Protecting Your Data

The files you save on your computer are valuable and can be costly or impossible to recover if your hard disc fails or your computer is damaged. Snow Leopard offers several options that make it easy for you to keep a second copy of the contents of your hard drive, allowing you to easily recover items that are might otherwise be lost if your computer or hard drive fails or disappears.

Starting up

There are no lesson files with this lesson, so you can get started right away.

See Lesson 5 in action!

Use the accompanying video to gain a better understanding of how to use some of the features shown in this lesson. The video tutorial for this lesson can be found on the included DVD.

Burning CDs and DVDs

You already know that the Finder is the primary way of accessing, organizing, and managing your files and applications. But when you need to back up data from your computer, the Finder can also burn files to a CD or DVD. You can use that disc as a backup, or to copy those files to another computer. Snow Leopard burns discs that can also be used in Windows and on other types of computers.

If your computer is equipped with a Combo drive, you can burn files onto CDs. If your computer has a SuperDrive, you can burn files onto either CDs or DVDs.

1 Insert a blank disc into the optical drive of your computer. A dialog box may appear, asking you to choose what you want to happen from the pop-up menu. You can also check *Make this action the default* if you want the same action to occur every time you insert a blank disc.

You can choose an action that you want to occur every time you insert a blank disc.

The disc appears on your desktop.

2 Double-click the disc to open it, then click-and-drag the files and folders you want into its window. The Finder creates aliases to the files in the disc's window, and will copy them onto the disc when it is burned. The original files are not moved or removed.

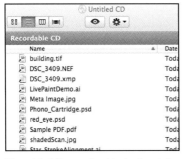

Your original files are aliased in the disc window, not moved or removed.

3   Organize and name the files exactly as you want them in the disc window.

When the disc is burned, the Finder will duplicate the names and locations from the aliases in the disc window. Once the disc is burned, you *will not* be able to change their names and locations on the disc.

4   Choose File > Burn Disc, and follow the instructions.

The aliased files are burned to the disc. In addition, if any folder you copied contains aliases, the original files for those aliases are also burned to the disc.

Follow the directions to choose a name, burn speed, and save location for your burn folder.

5   The Finder asks whether to cancel burning or to continue without an item if it can't find the original file for an alias. If you cancel, no files are burned.

6   If you eject the disc without burning it, the Finder creates a burn folder with the items you placed on the disc, and places that folder on your desktop.

If you eject a disc without burning it, the Finder creates a burn folder.

7   To burn a disc from the Finder sidebar, click the burn icon (⚆) that appears next to it.

8   Alternatively, you can hold down the Ctrl key as you click any disc icon and choose Burn Disc from the context menu that appears.

Create a burn folder by choosing File > New Burn Folder if you frequently burn the same items. Copy your items to the new burn folder, open the burn folder (if necessary), and click Burn.

Using Time Machine

Snow Leopard's Time Machine feature allows you to automatically back up your entire system. It keeps an up-to-date copy of everything on your Mac, and enables you to easily *go back in time* to recover files.

You'll now learn how to set up Time Machine to perform backups, restore items (or your entire system) from a backup, and use existing backups on a new Mac.

Setting up Time Machine for backups

Setting up Time Machine is as simple as connecting an external hard drive to your Mac, or connecting to a Time Capsule.

The Apple Time Capsule is a wireless network-attached storage device, combined with a wireless residential gateway router. It is designed to work in tandem with Time Machine.

If your Mac has a secondary internal disk (specifically, a disk that you don't boot up from), you can use Time Machine with that as well.

1   If you're connecting a hard drive for the first time, Time Machine asks if you'd like to use it as a backup drive (provided you haven't already specified a disk for this purpose).

Use a connected drive to back up data with Time Machine.

2 Press the Use as Backup Disk button to confirm that you want to use the disk for Time Machine backups.

Time Machine preferences allow you to select a backup disk and schedule.

3 Time Machine preferences open with this disk selected as your backup and Time Machine activated.

Depending on how much data you have, your first backup may take up to a few hours to complete. You shouldn't interrupt the initial backup, but you can continue to use your Mac while Time Machine is working.

4 After your initial backup is completed, Time Machine runs hourly backups of just the files that have changed on your Mac since the last backup (provided your backup disk is connected).

5 Time Machine stores hourly backups for 24 hours, daily backups for a month, and weekly backups until your backup drive is full.

Setting up Time Capsule for Time Machine backups

If you have a Time Capsule on your network, you can use it as a Time Machine backup disk.

1 Once your Time Capsule has been connected, open Time Machine preferences (in System Preferences) and press the Change Disk button.

2 In the window that appears, select the Time Capsule.

3 Enter the name and password you set for your Time Capsule.

Configuring Time Machine preferences

In Time Machine preferences (in System Preferences), you can press the Options button to adjust settings.

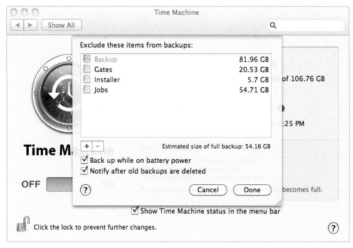

Options in Time Machine preferences allow you to exclude volumes from backup.

1 This window allows you to exclude files, folders, or mounted volumes from your backup schedule. This is useful when you want to avoid filling up your backup disk.

2 Selecting the Warn when old backups are deleted option lets you know when older backups are deleted from your backup disk to make space for more current backups.

Restoring files from Time Machine backups

Time Machine enables you to *go back in time* to restore files, or your entire system. To restore files, make sure your backup disk is connected and mounted. If it's not, Time Machine alerts you that the storage location for Time Machine backups can't be found when you open it.

1 Click the Time Machine icon in the Dock, and the Time Machine interface appears. You can literally see your windows as they appeared *back in time*.

The Time Machine interface shows windows as they appeared back in time.

2 Use the timeline, on the right side of the window, to reach a certain point in time. If you're not sure exactly when you lost a file, you can use the back arrow to let Time Machine automatically show you when that file last changed.

3 You can perform a Spotlight search in the Finder to locate a file. Type into the Spotlight search field, located in the upper right corner of the screen, and use the back arrow to have Time Machine search through your backups to find the desired item.

4 Before you restore a file, you can also use Quick Look to preview the file to make sure it's the one you want. Highlight the file and press the spacebar to bring up a preview.

Using Quick Look allows you to preview a file before restoring it.

6 To restore, select the file or folder and press the Restore button. The file is automatically copied to the desktop or appropriate folder.

You can restore all files and folders by using the Restore System from Backup feature of the Mac OS X Installer.

Using an existing Time Machine backup with a new Mac

If you've used Time Machine to back up your Mac, you can transfer your applications, files, and settings in their entirety from an existing backup to a new Mac. This can be done either when you start up your new Mac for the first time, or by using the Migration Assistant application, located in Applications > Utilities.

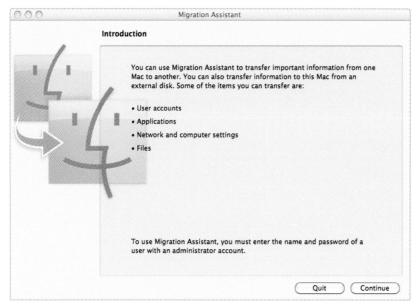

Use the Migration Assistant to transfer files from an existing Time Machine backup.

Deleting old backups

When your backup disk begins to reach its capacity, Time Machine smartly deletes the oldest backups to make room for newer ones.

If your backup disk fills up often, causing your oldest backups to not go as far back as you want, consider the following options:

- **Specify a larger disk for your backups.** Use Time Machine preferences to select the disk when you connect it for the first time.

- **Add to the "Do not back up" list** in Time Machine preferences to reduce the amount of information being backed up.

- **Delete files that are no longer needed** so that they will no longer be backed up.

- **Use Time Machine to find files that can be removed** from the backup disk to conserve space.

Using MobileMe

If you've purchased MobileMe, you have a free backup application waiting for you on your iDisk. Not surprisingly, it's called Backup. However, to use it, you have to download it to your Mac.

1   On either your desktop or the Internet interface, go to your iDisk, then go to the Software folder.

2   Inside that folder, locate another folder called Backup for Mac OS X 10.4.2 or later or 10.5.

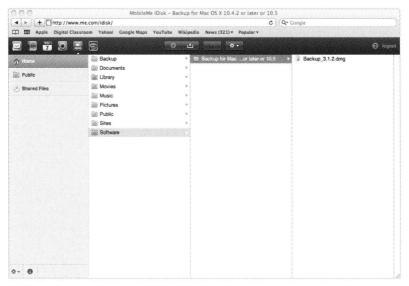

Find the Backup application on your iDisk and download it for use.

3   Open the folder and, if your iDisk is mounted on the desktop, drag the Backup.dmg file to a location on your hard drive.

4   If you're using the online MobileMe interface, click the Download button on the toolbar to download the file to your hard drive.

5 Once the file is on your hard drive, double-click it and follow the online instructions for installing it.

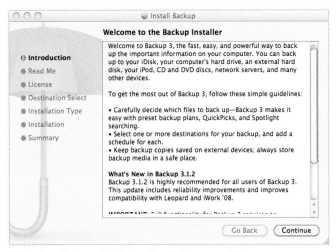

Follow the online instructions for installing Backup on your Mac.

Select your Backup type

1 From the Applications folder on your hard drive, launch the Backup application.

2 A window opens, allowing you to choose a Backup plan template. For this exercise, select Personal Data & Settings, and press Choose Plan to proceed.

Choose a Backup plan from existing templates, or create your own.

Choosing items to back up

1 Click the plus sign (+) under the top section of the Personal Data & Settings window that appears.

2 Select the Files & Folders button at the top of the next window, and find the files or folders you want to back up. For this example, you will select some of the images from my Pictures folder.

3 Choose *Include this folder* from the radio buttons below, then press Done.

Choose Items to Back Up as part of your Personal Data & Settings plan.

Scheduling a backup

1 After you choose the items you want to back up, you'll be taken to the plan window where you'll click the plus sign under the bottom section (Destination and Schedule).

2 The next window lets you select the destination (your iDisk, a hard drive, or a CD or DVD), as well as a time schedule for the backup to occur automatically. In this example, we have set the schedule for Every Day at 3:30 P.M.

3 Once you've set a schedule for the backup, press OK.

Schedule your backup and choose a destination.

Running your backup

1 Start your backup by pressing the Back Up Now button in the main window.

2 You can also wait for Backup to work automatically, following the time you entered on the scheduling window.

3 Once Backup starts working, you can monitor the backup with a progress bar that appears.

Using Disk Utility

Another backup process, using Disk Utility, produces a disk image of your entire Mac's contents. Disk Utility preserves the unique attributes of your files, and a disk image backup works well for archive-type, offsite storage.

Backing up to an external hard disk

1   Using FireWire or USB, connect an external hard drive that has enough free space to hold at least one full copy of the contents of your Macintosh hard drive.

2   Reboot your Mac from the Snow Leopard (Mac OS X 10.6) Install DVD. To do this, insert the disc, and then restart while pressing and holding the C key.

3   Select English as your language. (Do not begin an installation.)

4   Choose Utilities > Disk Utility.

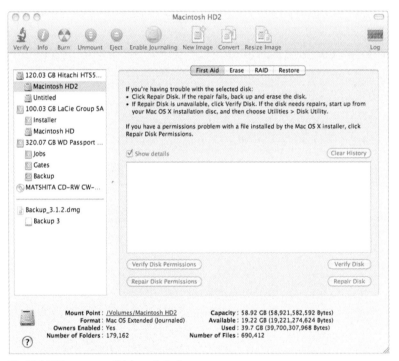

Use Disk Utility to create a disk image for backup.

5   Select the disk you want to back up from the pane on the left.

6   Press the New Image button in the toolbar.

7   Give your image a useful name, such as 08.07.09 HD backup. (Using a date in the name makes it easier to discern when the backup was made.)

8   Make sure the Save destination is a location on your external hard disk, then press Save to continue.

9   If prompted, enter your Administrator name and password. The imaging process begins. The time it takes to complete the imaging process depends on factors such as the amount of data on your disk. About 1GB per minute is imaged, depending on these factors.

10 When the process is complete, quit Disk Utility.

11 Press Command+Q to quit the Mac OS X installer. (You are prompted to restart.)

If your external disk does not have enough free space to hold future backups, consider using a different disk or deleting prior backups to free up space on the external disk.

Restoring the backup disk image to your internal disk

These steps overwrite data with the same name in the same location.

1   If necessary, reconnect the backup disk to your Mac.

2   Reboot your Mac from the Snow Leopard (Mac OS X 10.6) Install DVD. To do this, insert the disc, then restart while pressing and holding the C key.

3   Select English as your language. (Do not begin an installation.)

4   Choose Utilities > Disk Utility.

5   Select the internal Mac OS X disk that you want to restore to.

6 Select the Restore tab.

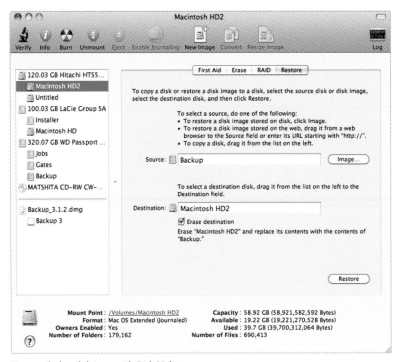

Restore a backup disk image with Disk Utility.

7 Drag your internal disk to the Destination text field.

8 Press the Image button next to the Source text field.

9 Navigate to the location of the backup you want to restore, located on your external disk.

10 Press Open to continue.

11 Press the Restore button. Confirm you want to Restore to Disk by Pressing Restore again. This replaces data on your Mac OS X volume with data from your backup.

12 If prompted, enter your Administrator name and password. The time it takes to restore from the image depends on factors such as the amount of data on your backup disk image.

Using Software Update

Subscribing to the belief that *an ounce of prevention is worth a pound of cure*, Apple frequently releases software updates that you can download. The Software Update feature in Mac OS X makes it very easy to determine and get exactly what you need.

Getting updates immediately

1 From the Apple menu (), choose Software Update.

2 Software Update checks for available updates. If there are any, a window opens, asking if you want to install them. Press Show Details for more information.

3 When the Software Update window opens, choose the items you want to install, and press the Install Items button. It's usually a good idea to install all available updates.

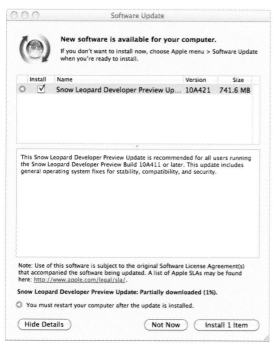

Check available updates in the Software Update window.

4 If prompted, enter an Administrator account name and password.

5 After the install is complete, restart the computer (if a restart is required).

Because some updates are prerequisites for others, you may need to repeat these steps several times to complete the update sequence.

Scheduling an update

The Software Update preference (in System Preferences) lets you schedule automatic checks for updates. It checks for updates weekly by default, but you can change the interval to daily or monthly, or you can deactivate scheduled checks if you want.

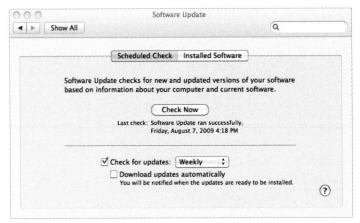

Automatic update checks can be set up in Software Update preferences.

Mac OS X 10.6 Snow Leopard can automatically run Software Update checks in the background and let you know when an update is available for your computer.

Using standalone installers from Apple Support Downloads

There are times when a standalone installer may be more useful than the automatic Software Update feature. For example, you may:

*   Need the file again later.
*   Have to install on multiple computers and need a portable file.
*   Have a faster Internet connection available to you at another computer.
*   Need an update but not have an Internet connection on that computer.

You can get standalone copies of many Apple software updates from the Apple Support Downloads web site, *support.apple.com/downloads*.

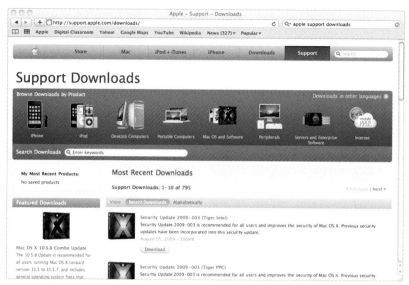

Get standalone copies of software updates from Apple Support Downloads.

It's important that you read the system requirements before using a standalone installer. Updates must be installed in the correct order when applicable, and only on compatible computers when applicable.

Self study

Try some of the different backup methods mentioned in this lesson to back up data from your Mac's hard disk. For example, burn selected files onto a CD, and use that CD to transfer those files to another computer. Use Time Machine to schedule an automatic backup, and then restore those files from the backup at a later date. If you have a MobileMe account, use it to download the latest version of Backup, and experiment with the settings in that application. Finally, try running successive Software Updates to ensure that you've completed the update sequence for your Mac.

Review

Questions

1 When burning a disc, what happens if a folder you've copied contains aliases to other files?

2 How can you search for a file among multiple Time Machine backups?

3 What must you have in order to use the Backup application on your Mac?

4 Why should you use caution when restoring a backup disk image to your Mac's internal disk?

5 Where can you get standalone installers to run in place of Software Update?

Answers

1 If any folder you copied contains aliases, the original files for those aliases are also burned to the disc.

2 You can perform a Spotlight search in the Finder to find a file. Type what you are searching for into the Spotlight search field and use the back arrow to have Time Machine search through your backups to find the desired item.

3 You must have a MobileMe account, *www.apple.com/mobileme*, to use the Backup application.

4 Restoring a backup image to your internal disk overwrites all data with the same names in the same locations.

5 Standalone copies of many Apple software updates are available from the Apple Support Downloads web site, *support.apple.com/downloads*.

What you'll learn in this lesson:

- Various types of Internet connections
- How to set up an Internet connection
- Features of the Safari web browser
- How to customize Safari

Connecting to the Internet and using Safari

In this lesson, you will learn how to set up an Internet connection on your computer and how to use the Safari web browser to look at content on the Internet.

Starting up

This lesson doesn't utilize any lesson files and therefore doesn't require any files to be copied onto your computer.

See Lesson 6 in action!

Use the accompanying video to gain a better understanding of how to use some of the features shown in this lesson. The video tutorial for this lesson can be found on the included DVD.

Internet access

Internet access refers to the ability of your computer to access the Internet, which allows you to browse web sites, check e-mail, and much more. The method by which you access the Internet from your home or office will vary from one location to the next, but will generally fall into one of the following categories:

- **Dial-up**—This type of Internet access is less common today and tends to be very slow; however, it is usually very inexpensive.

- **DSL** (Digital Subscriber Line)—This is a high-speed Internet connection usually provided by your phone company and utilizes your existing telephone line. It is generally more expensive than dial-up but is much faster.

- **Cable**—This is a high-speed Internet connection usually provided by your cable company and uses your existing TV cable. This is also more expensive than dial-up and usually more expensive than DSL, but it can have higher speeds than both.

- **Satellite**—Fairly new in comparison to the other Internet access methods, satellite provides Internet access through a satellite connection via a satellite dish mounted on the exterior of your home or office. Satellite Internet access is faster than dial-up and has comparable access speeds to cable and DSL. This connection method is often attractive to consumers who live in remote areas where cable and DSL access are unavailable.

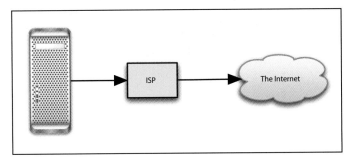

To obtain access to the Internet, you need to purchase it from an Internet Service Provider.

Of the Internet access types described here, all except for dial-up fall under the category of broadband Internet access. The Federal Communications Commission, or FCC, defines broadband as Internet access that exceeds 200 kilobits per second (Kbps). As a reference point, the maximum potential speed using dial-up Internet access is 56 Kbps. So when comparison-shopping, use this number as a reference point to determine what Internet speed you'd like to purchase. Most broadband connections can exceed 1 Megabit per second (Mbps), or 1024 Kbps. See the sidebar *Kilo what?* on the next page for more information.

Kilo what?

Don't get caught up in the confusing numbers that are released by ISPs to lure you into buying their product. Internet transmission speeds are rated using bits per second (bps). Due to the overall increase in transmission speeds over the years, the ratings are simplified by using other units to make it easier to understand. Below is a table that explains commonly used measurements when describing Internet transmission speeds.

1 Kilobit = 1024 bits

1 Megabit = 1024 Kilobits

1 Gigabit = 1024 Megabits

Don't confuse these with the Megabytes and Kilobytes that are typically used to refer to the amount of memory or the amount of hard drive space on your computer. Bytes are much larger units of measurement and are not used to describe Internet transmission speeds.

Internet service providers

In order to obtain Internet access, your first step is to contact an Internet Service Provider, or ISP. An ISP sells you a package that provides Internet access to your home or office using one of the connection methods listed earlier. You need to do some investigating by contacting ISPs in your area to find out what Internet options are available to you and their respective prices. ISPs often offer first-time customer promotions that include discounted rates for an initial period of time. Make sure you understand the plan you are purchasing before you agree to buy. Price, speed, and connection type vary, depending on where you live.

Setting up your Internet connection

Once you've contacted an ISP and have purchased a package, you are sent instructions from your ISP on how to connect your computer to the Internet. These instructions usually include a username and password required to complete the setup process. Make sure you keep this information in a safe place, as you need it to set up your Internet connection. Also, once you've completed the setup process, you'll need it if you ever purchase a new computer or have to reconfigure your computer for some reason.

Due to the various processes required by each ISP, this book cannot cover all potential variables involved in the setup process, but the information provided here should work in most cases. If you encounter problems during the setup process, call your ISP for assistance.

Setting up a dial-up connection

Although dial-up is not as common as it once was, it is often the best choice for people who require limited access to the Internet and don't require high connection speeds. Dial-up uses a standard telephone line to connect to the Internet and therefore renders the telephone line unusable while you are connected to the Internet. In the following exercise, you'll learn how to configure a dial-up connection to the Internet.

You need a dial-up modem (internal or external) connected to your computer to perform this exercise. As of this writing, none of the currently shipping Mac computers contain an internal modem, and so this lesson assumes that you are using an external modem.

1   From the Apple menu (), choose System Preferences.

2   Click the Network button under the Internet & Wireless category to open the Network preference pane.

3   Click the External Modem icon along the left side of the window to select it. The current status at the top of the screen indicates that the modem is currently not configured.

Select the External Modem icon in the sidebar to configure the options for the modem.

4   From the Configuration drop-down menu, choose Add Configuration. In the resulting dialog box, type **Snow Leopard dialup**. Press Create. This saves this configuration for future use and is helpful if you connect to multiple ISPs.

5   In the Telephone Number text field, type the phone number provided by your ISP.

6   In the Account Name text field, type the name provided by your ISP.

7   In the Password text field, type the password provided by your ISP.

8   Press the Apply button to save these settings.

9   The Show modem status in menu bar check box displays an icon in the menu bar that allows you to easily establish a connection from that icon. For now, leave this check box unchecked.

10 Press the Connect button. You should hear a dial tone followed by the dialing of the telephone number that you entered in step 5. You should also hear a connecting sound, and if the connection is successful, the Status at the top of the Network preference pane indicates that you are connected and can now browse the Internet.

After you click the Connect button, the Status indicates
that you are now connected to the Internet.

The Advanced button at the bottom of the Network preference pane provides advanced settings that your ISP may require you to configure in order to connect to their service. If you experience problems connecting to the Internet after following these steps, contact your ISP for further assistance.

11 To disconnect the connection, simply press the Disconnect button in the Network preference pane.

12 Choose System Preferences > Quit System Preferences.

Setting up your broadband connection

The process of configuring your broadband connection (DSL, cable, or satellite) differs, depending on the ISP that is providing your Internet service. After signing up for service through your ISP, you will probably be sent a welcome kit that includes a modem, router, or modem/router combination. If you are using a DSL service, you may also need to install DSL filters on all devices in your home or office that use the same telephone line that the DSL service is using.

Regardless of the type of broadband connection you are using, you need a broadband modem that establishes the connection to your ISP. This is typically provided in your welcome kit. A router is a device that allows multiple computers to share that same Internet connection. Specifics on setting up your modem and/or router are beyond the scope of this book and therefore will not be covered. If you need assistance configuring your modem/router, contact your ISP for help.

Wired connections

As their name implies, wired connections require a cable to be connected from your modem or router to your computer. This cable is called an Ethernet cable and allows your computer to communicate with your modem/router and therefore to the Internet. Let's explore how easy it is to set up your Ethernet connection.

1 From the Apple menu (), choose System Preferences.

2 Click the Network button under the Internet & Wireless category to open the Network preference pane.

3 Click the Ethernet icon in the sidebar to select it. Depending on your computer's hardware configuration, it may say Ethernet 1 or Ethernet 2. Choose the port that you'll be plugging an ethernet cable into.

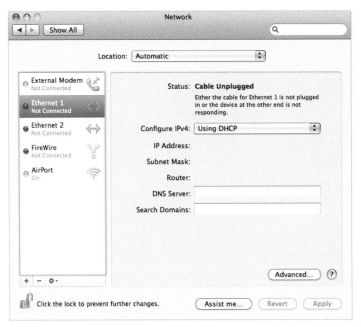

When no Ethernet cable is plugged into your computer, the Network preference pane indicates this.

4 If you don't have an Ethernet cable plugged into your computer, the Network preference pane indicates that the cable is unplugged. At this point, plug your Ethernet cable from your modem/router into your computer, as per the instructions provided by your ISP.

5   After you connect a cable from your modem/router to your computer, the Network
preference pane should indicate that you are connected and can now browse
the Internet.

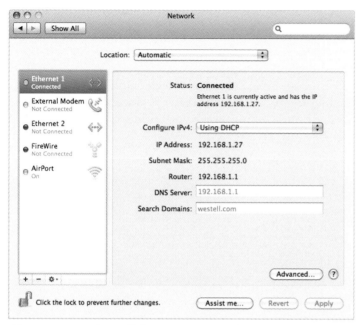

*After you connect an Ethernet cable between your computer and the modem/router, the Network
preference pane indicates that you are connected to the Internet.*

Most modem/routers come preconfigured with a setting to automatically dispense an IP
address to your computer called DHCP (Dynamic Host Configuration Protocol). It is
important that your computer has an IP address, as without one, you cannot connect to
the Internet. If the Network preference pane indicates that your cable is plugged in but a
connection to the Internet can't be established, contact your ISP for further assistance.

6   Choose System Preferences > Quit System Preferences.

Wireless connections

A common approach to connecting to the Internet is via a wireless Internet connection. For
the most part, the initial setup process from your ISP is the same; however, when you connect
to your modem/router, it uses a wireless connection instead of a wired one. Apple refers to its
wireless technology as *Airport*, and it comes standard on all currently shipping Apple computers.

As its name implies, a wireless connection uses wireless technology to communicate with
your modem/router, which in turn communicates with your ISP, thereby providing Internet
access to any computer. One advantage of a wireless connection is that there are fewer wires
connected to the back of your computer. Another advantage, in the case of a laptop computer, is
that you can move just about anywhere in your home or office to browse the Internet. So you
could sit at the kitchen table and check your e-mail while you eat your breakfast!

Factors, such as the wireless technology being used, as well has how many walls the wireless signal must travel through to reach the modem/router, determine how far from the wireless modem/router you can be while still receiving a wireless signal.

The process of configuring your wireless modem/router is beyond the scope of this book and therefore will not be covered. If you need assistance configuring your wireless modem/router, call your ISP or the manufacturer of the modem/router for additional help. To complete the lesson, this book assumes that you've already configured the wireless setup on the wireless modem/router.

1   From the Apple menu (), choose System Preferences.

2   Click the Network button under the Internet & Wireless category to open the Network preference pane.

3   Click the AirPort icon in the sidebar to select it. If this is your first time using AirPort, the Status section at the top of the screen indicates that AirPort is currently off.

The AirPort status is currently off.

4   Press the Turn AirPort On button. Simply turning AirPort on does not provide Internet access yet, as you need to connect to a wireless network to establish Internet access.

After turning AirPort on, the status indicates that it is on, but not connected to a wireless network as indicated by the yellow icon..

5   From the Network Name drop-down menu, choose the name of the network that was configured during the modem/router setup process. You may be asked for a password to access the network. Call your ISP for assistance if you have difficulties with or don't remember your password.

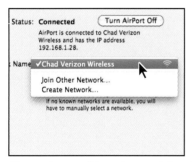

Choosing the name of the wireless network from the list.

6 Once connected, the Network preference pane shows your connection status and also indicates that you are now connected to the wireless network. You can now access the Internet.

Once connected to a wireless network, the status indicates that you are connected and can now access the Internet.

7 Choose System Preferences > Quit System Preferences.

Wireless access and passwords

So why do you need a password when accessing your own wireless network? Well, unlike wired networks, it's difficult to restrict who sees your wireless network and who doesn't. Therefore, if you don't password-protect your wireless network, at the very least, you're providing other people with free Internet access. If that person is your friend, that's fine, but if not, you could be footing the bill for a stranger's access to the Internet. At the very worst, you are providing anyone with potential access to your computer and the files on your computer.

This is why it's important to use a password when setting up your wireless modem/router. You can still share your Internet connection with your friends; you'll just have to provide them with the password to gain access to the Internet. Better safe than sorry.

Using Safari

Snow Leopard introduces a brand-new version of the Safari web browser. Safari, now at version 4, introduces significant speed improvements and takes advantage of the latest hardware found on the new Apple computers, resulting in a better Internet experience for you, the user. Because of the new improvements to Safari, you should experience fewer crashes and an overall more stable web browser. Let's explore how Safari can make your Internet experience better.

To perform this exercise, you need an established Internet connection.

The toolbar

The toolbar is the top-most portion of the Safari interface where you'll do most of your site navigation in Safari.

The Address bar

1   Launch Safari on your computer by clicking the Safari icon in the Dock.

The Safari web browser icon.

2   When you launch Safari, it displays the default Home page defined in the Safari preferences.

3   Choose Safari > Preferences. Click the General button at the top of the window, then type **www.digitalclassroombooks.com** in the Home page text field to set the new default Home page. Close the preferences window by pressing the Close button (⊗).

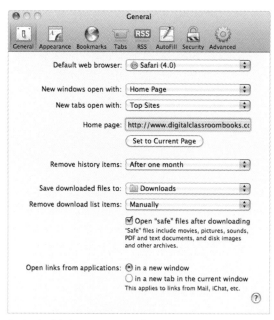

Setting the default Home page in Safari.

4   From the History menu, choose Home to display the current default Home page.

5   You can navigate to any web site by typing it in the Address bar at the top of the Safari interface. Type **www.apple.com/macosx** in the Address bar and press Return on your keyboard to display the new web page.

Typing an address in the Address bar displays that web page in Safari.

6   Press the Back button (◄) to go back in the list of web pages that you've visited.

7   Press the Forward button (►) to go forward in the list of web pages that you've visited.

Google search

Safari contains a built-in text field to search using the Google search engine. Instead of first navigating to the Google web page, you can simply initiate your search directly from the Safari interface.

1   In the Google search text field in the upper right corner, type **Snow Leopard** and then press Return on your keyboard. The Google search results are immediately displayed.

Safari's built-in Google Search bar.

2   The search for Snow Leopard displays some relevant information about Snow Leopard the operating system, but also displays results about the animal. Let's refine that by typing Snow Leopard + os x. Because this search is more specific, your search yields only results having to do with Snow Leopard the operating system.

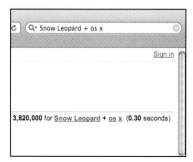

A more specific search yields better results.

3   Click the X at the right of the Google search text field to clear the text of the last search you performed.

Bookmarks

Bookmarks are saved web site locations that you can store for later access in Safari. When you browse the Internet, you often arrive at a web page that you may want to visit later or even on a regular basis. You can bookmark that web page for later viewing.

1   Press the Show All Bookmarks button (📖) on the left side of the toolbar at the top of your screen. A new screen appears, showing different collections of bookmarks on the left, starting with History. History is simply the history of sites that you've visited, organized by each day. By default, Safari stores up to one month of web site visits in the History collection.

2   Click the Bookmarks Bar entry under the Collections section on the left side of the Safari window. The Bookmarks Bar directly correlates to the Bookmarks listed at the bottom of Safari's toolbar.

3   In the Address bar, type **www.digitalclassroombooks.com** and press Return on your keyboard.

4 To add a web site to your Bookmarks Bar, drag the icon to the left of the web address and drag it below the Address bar. The existing bookmarks in the Bookmarks bar move to make room for the new bookmark. Release your mouse when your cursor is at the desired position.

Click and hold the icon to the left of the web address and drag it into the Bookmarks bar.

5 A dialog box appears, asking you to name your bookmark. Type **Digital Classroom** in the text field and press OK. The new bookmark is added to the Bookmarks Bar.

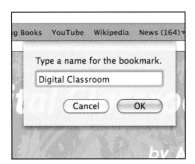

Naming the bookmark.

6 Press the Show All Bookmarks button (📖) again; notice that the Digital Classroom bookmark is listed at the bottom of the screen in the list of bookmarks, as well as in the Bookmarks Bar.

7 Type **www.agitraining.com** in the Address bar and press Return on your keyboard to display the web site.

8 From the Bookmarks menu at the top of the screen, choose Add Bookmark. In the resulting dialog box, type **AGI Training** and choose Bookmarks Menu from the drop-down menu. Press Add.

9 Click the Bookmarks menu again, and you now see the AGI Training bookmark that you added in step 8.

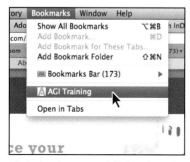

The bookmark is now available from the Bookmarks menu.

10 Press the Show All Bookmarks button (▣) again, and you see the AGI Training bookmark when you click the Bookmarks menu collection on the left side of the screen.

11 You can further organize your bookmarks by putting them inside of bookmark folders. With the Show All Bookmarks screen displayed and the Bookmarks Menu category highlighted, click the rightmost plus sign at the bottom of the screen.

12 A new folder is created, with the name highlighted so that you can type a new name for the folder. Type **Training and Learning** and then press Return on your keyboard.

13 Drag the AGI Training bookmark on top of the Training and Learning folder, and then release your mouse button. The AGI Training bookmark is now an item within the Training and Learning folder.

14 Under the Bookmarks menu, choose Training and Learning; you see the AGI training bookmark listed as a sub-item of the Training and Learning folder. Select the AGI Training bookmark to display the web site.

Bookmarks make quick work of accessing frequently visited web sites on your computer. Bookmark folders make it easy to organize those bookmarks into logical categories for fast retrieval of web pages.

Installing the Silverlight plug-in

Siliverlight is an increasingly popular platform for viewing video, games, and interactive content on-line. It is used on sites such as NBC Sports for streaming live Olympic video coverage or live football coverage, and by Netflix for subscribers who want to watch movies on-line. Fortunately it takes less than a minute to download and install.

1   With Safari open, navigate to *www.DigitalClassroomBooks.com*. Click the Get Microsoft® Silverlight™ icon on the right side of the screen.

Click the Get Microsoft® Silverlight™ icon.

 If you can see the video, then your browser already has the Silverlight Plug-in installed.

2   Press Continue in the alert window that indicates, *This package will run a program to determine in the software can be installed.*

Press Continue in the alert window.

3   Press Continue in the Install Microsoft Silverlight Browser Plug-In window, and also Press Continue in the following window to accept the software license agreement.

4   Press Install to accept the installation location. If necessary, enter the password on your computer to install software. When the installation is successful, a message is displayed.

The installation was successful.

6   Quit Safari by choosing Safari > Quit Safari.

7   Start Safari and return to *www. DigitalClassroomBooks.com.* The video tutorial in the upper right corner displays. Click the video to view it and confirm that the Silverlight plug-in has been correctly installed.

The video can now be seen on the web site.

Top Sites

Top Sites is a new feature in Safari 4 that displays a wall of recently visited web sites and a thumbnail of each site for easy identification of those sites. As you browse the Web, Safari learns which web sites are your favorites and displays them in the Top Sites screen. One of the amazing new features of Safari 4, Top Sites makes it easy to access sites with just a few clicks.

1   Press the Top Sites button in the toolbar (⊞) to display the Top Sites screen. You may see a couple of pages that you've recently visited. These pages become more accurate as you continue browsing the Web.

The Top Sites screen.

2   As you move your cursor around the screen, each site is highlighted and its title is displayed at the bottom of the screen. Click any site to display the related web page.

3   Press the Top Sites button again to display the Top Sites screen.

You can also customize the sites available in the Top Sites screen by manually entering addresses that you frequently access.

4   Press the Edit button in the lower-left corner of the Top Sites screen. Each thumbnail now has an X and a pushpin button, which allow you to either remove a site or make it permanent, respectively.

5   Press the pushpin button in the upper-left corner of the AGI Training thumbnail to make it a permanent entry in the Top Sites screen.

6   In the Address bar at the top of the screen, type **www.macworld.com**, but don't press Return on your keyboard. Drag the icon to the left of the address into the Top Sites window.

7   As you drag, the thumbnails in the site window move to make room for the new Top Sites entry. Release your mouse button to add the site to the Top Sites screen. The Macworld web site is automatically set as a permanent item in the Top Sites screen.

Dragging the icon to the left of the address into the Top Sites screen makes it a permanent site.

8   You can change the size and therefore the quantity of thumbnails displayed in the Top Sites screen by clicking on the Small, Medium, and Large buttons in the lower-right corner of the Top Sites screen. For now, leave them set to Medium.

9   Press the Done button in the lower-left corner of the screen to exit the editing mode of the Top Sites screen.

10 Press the Back button (◄) to return to the last viewed web page.

Tabs

Very often when browsing web sites, you'll find that you'd like to go to a new web page, but you still want the ability to return to the web page that you are currently viewing. You certainly could open a new browser window, which gives you two completely separate windows in which to view web pages, but this method becomes clumsy and it is difficult to efficiently view multiple web pages. Safari solves this problem by offering tabbed browsing. Tabbed browsing allows you to open multiple sites in their own individual tabs but within the same overall browser window. This allows you to quickly switch between multiple web pages but keeps those web pages organized for easy access. Let's see how tabbed browsing works.

1   With Safari still open on your computer, type **www.digitalclassroombooks.com** in the Address bar and press Return on your keyboard.

2   Choose File > New Tab. A new tab is displayed with your Top Sites screen active.

3   Click the AGI Training thumbnail in the Top Sites screen to open that web page.

4   Press Command+T on your keyboard to create another tab. Type **www.apple.com/macosx** in the Address bar and press Return on your keyboard.

5   You now have three separate tabs below the toolbar. Each one contains a separate web site. Click the different tabs to display the different sites contained in each tab.

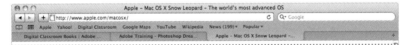

Tabbed browsing allows you to put web sites in their own individual tab within the same browser window.

6   Tabs can be closed just as easily as they are created. Hover your cursor over one of the tabs, and you see an X on the left side of the tab. Click the X to close the tab. Repeat until there are no tabs remaining.

7   Choose Safari > Quit Safari.

Congratulations! You've completed Lesson 6.

Self study

Spend some additional time exploring and becoming familiar with Safari. People are spending an increasing amount of time accessing the Internet, and it will benefit you to become proficient using Safari. The more familiar you are with Safari, the easier it will be for you to browse and navigate to different web sites. Configure Top Sites so that all the sites that you visit frequently are a click away, and don't forget to bookmark sites for future access.

Review

Questions

1 What is broadband Internet access?

2 How can you specify the default web page that is displayed when Safari is first launched?

3 How can you add a bookmark to the Bookmarks Bar?

Answers

1 The FCC defines broadband access as an Internet connection with transmission speeds exceeding 200 Kbps. However, more generally, broadband simply refers to cable, DSL, satellite, and other types of high-speed Internet access.

2 With Safari open, choose Safari > Preferences and in the General section, type a new address in the Home page text field.

3 Simply drag the icon to the left of the address in the Address bar, and drag it down to the Bookmarks Bar. Name the bookmark using a name of your choice, and press OK.

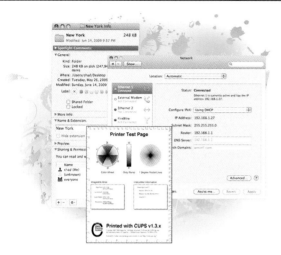

What you'll learn in this lesson:

* Setting up a basic network

* Sharing your files and computer's screen with computer users

* Sharing your printer

* Creating a basic web server

Creating and Using Your Own Network

In this lesson, you will learn how to set up a basic network on your computer and how to share files with people on other computers.

Starting up

You will work with several files from the sl07lessons folder in this lesson. Make sure that you have copied the contents of the sl07lessons folder into the Pictures folder of your Home folder from the Digital Classroom DVD. There are three folders to copy: New York, Creative, and Nature. This lesson may be easier to follow if those folders are in your Pictures folder.

See Lesson 7 in action!

Use the accompanying video to gain a better understanding of how to use some of the features shown in this lesson. The video tutorial for this lesson can be found on the included DVD.

What is a network?

A network consists of two or more computers connected to each other using either a physical cable or a wireless connection. The most popular network in use today is the Internet. At its most basic level, the Internet is millions of computers connected to each other using a combination of network technologies that allow them to communicate with each other. This, of course, is an oversimplification of the complexities of the Internet; however, it is a good example of a network.

Why create a network?

You probably don't need a network as complex as the Internet; however, you may have more than one computer in your house or office at work that you'd like to connect so that you can share files with one another. You may even want to share a single printer so that each person can print to it. A network opens up several possibilities and can save you time and money by making resources available to several computers instead of purchasing duplicate resources for each computer. When configured properly, a network also allows you to share a single Internet connection with other computers on the network, giving each computer access to the Internet. Let's explore how to set up a network.

Creating a network

This lesson will go through the general steps required to create a network, including both a wired and wireless network. You'll start by creating the most basic type of network possible, and then move on to a slightly more complex, but versatile network.

Creating a basic network

The most basic type of network is called a *peer-to-peer network*. This type of network involves connecting a network cable between two computers. Although this type of network has its limitations, it's often sufficient for use in a home environment.

Performing this exercise will require that you have an Ethernet cable, sometimes referred to as a Cat5 cable. An Ethernet cable can be purchased at any home electronics store or computer store. All current Apple computers ship with a built-in Ethernet port for connecting to a network. The Ethernet port on your computer looks like a phone jack but is larger; this is the port you will use in this exercise to create a network.

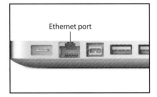

An Ethernet port.

You will also need a second computer to create the network in this exercise. Although this exercise illustrates connecting two Mac computers, you can also create a network between a Mac and Windows computer. When appropriate, the settings for creating a Mac/Windows network will be listed.

1   Begin by plugging the Ethernet cable into the Ethernet port of each computer that is being networked.

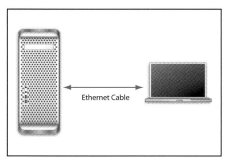

Connecting two computers using an Ethernet cable creates a basic peer-to-peer network.

Once two computers are connected, they need a unique number that identifies each computer on the network; this number is called an *IP address*. Think of this as a phone number for your computer. Just as you need each person's unique phone number in order to call them, computers need a unique IP address to communicate with one another. Fortunately, Snow Leopard makes this process very easy. Networks often utilize a technology called DHCP (Dynamic Host Configuration Protocol) that automatically assigns a unique IP address to each computer. Snow Leopard utilizes a type of DHCP called Bonjour that creates a self-assigned IP address for you.

2   From the Apple menu (), choose System Preferences.

3   Click the Network icon in the Internet & Wireless section to display the Network preference pane.

4 Highlight the Ethernet connection on the left side of the window to select it. You see that the Status to the right indicates that you are connected and that your computer has a self-assigned IP address and will not be able to connect to the Internet. Also note the IP address that has been assigned to your computer. This numbering scheme is the type of address that is used by Bonjour. Both computers should have a similar but unique address.

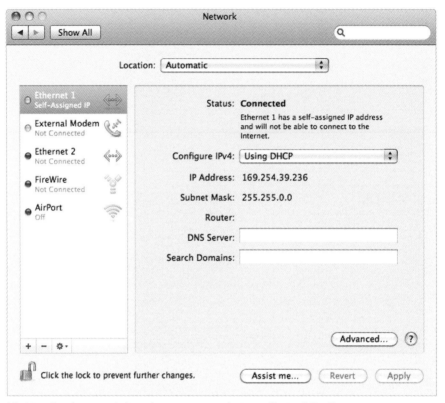

The Network preference pane indicates that you are connected using a self-assigned IP address.

5 Choose System Preferences > Quit System Preferences. You've just created a basic network.

Creating a Local Area Network

A *Local Area Network*, or LAN, goes beyond the basic peer-to-peer connection by adding hardware called a network device to expand the capabilities of the network. A local area network is a computer network covering a small physical area, like a home, office, or small group of buildings, such as a school, or an airport. The defining characteristics of LANs, in contrast to wide-area networks (WANs), include their usually higher data-transfer rates, smaller geographic place, and lack of a need for leased telecommunication lines. Creating a LAN isn't as difficult as it may sound and can be accomplished by adding devices that can add functionality to a network, such as hubs, switches, and routers.

Switches and Hubs

A hub is a network device that contains multiple Ethernet ports connecting computers together. A hub lets several connected computers or devices share information. Hubs are quickly being replaced by devices that look identical but include additional intelligence that helps data find the correct location on the network. Switches help avoid data from colliding with each other, allowing for more efficient transfer of data. A switch is like a hub with a traffic cop, directing network traffic to a specific destination—whether a different computer, server, or router.

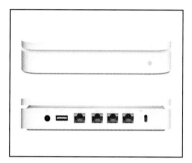

A wireless switch/router for home networking.

Router

A router is a network device that typically connects your home or office network to another network—such as the Internet. A router lets you share an Internet connection between several computers on a network. A router may include Ethernet ports for connecting computers together and also includes a wireless connectivity for sharing data between computers using radio waves—there is more information on wireless networks in the next section, Connecting to a wireless Local Area Network.

Many network devices that are provided to you when you purchase Internet access from an ISP include a combination of a router and switch in the same device. This provides the best of both worlds, allowing you to connect several computers to the device as well as share your Internet connections with all computers that are connected to the device.

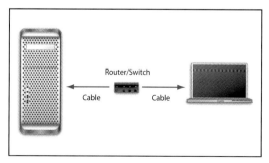

A Local Area Network configuration.

This exercise requires that you have a switch in which to connect all the computers, as well as a separate Ethernet cable to connect each computer to the switch. Due to the differences between manufacturers and models of switches, you may need to contact the manufacturer of the switch for more detailed instructions on how to configure your switch or switch/router.

1 Connect an Ethernet cable from each computer to an Ethernet port on the switch.

Most switches have DHCP capabilities that will assign an IP address to each computer on the network. For help setting up DHCP, contact the manufacturer of the switch. If your switch doesn't have DHCP capabilities, Bonjour will automatically provide each computer with a self-assigned IP address.

2 From the Apple menu (), choose System Preferences.

3 Click the Network icon from the Internet & Wireless section to display the Network preference pane.

4 Highlight the Ethernet connection on the left side of the window to select it. You see that the Status to the right indicates that you are connected and that your computer has an IP address. Also note the IP address that has been assigned to your computer. This numbering scheme is the type of address that is often used by DHCP. Both computers should have a similar but unique address.

The switch is providing an IP address to each computer using DHCP.

5 Choose System Preferences > Quit System Preferences.

IP addresses

IP (Internet protocol) addresses are used to identify each computer on a network. The IP address that you see in your Network preference pane may look different from the one in the previous figure. The IP address that is provided from your switch or switch/router is a private IP address. This means that the address cannot be routed on the Internet without additional technology, and is reserved for private networks such as internal LANs. Private IP addresses can be in the following ranges:

- 10.0.0.0 – 10.255.255.255
- 172.16.0.0 – 172.31.255.255
- 192.168.0.0 – 192.168.255.255
- The IP address being provided by the DHCP server on your switch/router should be within these ranges.

Bonjour addresses, or Link-local addresses, are used when a DHCP server is unavailable and uses an IP address in the range of 169.254.0.0 to 169.254.255.255. These are also private IP addresses and cannot be routed on the Internet.

Public IP addresses are used on the Internet. These addresses can be within a very wide range. Every web site that you visit on the Internet has an underlying IP address that identifies the computer that hosts the web site on the Internet.

Connecting to a wireless Local Area Network

So far in this lesson, you've seen how to create a wired network using Ethernet cables to connect computers to that network. Wireless networks use the same idea as wired networks, but without the cables. Wireless networks use radio waves to send data to and from other computers on the network.

A wireless network is created by either attaching a Wireless Access Point (WAP) to an existing network, or wireless router to share an Internet connection. Once these are connected and set-up, you can connect your Mac to the wireless network. Advantages of wireless networks include:

- **Mobility**—Users can walk around while using their computer as long as they remain within range of the wireless switch/router.
- **Cost**—You can create a basic wireless network at a very reasonable cost.
- **Expandability**—It's easy to expand a wireless network by adding additional access points to extend the range of the wireless network.

Disadvantages of wireless networks include:

- **Security**—Because data is being sent wirelessly, it's possible for other users to intercept data and to gain access to your Internet connection. When establishing a wireless network, it is important to create a password to access the wireless network.

- **Range**—The distance that you can be from the wireless switch/router while still accessing a signal will vary depending on your home/office and factors such as how many load-bearing walls the signal must travel through. Interference from other components that use radio waves, such as microwaves and cordless phones, can also affect the range.

- **Speed**—Wireless transmission speeds are often 10 to 25 percent as fast as wired transmission speeds, depending on which wireless implementation is being used. If you frequently copy large amounts of data to and from a server, a wired Ethernet connection is typically the best method of connecting the computer and server.

To complete this lesson, you will need to have already configured a wireless switch/router for wireless access and have created a wireless network. Configuring a wireless switch/router is beyond the scope of this book. Contact the manufacturer of the switch/router for help setting up a wireless network. In addition to setting up a wireless network, you need to ensure that your computer has an AirPort card installed. As of this writing, all current Mac models ship with a built-in AirPort card.

To check if your computer has an AirPort card:

1 From the Apple menu (), choose About This Mac.

2 In the About This Mac window, press the More Info button. This launches System Profiler and displays the current configuration of your computer.

3 On the left side of the System Profiler window, click the AirPort entry under the Network section. If a Card Type is listed, you have an AirPort card; if no items are listed, you do not. Contact your local Apple Reseller to see if you can have one installed in your computer.

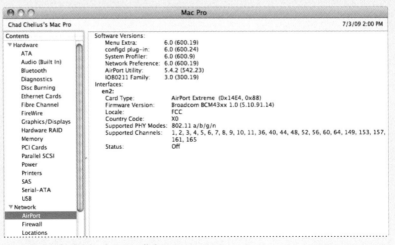

An AirPort card is listed as being installed.

4 Choose System Profiler > Quit System Profiler.

Connecting to a wireless network

1 From the Apple menu (), choose System Preferences. Click the Network icon from the Internet & Wireless section to display the Network preference pane.

2 Highlight the AirPort connection on the left side of the window to select it. If the Status in the main window displays Off, press the Turn AirPort On button. You see that the Status changes to indicate that AirPort has been turned on but is not connected to a network.

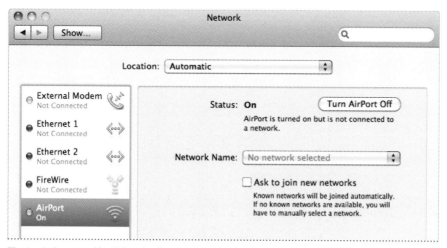

Turning AirPort on enables AirPort, but doesn't connect it to a network.

3 Click the Network Name drop-down menu. Any wireless networks in range are displayed in the list. Any networks that are password-protected display a padlock icon to the right of the network name.

Any wireless networks in range display in the Network Name list.

4 Select the wireless network that you set up when you configured your wireless switch/router. Enter the username and password you used when you set up the network (if applicable). Press OK.

5 Press the Apply button to save your changes. The status now indicates that you are connected to the network and the IP address of your computer displays within the status area of the Network preference pane.

6 Choose System Preferences > Quit System Preferences. At this point you should have one of the above types of networks created and now have two or more computers connected to each other.

File sharing

Regardless of what type of network you are connected to, you can enable file sharing from one computer to the other. This is useful if you have files that you would like to share with someone on another computer. In the following steps, you'll learn how to enable file sharing so users on other computers on your network can access files on your computer. These steps will need to be performed on both computers if you want bi-directional sharing of files. If you only enable file sharing on your computer, other users can see your information but you can't see theirs.

1 From the Apple menu (), choose System Preferences and click on the Sharing button in the Internet & Wireless section to display the Sharing preference pane.

2 The Computer Name field at the top of the Sharing preference pane is the name of your computer and will be what other users see when they connect to your computer. Feel free to change this name but try to keep the name simple.

3 Select the File Sharing entry on the left side of the preference pane to highlight it, and then click the check box to enable File Sharing. By default, only the user's Public folder is shared.

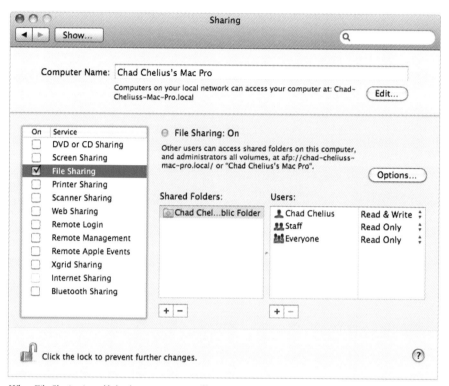

When File Sharing is enabled, other users can access files on your computer.

4 Press the plus icon (+) beneath the Shared Folders section of the Sharing preference pane to add a new shared folder.

5 Select the Pictures folder within your Home folder and press the Add button.

By default, any new folder you add to the Shared Folders list will give Read & Write permissions to the user who is currently logged in and No Access permissions to everyone else. You'll change this in the next steps.

6   Select the Pictures folder in the Shared Folders list to select it; then, in the Users section to the right, choose Read & Write from the drop-down menu to the right of Everyone. This gives any user access to the shared folder.

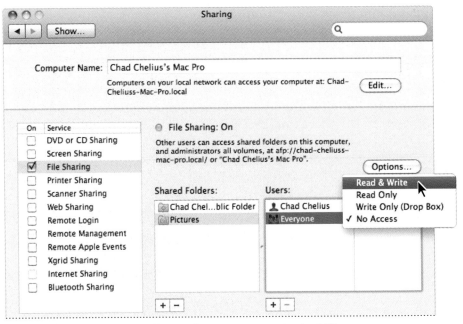

Assigning Read & Write permissions to Everyone allows any user access to that shared folder.

7   Press the Options button to display the file sharing options window.

8   The file sharing options window allows you to enable sharing via FTP (File Transfer Protocol) using SMB (Server Message Block) for Windows users.

9 If you'd like to share files with Windows users, click the Share files and folders using SMB checkbox, then click the checkbox next to the account at the bottom of the window that you'd like to provide access to. When you do this, you're asked to enter the password for the user account that you've enabled. Enter the password and press OK. For this reason, you may want to create a sharing only account and enable access using that account. For more on setting up user accounts, refer to Lesson 6, "Connecting to the Internet and using Safari."

Enabling sharing using SMB will allow Windows users to access files in your Shared folder.

10 Press the Done button to close the file sharing options window.

11 Choose System Preferences > Quit System Preferences.

Testing File Sharing

Now that you've enabled File Sharing on your computer, you'll want to test the File Sharing from another computer on your network. If you don't have another computer to test this feature, simply read on, as the examples will display what you can expect to see when sharing has been enabled.

1   From another computer on your network, open a new Finder window and set the view to Column view.

2   In the sidebar, there is a new category called Shared. Click the disclosure triangle to the left of the word Shared, if necessary, to display the shared computers available on the network.

3   Click the name of the computer on which you enabled file sharing in the previous exercise to select it. You see the Public and Pictures folders that have been shared on that computer.

4   Select the Pictures folder to display its contents. The lesson files that you copied at the beginning of this lesson are displayed.

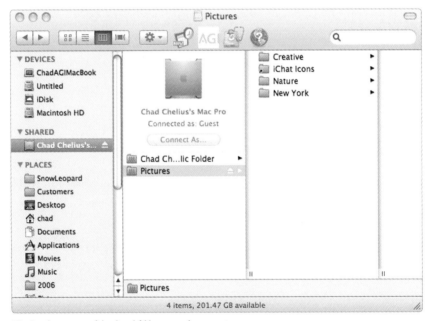

Viewing the contents of the shared folder on another computer.

5 Select the New York folder and drag the folder to the desktop of the computer you are currently working on. The New York folder is copied to your desktop and you can modify those files as needed.

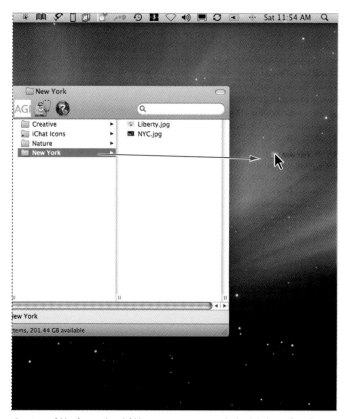

Copying a folder from a shared folder on one computer to the local desktop of another computer.

Changing permissions

Privileges and permissions can become a very complex topic when dealing with file sharing on a network. A lengthy discussion of privileges is beyond the scope of this book but it's important to have a basic understanding of permissions. When you copied the New York folder to your local desktop, permissions were changed to give you ownership.

1 Select the New York folder, and choose File > Get Info. The Info window displays information about the selected folder.

2 Click the disclosure triangle to the left of the Sharing & Permissions section. The permissions for the New York folder are currently set so that everyone has read & write access to the folder. When a file or folder is copied to another computer, the permissions are updated to give all users read & write access to the files. Close the info window.

3   On the computer where the files are being shared, select the NYC.jpg file and choose File > Get info.

4   In the Sharing & Permissions section of the info window, change the Privilege for staff and everyone to Read Only. Close the info window.

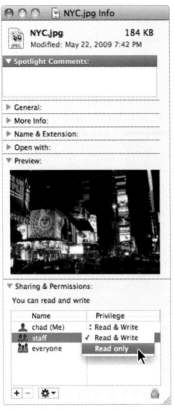

Changing the file permissions for the NYC.jpg file.

5   On the computer that is not sharing the files, right-click or Ctrl+click the NYC.jpg file on the computer that is sharing the files and choose Open with. Select Preview from the resulting list to open the NYC.jpg file using the Preview application.

6   Choose Tools > Adjust size. Type **12** in the width text field and press OK to adjust the size of the file.

7   Choose File > Save. A window appears indicating that the file is locked. Press the overwrite button.

8 A message appears indicating that you do not have appropriate privileges to save the file. This is because you don't have write access to the file, only read access. Press OK.

Because everyone except the owner of the file has read only access, changes can not be made to the file by anyone except the owner.

9 Choose File > Quit Preview. Press the Don't Save button.

This exercise demonstrates how you can limit access to files on your computer so that they can't be modified. Although you probably won't need to modify permissions extensively, its useful to understand how to do so.

Privileges versus permissions

Privileges and permissions can often be confusing when discussing security and access on a computer or network. The terms are often used interchangeably, but there is a difference.

Privileges refer to the access that a user has to a file or folder (i.e., read only, read & write, etc.). Permissions, on the other hand, refer to the assignment of privileges to the various users of a computer.

Clean up

If you no longer want to share the Pictures folder with other users on your network, you can easily stop sharing that folder at any time.

1 On the computer that has the Pictures folder shared, select the Pictures folder in the sidebar of any Finder window.

2 Press Command+I to display the Info window of the Pictures folder.

3 Uncheck the *Shared folder* checkbox and close the Info window. The folder is no longer shared. This can also be done in the Sharing preference pane.

Screen sharing

In addition to sharing files with other users on a network, Snow Leopard makes it possible to share your screen with other users running Mac OS X 10.5 or later (Leopard or Snow Leopard). When a user needs assistance on their computer, you can connect to their computer via screen sharing, and give them the assistance that they need without ever having to leave your computer! It is also possible to share someone's screen even if they are not on your local network; they could be in another state, and screen sharing could be used. To perform screen sharing outside of your local network, advanced setup and configuration is required, so we are not covering it in this book. This exercise will focus on how to enable screen sharing within a local area network.

1 From the Apple menu (☺), choose System Preferences and press the Sharing button.

2 Click the Screen Sharing entry on the left side of the preference pane to highlight it; then click the checkbox to enable Screen Sharing. By default, only Administrators on the computer in which you are enabling Screen Sharing can share your screen.

   You can add additional users in the Allow access for section of the Sharing preference pane, which will give other users the ability to see your screen anytime your computer is turned on. In this lesson, you'll limit that access to only when a user definitely wants their screen shared.

3 Click the Computer Settings button. In the resulting window, click the checkbox next to *Anyone may request permission to control screen*. Press OK. This will allow anyone on your network to request permission to control your screen; however, the user of the computer whose screen is being shared will need to grant permission to do so each time. This is a bit more secure than allowing people to share your screen anytime.

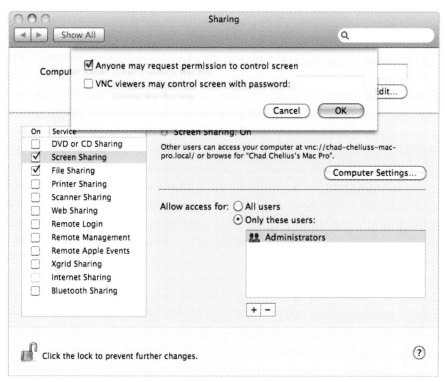

Clicking the Anyone may request permission to control screen *check box requires you to grant permission to any user who wants to control your screen.*

4 The Screen Sharing status now indicates that it is on, and there is a green icon to the left. Choose System Preferences > Quit System Preferences.

Sharing a computer's screen

Now you need to go to another computer on your network to access the computer that has Screen Sharing enabled to test screen sharing.

1 Open a new Finder window and set the view to Column view. In the sidebar under the Shared section, select the computer that has Screen Sharing enabled.

2 In the first column, click the Share Screen button to initiate the session.

3 In the Connect section of the resulting dialog, click the *By asking for permission* radio button, then press the Connect button.

Clicking the By asking for permission *radio button sends a request to the computer you are connecting to, asking for permission to share that computer's screen.*

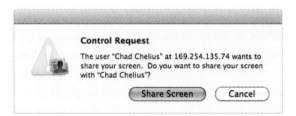

The user of the computer whose screen is being shared needs to click the Share Screen button to grant the connecting user permission to share the screen.

4   Press the Share Screen button. The Screen Sharing application is launched on the connecting user's computer, and they now see the computer that has screen sharing enabled. The name of the computer that you are connected to is listed at the top of the Screen Sharing window.

When you connect to another computer using Screen Sharing, the Screen Sharing application is launched and displays the name of the computer at the top of the window.

5   Double-click the hard drive of the computer you are connected to, to open a new Finder window. You can do anything on this user's computer, as if you were sitting right there in front of the computer.

6   Choose Screen Sharing > Quit Screen Sharing.

Screen sharing on other operating systems

Screen sharing is a fantastic tool as long as both computers are running Mac OS X 10.5 or 10.6 (Leopard or Snow Leopard). But what if some of the computers are running an older version of OS X or another operating system altogether? Does that mean you're out of luck? Absolutely not!

VNC (Virtual Network Computing) is open source software that allows computers running virtually any operating system, including Windows, Linux, Unix, and more, to remotely share screens across those different operating systems. If you are running an operating system that currently doesn't have screen-sharing capabilities, simply do an Internet search for VNC and you'll find a lot of information on the topic.

To allow users other than Leopard and Snow Leopard users to access your computer, simply go back to the Sharing preference pane, and in the Screen Sharing section, click the Computer Settings button and check the *VNC viewers may control screen with password* check box. Now anyone on your network can launch their VNC client and connect to your computer as long as they have the password to an account on your computer. You may want to create a Sharing Only account specifically for this reason.

That's all there is to sharing the screen of another computer on your network. Try connecting to another computer that has screen sharing enabled to practice sharing other users' screens.

Printer sharing

Printer sharing allows you to share a single printer that is already set up on a computer with other users on your network. This allows the budget-conscious consumer to avoid buying a separate printer for each computer in a home or office environment. This exercise requires that you already have a printer installed on one computer on your network that is running Snow Leopard. For more information on how to install a printer, see Lesson 8, "Printing."

1   From the Apple menu, choose System Preferences, and press the Sharing button.

2   Click the Printer Sharing entry on the left side of the preference pane to highlight it, and then click the check box to enable Printer Sharing. By default, anyone on your network will be able to print to this printer.

Now that Printer Sharing is enabled, you need to ensure that the specific printer you want to share is enabled.

3 In the Printers section of the Printer Sharing preference pane, click the check box next to the printer that you want to share. In this example, the Epson Stylus Photo RX500 is enabled.

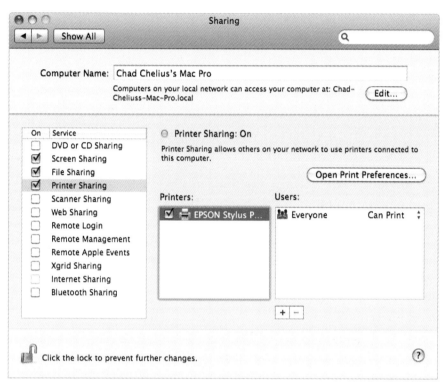

Be sure to click the check box next to each printer that you want to share on your network.

4 If necessary, you can add and remove users who you want to allow to print to this printer in the Users section of the Printer Sharing preference pane. Leave this at the default setting for this lesson.

5 Choose System Preferences > Quit System Preferences.

Adding the printer to another computer on the network

This part of the lesson requires you to be on a different computer than the one in which you enabled printer sharing. Although this exercise assumes that you are running Snow Leopard on the computer that is connecting to the shared printer, this is not a requirement.

1 From the Apple menu (), choose System Preferences, then click the Print & Fax button in the Hardware section of the System Preferences pane.

2 Click the plus sign (+) in the lower-left corner of the Print & Fax preference pane to add a printer to this computer.

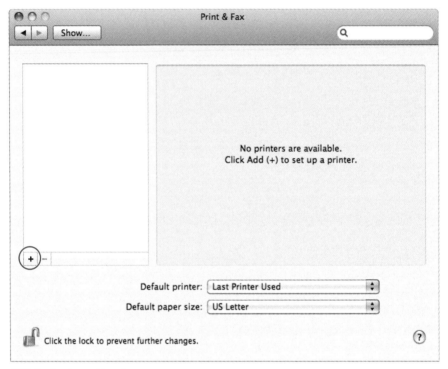

Click the plus sign to add a printer.

3   In the Add a printer dialog, you see the name of the printer that has been shared, as well as the name of the computer that is sharing the printer and possible other shared printers on your network. Select the printer you shared in the previous exercise and press the Add button. The new printer is added to the list in the Print & Fax preference pane.

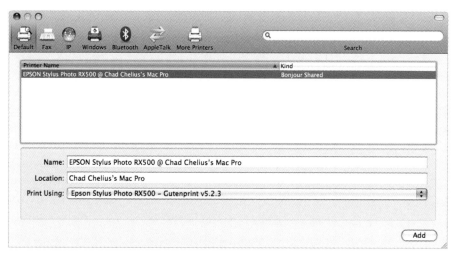

Select the printer that you shared and press the Add button.

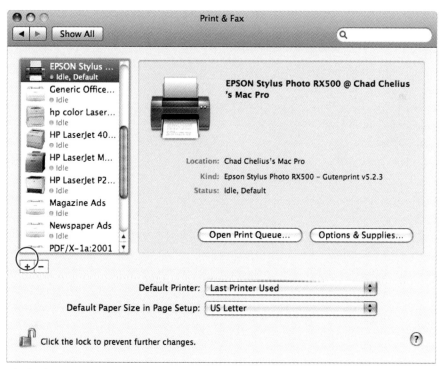

The shared printer is now added to the printer list.

Testing the printer

Now that you've added the shared printer to another computer, you should test it to make sure you can print to it.

1   Select the printer from the list on the left side of the Print & Fax preference pane and press the Open Print Queue button. A print queue window for the selected printer is displayed.

2   Choose Printer > Print Test Page. A file called testprint.ps is added to the print queue and the test page prints on the shared printer.

Printing a test page ensures that the shared printer is working properly.

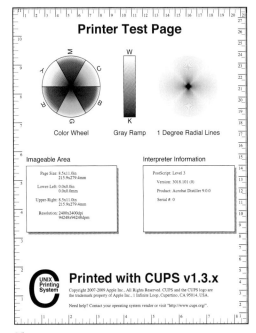

The test page.

If the test page does not print, make sure that your computer is still connected to the network and that the computer that is sharing the printer is on and has not been put to sleep.

3 Close the printer window.

Now that you know how to enable printer sharing in Snow Leopard, add the shared printer to other computers on your network so they can also print to the shared printer.

Your Mac as a web server

Believe it or not, every copy of Snow Leopard ships with a very powerful web server built right into the operating system, called Apache. You can find out more about the Apache web server project at *www.apache.org*. According to a survey done by Netcraft, as of January 2009, Apache was the most widely used web server software in the world.

A web server is simply software that runs on your computer. Its job is to provide web pages to other computers on your immediate network and even potentially the entire Internet. Every web page that you visit on the Internet is being served by one form of web server software or another. This exercise will focus on sharing web pages within your private network. This is useful for providing information within your office environment or even to provide information to members of your family, such as one member's sports schedule or family photos. The possibilities are endless.

This exercise will walk you through the basics of enabling the web server on your Mac and accessing that web server from other computers on your network. Let's get your web server up and running.

1 From the Apple menu (), choose System Preferences, and click the Sharing button.

2 Click the Web Sharing entry on the left side of the preference pane to highlight it, then click the checkbox to enable Web Sharing.

Once Web Sharing is enabled, your computer's web server is available to everyone on your local network. In addition, the URL (Uniform Resource Locator) or web address of your computer is listed on the right side of the Web Sharing preference pane. There are two addresses listed: One address is for the computer itself and the other is for your own personal web site. Each user account on a computer gets his or her own personal web page in addition to the main web server for the computer.

With Web Sharing enabled, the URL of the web server is listed in the Web Sharing preference pane.

Test the web server

1 On another computer on your network, open the web browser and type the URL of the computer's web site in the address bar. This is the bottom-most address listed in the Web Sharing preference pane.

After entering the URL, a web page displays the text, "It works!" This is the default web page for your computer's web server.

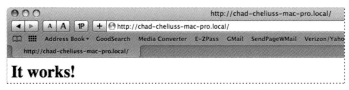

After entering the computer's URL, a web page displays, indicating that it works!

2 Now type the URL of your personal web site, which is the top address listed in the Web Sharing preference pane. A new web page displays, called "Your website."

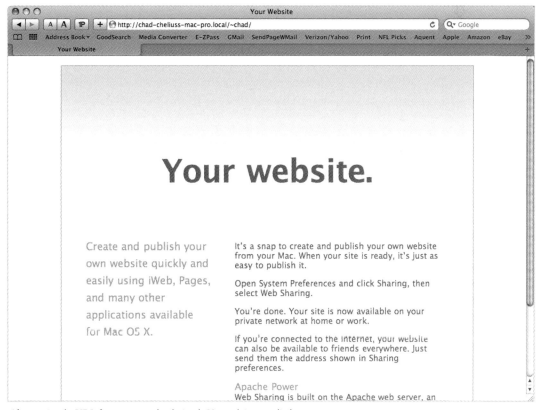

After entering the URL for your personal web site, the Your website page displays.

Editing your web site

Although creating a web site and writing XHTML code is beyond the scope of this book, you'll now make a minor change to your personal web site to see how easy it is to do so. If you want detailed instructions on editing and creating web sites, *Adobe Dreamweaver CS4 Digital Classroom* can help get you up-and-running quickly. When you access a web site, your browser is simply reading an XHTML file that resides in a folder on your computer. The locations for the web sites located on your computer are as follows:

- The computer's web site is located at: /Library/Webserver/Documents
- Each user's personal web site is located at: ~/Sites (the Sites folder in each user's Home folder).

Regardless of which location you access, there is an index.html file that contains the contents of the web page that is first displayed when you access the site (this is also called the Home page). Let's make a small change to your personal web site to see how easy it is.

1　On the computer where you enabled Web Sharing, launch the TextEdit application located in your Applications folder. This is one application that you can use to edit a web page.

2　Choose File > Open and navigate to ~/Sites (the Sites folder inside your Home folder).

3　Select the index.html file, click the checkbox at the bottom of the window to Ignore rich text commands, and press Open.

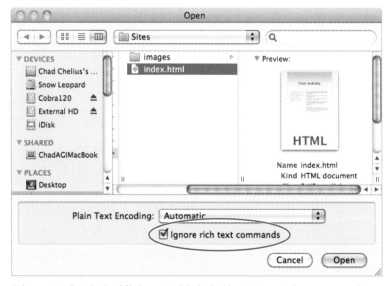

When opening the index.html file, be sure to click the checkbox to Ignore rich text commands.

If you're not used to looking at XHTML code, the code in this window may look intimidating. Don't worry, though; it's actually quite easy to make changes here.

4　Scroll down in the window and search for a line in the code that looks like this: <h3>Your website.</h3>. The h3 indicates a third-level headline. This is the line of text you're going to change.

5　Change that line of text so it reads: **<h3>This is my first website!</h3>**

```
{ color: #666; text-decoration: underline; }
e>


utline">
img src="images/gradient.jpg" alt="" height="
div id="title">
        <h3>This is my first website!</h3>
/div>
div id="caption">
        <h1>Create and publish your own websit
ns available<br />
                for Mac OS X.</h1>
/div>
```

Making a change to a line of text in the XHTML file.

6　Choose File > Save to save the document.

7　Choose TextEdit > Quit TextEdit to close the application.

8　If System Preferences is open, close it by choosing System Preferences > Quit System Preferences.

Now you'll check to make sure that the changes you've made are reflected when other users visit your web site.

9　On another computer on your network, launch the web browser and type your personal web site address. If the web site is still open from the previous exercise, simply press the Refresh button. The changes that you've made to the index.html file are reflected in your web browser.

This is my first website!

Create and publish your
own website quickly and

It's a snap to create and publish your own website
from your Mac. When your site is ready, it's just as
easy to publish it.

The updated web page.

Congratulations! You've completed Lesson 7, "Creating and Using Your Own Network."

Self study

You've learned a lot about sharing in this lesson. Go back and practice file sharing with other users on your network. Show other users how they can create their own personal web sites and share them with other users, as well. You may want to look at other Digital Classroom books in the series, such as the Dreamweaver Digital Classroom, that will help you understand how to build and edit web sites. Check them out at *digitalclassroombooks.com*. If you have additional printers at your office or home, share them so that everyone on the network can access them. It's a great way to utilize the resources at your disposal.

Review

Questions

1   What feature in Snow Leopard allows other users on the same network to control your computer's screen?

2   How can you allow a person on the same network to access files on your computer?

3   What server software is used by Snow Leopard to provide web sharing?

Answers

1   Screen Sharing allows a user on the same network to share your screen.

2   By enabling File Sharing. You can even create a sharing-only account for that user for even more control.

3   The Apache web server.

Lesson 8

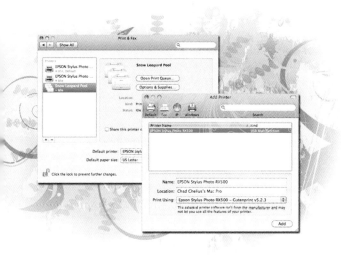

What you'll learn in this lesson:

- The purpose of a printer driver
- Installing a printer
- Managing the Print Queue
- Conserving ink
- Printing to a file

Printing

In this lesson, you will learn how to install a printer, configure its settings, and print to that printer using Snow Leopard.

Starting up

This lesson doesn't utilize any lesson files and therefore doesn't require any files to be copied onto your computer.

See Lesson 8 in action!

Use the accompanying video to gain a better understanding of how to use some of the features shown in this lesson. The video tutorial for this lesson can be found on the included DVD.

Printers

Printers come in varying shapes, sizes, and configurations. As the primary output device on your computer, the printer becomes an important tool for converting the digital information on your computer to ink on paper. As much as we've become a digital society, there's still a significant need to print content to a physical medium, from party invitations, name tags, directions, photos and more.

Printer types

There is a wide assortment of printers available to you as a consumer, and you'll need to decide what type of printer meets your specific needs. Printer types include inkjet, laser, dot-matrix, thermal, and many more. In today's market, consumer printers generally fall into two categories: laser and inkjet. Let's take a look at these two options.

Laser printers

Laser printers work by heating toner (a dry, powdery substance that is electrically charged so that it adheres to a piece of paper) and adhering it to the paper. Laser printers generally have very good text and line art quality, but lower photo quality. The cost for laser printers is much higher than that of inkjet printers, but they are usually built better because of their expected output requirements. The toner cartridges can be expensive, but the price per page is generally pretty low. Laser printers usually have a pretty fast ppm (pages per minute) rating and are a good choice if you tend to print a lot of letters, reports, forms, and so on. Color laser printers are also a good choice for printing reports that contain charts and graphs for presentation purposes, but the cost per page of a color laser printer is certainly higher than that of a black-and-white laser printer.

Inkjet printers

Inkjet printers and their underlying technology have significantly improved over the past several years. Because of their low initial cost (stores often include them with the purchase of a computer), they are usually the first choice for budget-minded consumers. Inkjet printers work by spraying droplets of ink onto the paper during the printing process. Because of this technology, photos look outstanding, but you obtain the best photo results when printing on coated paper. Inkjet printers usually have very good photo quality, but lower text and line art quality. Although the overall cost of the printer is fairly low, the consumer needs to use caution, as the ink can sometimes be very costly. Some inkjet printers can contain six or more color cartridges.

Installing a printer

Regardless of what type of printer you choose, the printer needs to be installed on your computer. The installation process may vary, based on the manufacturer and type of printer you are installing, but this lesson will guide you through the general steps required to install your printer. Always consult the instructions provided with your printer to verify the installation process for that printer. The general steps to installing a printer on your machine involve installing the appropriate printer drivers on your computer and then adding the printer to the printer list so that Snow Leopard can access it.

Printer drivers

A printer driver is a piece of software written for a particular printer that allows the computer to communicate with that specific printer. Printer drivers are usually supplied on a disk that is included with the printer. As a general rule, it's a good idea to check the manufacturer's web site for the latest version of the printer driver to ensure the best performance from your printer.

Printer drivers are written for the operating systems that are current on the release date of the printer. Therefore, older printers may not have printer drivers for operating systems that are released after the shipping date of those printers. Generally, printer manufacturers only release printer drivers for new operating systems for certain older printers. You may find that this is the case for Snow Leopard if you are trying to connect an older printer to your computer.

Fortunately, you're not completely out of luck if you own an older printer and are not yet ready to part with it. Snow Leopard ships with a complete package of Gutenprint printer drivers for older printers that do not have current printer drivers from the manufacturer. Gutenprint is open-source software. Open-source means that a group of dedicated software developers have invested their time and energy to write software for people to use free of charge. Gutenprint (formerly called Gimp-Print) drivers are often even more robust and feature-rich than the drivers supplied by the manufacturer! For more information on Gutenprint and open-source software, go to *gutenprint.sourceforge.net*.

Installation

1 Connect your printer to your computer using your preferred connection method. Usually this is a USB cable if you are connecting the printer directly to your computer, or an Ethernet cable if you are connecting the printer to a network.

2 If you have received a disk with your printer that contains the latest drivers, insert the CD and follow the instructions to install the printer drivers. If you've downloaded the drivers from the Internet, the installer will be located in your Downloads folder or your Desktop depending on your browser preferences. Launch the installer and follow the instructions on the screen. For more information on installing Mac OS X software, see Lesson 12, "Installing Snow Leopard and Applications."

3 Now it's time to add the printer to the printer list. Choose System Preferences from the Apple menu (🍎) and press the Print & Fax button in the Hardware section of the System Preferences pane.

4 Click the plus sign (+) in the lower left corner of the Print & Fax preference pane.

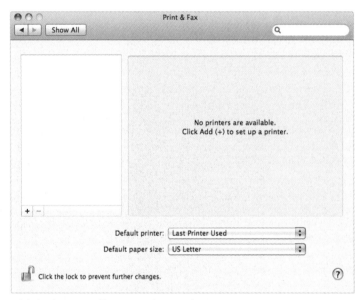

Click the plus sign to add a printer to the printer list.

5   In the toolbar of the Add Printer window, make sure that Default is chosen. Your printer
    is displayed in this category.

    There are three other categories that you can choose from in the toolbar of the Add
    Printer window:

    •   **Fax** is used to set up your modem or Bluetooth device to send and receive faxes.

    •   **IP** is used when you want to add a printer based on its IP address or DNS name. This is
        usually a network printer.

    •   **Windows** is used when you want to add a shared printer that is located on a Windows
        workgroup.

6   Select your printer from the list. After a few minutes, the bottom of the Add Printer
    window displays the default name, location, and the printer driver being used to print to
    the selected printer.

    Feel free to change the name or location to something more relevant. The printer in
    this example is using the Gutenprint drivers because the manufacturer has not released
    drivers compatible with Snow Leopard yet. If you've installed printer drivers from the
    manufacturer, but those drivers are not selected in the Print Using drop-down menu,
    you can choose specific drivers by clicking on the Print Using drop-down menu and
    choosing the drivers supplied by the manufacturer.

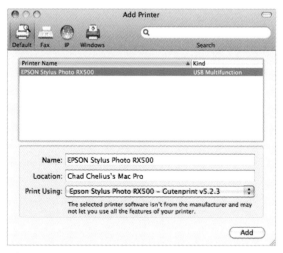

*After selecting the printer, you can customize the name and location, and
choose a specific printer driver to use.*

7 Press the Add button. The Print & Fax preference pane appears, and the printer is added to the printer list on the left side of the pane.

The features available to you depend on the model of printer that you have, as well as which printer drivers have been installed for use with this printer. Although the figures in this lesson show an all-in-one printer (printer/scanner/copier), this lesson will focus on the general features that are likely to be found on most printers.

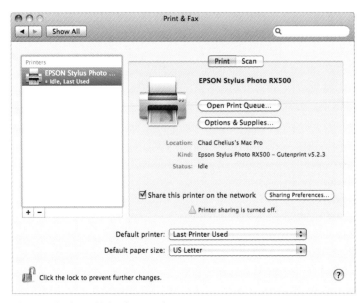

The printer has been added to the printer list.

8 Notice that by default, the *Share this printer on the network* checkbox is enabled but is not being shared because, by default, printer sharing on the computer is turned off. Uncheck this checkbox to disable printer sharing for this printer. For more on sharing a printer, refer to Lesson 7, "Creating and Using Your Own Network."

9 At the bottom of the Print & Fax preference pane, there's a drop-down menu where you can choose the default printer. The default setting is Last Printer Used. Change this to the printer that you just added. This feature is useful if you have more than one printer installed and would like to print to one specific printer most of the time. When you print from any application, the printer that you choose here is automatically selected.

10 You can also choose the default paper size from the drop-down menu at the bottom of the Print & Fax preference pane. For now, leave this set to US Letter; however, if you are using a printer for a specific purpose, such as envelopes, you can choose that size here.

The Print Queue

Each printer that has been added to the printer list has a Print Queue. A Print Queue is a temporary storage location that is used when you print to a printer. When you print to a printer, the information is sent to the Print Queue, where it waits until the printer is ready before sending the information to the printer. If you send multiple files to the printer or if multiple users print to the printer at the same time, the print files wait in the Print Queue until the printer is finished processing the last job and then releases the next file in the queue for printing.

1 If the Print & Fax preference pane isn't open, choose System Preferences from the Apple menu (🍎) and press the Print & Fax button to display the Print & Fax preference pane.

2 Select a printer in the Printers list and press the Open Print Queue button in the main area of the Print & Fax preference pane. The Print Queue for the selected printer is displayed.

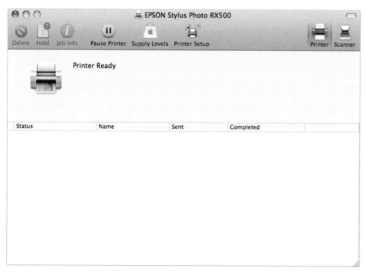

The Print Queue for the selected printer.

3 Confirm that the printer is working by printing a test page. From the Printer menu, choose Print Test Page.

Selecting Print Test Page with the Print Queue window open sends a test page to the printer.

4 A print file is added to the Print Queue and the status of the current page is displayed.

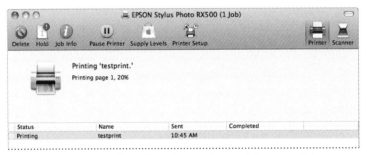

After printing a test page, the file is added to the Print Queue and the status is displayed.

Managing the Print Queue

The Print Queue allows you to manage jobs that are sent to the printer for maximum efficiency.

1 Press the Pause Printer button in the toolbar of the Print Queue window. Users can still print to the printer; however, they will wait in the Print Queue because it is paused.

2 Launch the Safari Web browser and go to *www.apple.com*.

3 Choose File > Print.

4 Make sure that the printer of the Print Queue that you paused in step 1 above is selected, and click the Print button. You see a window indicating that the printer has been paused; click the Add to Queue button.

5   Go to *www.digitalclassroombooks.com* and repeat steps 2 and 3 above.

6   Go to *www.agitraining.com* and repeat steps 2 and 3 above.

7   Quit Safari.

8   In the Print Queue window, you can see that there are three jobs on hold in the queue to be printed and they are ordered from top to bottom in the list. Select the Apple print job and press the On Hold button in the toolbar. The status of the job to the left of the job name now indicates that the job is on hold.

9   You've decided that you no longer need to print the AGI training web site, the last one in the list. Select that job, and press the Delete button in the toolbar to remove it from the queue.

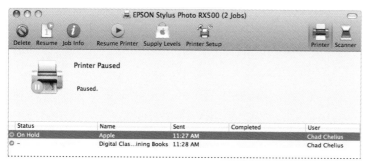

The Print Queue allows you to hold and delete jobs for better control of what is printed on the printer.

If you prefer not to print any jobs on your printer, do not perform steps 10 and 11 below. Instead, simply select each print job in the Print Queue and click the Delete button in the toolbar.

10 Press the Resume Printer button in the toolbar to put the printer online. Printing begins. Because the Apple print job was put on hold, the Digital Classroom Books job begins printing.

11 To resume printing of the Apple job, select the job in the Print Queue and press the Resume button in the toolbar. The Apple job will begin printing after the Digital Classroom job is finished.

12 If you decide at any time that you prefer not to print a job that is sent to the printer, simply select each job in the Print Queue window and press Delete in the toolbar.

Viewing jobs that have already been printed

It can be useful to view jobs that have been printed on your printer for both verification and troubleshooting purposes.

1   With the Print Queue window still open on your screen, choose Jobs > Show Completed Jobs. All of the jobs that have been sent to this Print Queue are listed.

2   Choose Jobs > Show Everyone's Jobs. This displays each job, with the user who printed the job listed in a column on the right side of the Print Queue window. This is useful if you are sharing your printer with other users and would like to analyze the printer usage.

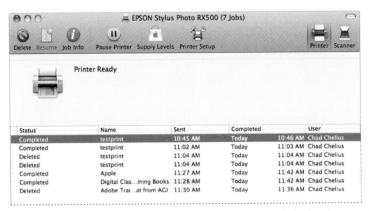

Choosing Show Completed Jobs and Show Everyone's Jobs displays the jobs that have been printed on this printer as well as who printed them.

3   Choose Jobs > Hide Completed Jobs and choose Jobs > Show My Jobs to set the Print Queue window back to its default state.

4   Press the Close button (●) in the upper-left corner of the Print Queue window to close the window.

5   Choose System Preferences > Quit System Preferences.

The print dialog

Whenever you need to print a file to a printer, regardless of which application you are using, you almost always need to use the print dialog to do so. The print dialog allows you to control various aspects of how the document is printed on your printer. Although the print dialog varies, depending on which application you are using, the general parameters are consistent throughout the different applications. You'll be using Safari to print the files to your printer. This exercise will help to demystify the options within the print dialog box giving you better control of your print output.

1   Launch Safari on your computer and go to *www.digitalclassroombooks.com*.

2   Choose File > Print to display the print dialog.

3   In the Printer drop-down menu, choose the printer that you want to print to.

4 By default, the print dialog is minimized. Click the blue triangle to the right of the Printer drop-down menu to expand the print dialog to show more options.

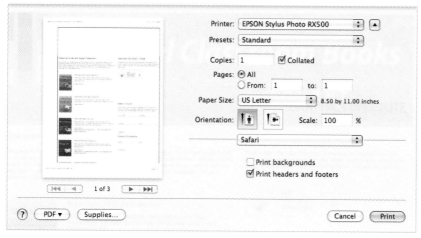

The print dialog, minimized and expanded.

5 The preview section on the left side of the print dialog shows you how your document will be printed on your printer. You can click the arrow buttons below the preview to view each page that will be printed.

6 The Copies field allows you to enter how many copies you'd like to print on the printer. Leave this set to 1. When you select the Collated check box, this feature collates, or orders, the pages appropriately when the document is printed, however, your printer may not have this option.

7 The Pages area allows you to designate a specific range of pages to print, or all the pages. Leave the All radio button checked.

8 Paper size allows you to choose the paper size that your document is printed on. Your printer determines what options are available in this list. Choose US Letter from the drop-down menu.

9 The orientation section allows you to choose Portrait (shortest edge as the width) or Landscape (longest edge as the width). Select the Landscape orientation and notice that the preview on the left side of the print dialog changes.

10 If you are printing a document that is a different size than the paper, you can adjust the value in the Scale field to increase or decrease the size of the document on the paper. Leave the Scale field set to 100 percent.

Advanced print options

The Print Options drop-down menu, located directly below the Orientation section of the print dialog, provides features related to the application you are printing from or the options for the chosen printer. Because of this, the options in this drop-down menu will not be discussed here.

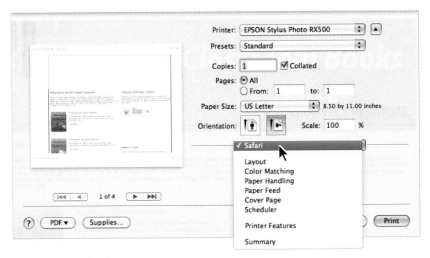

The Print Options drop-down menu.

1 Currently, Safari is chosen in the Print Options drop-down menu. When Safari is chosen, options related to printing from Safari are listed below the drop-down menu. Deselect the *Print headers and footers* checkbox.

2 Choose Layout from the Print Options drop-down menu. This option allows you to print multiple pages on each sheet to conserve paper. Leave these settings unchanged.

3 Choose Scheduler from the Print Options drop-down menu. This allows you to print a document at a later date specified by you. The file is sent to the Print Queue but remains on hold until the time that you specify.

4 Choose the Summary option from the Print Options drop-down menu. This displays a summary of the various options chosen in the Print Options drop-down menu. Click the disclosure triangle to the left of each item in the Summary window to view the settings.

Presets

You've just spent a fair amount of time configuring the settings in the print dialog so that your job prints to your specifications. It would be a waste of time to do this each and every time you had to print a job. Presets solve this problem by allowing you to save the settings for reuse when you have similar jobs to print. Let's see how you can save some time.

1   With the print dialog still open, click the Preset drop-down menu and choose Save As. The Save Preset As window appears.

2   In the Preset Name text field, type **Safari web pages**. You can make this preset available for the currently selected printer or for all printers. Because these settings are specific to the printer that you have selected, check the *Only this printer* radio button. Press OK.

```
                   Save Preset As:

  Preset Name:  Safari web pages

Preset Available For:  ⦿ Only this printer
                       ○ All printers

                         ( Cancel )  ( OK )
```

The Save Preset As window allows you to save settings for future use in the print dialog.

3   The Safari web pages preset is now active in the Presets drop-down menu.

4   If you create a preset and later decide that you want to remove it, you can simply select it from the Presets drop-down menu, then choose Delete from the Presets drop-down menu.

5   Press the Print button if you'd like to see how this job prints on your printer; otherwise, press the Cancel button.

Conserving Ink

Modern inkjet printers operate by applying very small droplets of ink to a substrate (i.e. paper, mylar, CD/DVD) during the printing process. In order to replicate the intended color, the printer will mix varying amounts of cyan, magenta, yellow, black, and sometimes additional colors such as light cyan and light magenta ink to achieve that intended color.

Believe it or not, even when you print a document that is black only, many modern inkjet printers will reproduce that black color using combinations of all inks in the printer. This wastes valuable and often expensive ink that could be used for printing color documents on your printer. Many users have experienced the need to replace their color ink cartridges when all they ever print is black only documents.

Most print drivers will have an option available that allows you to print using only black ink when desired. This setting usually is found under the color setting of the Print dialog and will be listed as black only or grayscale. Choosing this option will usually tell the printer to use only black ink instead of a combination of all inks in the printer saving those color inks for when you actually need them.

Printing to a PDF file

In addition to printing jobs to a physical printer, you can also print jobs to a PDF file. PDF stands for Portable Document Format and is probably the most widely used format for distributing files electronically. Snow Leopard gives you this capability right out of the box and allows you to print virtually any file to a PDF file. A PDF file is useful if you want to send someone a document that is currently in a format that the other person may not be able to read. For instance, let's say you have a Microsoft Word file but someone who you want to send the file to doesn't own Microsoft Word and therefore cannot open it. Printing the Word file to a PDF file allows them to read the file. If they are using a Mac, they can open the file using the included Preview application. Otherwise, they can download the free Adobe Reader application from *www.adobe.com* for any platform (Mac, Windows, Linux, and so on), which provides the ability to read the PDF file.

A PDF file can also be useful if you want to look at the contents of a web site when you're traveling or don't have an Internet connection. Simply make a PDF of the web site, and you can look at it anytime and anywhere. In this exercise, you'll make a PDF file of the Digital Classroom Books web site for later viewing.

1 Open Safari and go to *www.digitalclassroombooks.com*.

2 Choose File > Print to open the print dialog.

3 Press the PDF button in the lower-left corner of the print dialog. Several options are listed in this menu that allow you to perform specific tasks with the PDF document. Choose Save as PDF. The Save window appears.

4 Click the blue triangle next to the Save As field to expand the window.

5 In Save As text field, type **DCBooks** and click Desktop in the Sidebar to indicate where the PDF file will be saved.

6 The Title, Author, Subject, and Keywords text fields provide a location for detailed information about the PDF file. This information is called *metadata*. Leave Title and Author as is, but type **Digital Classroom web site** in the Subject text field and **Books** in the Keywords text field.

The Save window allows you to name the PDF and enter metadata about the file.

7 Press the Security Options button at the bottom of the Save window. The PDF Security Options window appears. This window allows you to require a password to open the document, copy content, or print the document. This is useful if you are sending a PDF containing sensitive information. You won't be protecting this document, so press the Cancel button.

The PDF Security Options window allows you to password-protect the document.

8   Press the Save button, and a PDF file of the web site is saved to your desktop.

9   Choose Safari > Hide Safari.

10   Double-click the DCBooks file on your desktop to open it in Preview. When the document opens, you can click each page of the PDF file in the Sidebar on the right of the window to look at each page.

If you have Adobe Reader installed on your computer, the PDF may open using that program. Both Preview and Adobe Reader can read PDF files.

11   Choose Preview > Quit Preview to close the Preview application.

12   Click the Safari icon in your Dock to display the web page on your screen.

Printer pools

If you work in an environment where there are several printers on which to print your documents, you may want to consider printer pools. Printer pools allow you to group several printers together so that when you send a document to the pool, the first available printer is used to print your document. Let's say that a coworker or household member just sent a 30-page document to the printer. That printer will be tied up for quite a long time; however, you may not be aware that the printer is in use. So if you send your job to the same printer, you'll have to wait until the 30-page document is finished printing before your document prints. With printer pools, you group several printers together so that your job is sent to the printer that currently is not busy, thereby printing your job sooner with no hassles. In this exercise, you'll add the same printer that you added earlier in this lesson to gain an understanding of how printer pools work. If you have two printers at your disposal, you can create a printer pool using those printers.

1   Choose System Preferences from the Apple menu (); then select the Print & Fax button to display the Print & Fax preference pane.

2   Click the plus sign (+) at the bottom of the printer list to add a new printer. If you have two printers, select a different printer from the one that you added earlier in this lesson. Otherwise, select the same printer.

3 Press the Add button to add the printer to the Printers list. A window appears, indicating that a queue for this printer already exists. Press Continue. A new printer is added to the list with –1 appended to the name of the printer.

4 Click the first printer at the top of the Printers list, then Shift-click the second printer in the Printers list to select both printers at the same time. The Print & Fax preference pane changes and indicates that multiple printers are selected.

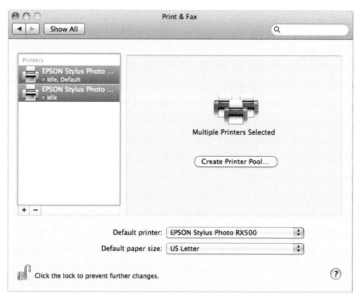

When multiple printers are selected, the Print & Fax preference pane changes to reflect this.

5 Press the Create Printer Pool button. In the resulting dialog, type **Snow Leopard Pool** or whatever name you prefer. Press OK.

6   The printer pool is added to the Printers list and can be shared on the network and controlled as if it were a single printer.

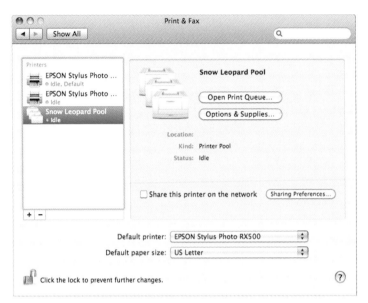

The printer pool is added to the Printers list.

As you can see, printer pools are very easy to add and configure in Snow Leopard. They make printing a more efficient process in your home or office.

7   Choose System Preferences > Quit System Preferences.

CUPS

CUPS stands for the Common UNIX Printing System. It is a system that allows you to manage, add, and control printers on your computer, and even on other computers on your network. CUPS makes it very easy to maintain printers. Although you don't have to use CUPS to add and manage your printers, it's often useful because it provides a nice interface for doing so. This exercise will cover the basics of CUPS, but if you'd like to dive in deeper, there's a wonderful help section available on the CUPS page that provides more information. The CUPS interface is accessed from any Web browser. Let's take a look!

1   Open Safari, type **localhost:631** in the Address bar, and press Return on your keyboard. The CUPS home page appears. The CUPS home page provides quick access to information and features of the CUPS system.

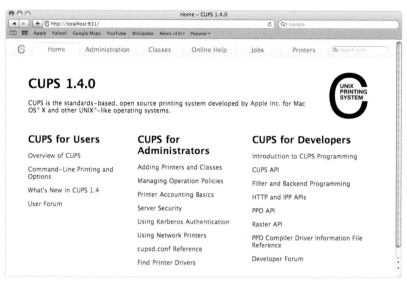

The CUPS home page.

2   Click the Administration tab at the top of the page. This section provides a convenient way to add printers, add classes (printer pools), and manage jobs. It also provides a way for you to share printers and control what users can do with jobs in the print queue.

3   Click the Classes tab at the top of the page. The printer pool that you added earlier in this lesson is displayed here.

4   Click the name of the printer pool (Snow_Leopard_Pool), and you see additional options that are available for managing this pool, such as seeing what jobs have been completed.

5   Click the Online Help tab at the top of the page. If you want to know the answer to certain questions about CUPS or simply want more information, you can find it here.

6   Click the Jobs tab at the top of the page. This displays any jobs in any of the Print Queues on your computer.

7   Click the Show Completed Jobs button in the upper-left corner of the page. All jobs that have been printed are listed with very detailed information, such as the user who printed the job, when it was printed, and what the name of the job was. Very useful!

8   Click the Printers tab at the top of the page. This displays all the printers installed on your computer. Click the name of the first printer in this list to display more detailed information about the printer.

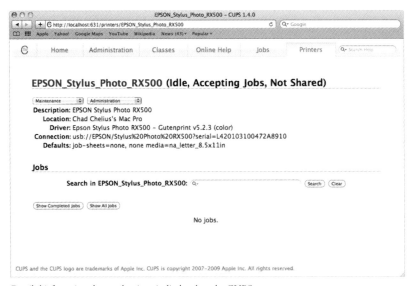

Detailed information about each printer is displayed on the CUPS page.

9   Click the Maintenance drop-down menu. From this menu, you can use all of the features that you could from within the Print & Fax preference pane, and then some. Choose the Print Test Page option. A test page prints on your printer and the CUPS Web page refreshes to show you the status of the print job. This menu also allows you to perform functions such as cleaning the print head, cancelling jobs, moving jobs to another printer, and much more.

10   Choose Safari > Quit Safari.

CUPS makes managing either a single or multiple printers a very easy process. The ability to manually move a job from one printer to another is a great feature if you don't have a printer pool configured and are waiting for another job to finish printing. You can also pause and resume any printer as needed.

Congratulations! You've finished Lesson 8, "Printing."

Clean up

To restore your system back to the state it was in prior to this lesson, follow these steps.

1 Drag the DCBooks file on your desktop to the trash.

2 Choose Finder > Empty Trash.

3 Choose System Preferences from the Apple menu (🍎) and press the Print & Fax button to display the Print & Fax preference pane.

4 Select any printers in the Printers list that you'd like to remove from your computer.

5 Click the minus (–) sign at the bottom of the Printers list to remove the printer.

6 Repeat steps 4 and 5 for any other printers or for the printer pool that was created earlier in the lesson.

Self study

Being able to set up and configure your printer is of prime importance for most computer users. Go back and add another printer to your computer, and create a printer pool to limit the amount of time you have to wait when printing a file. Go back and reference the printer sharing section in Lesson 7, "Creating and Using Your Own Network," to see how easy it is to share your printer with other users on your network. Use Snow Leopard's ability to create a PDF file of any document on your computer. This is a great way to share information with other users.

Review

Questions

1 What is the software called that allows a computer to communicate with a specific printer?

2 How do you configure several printers so that if one printer is busy, it prints to another available printer?

3 How do you share a proprietary file with a user that doesn't have the program to open that proprietary file?

4 How do you get to the CUPS administration page?

Answers

1 The printer driver.

2 Create a printer pool.

3 Print the file to a PDF and give the user the PDF file. They can open it in the Preview or Adobe Reader application.

4 Open a web browser and type **localhost:631** in the Address bar.

What you'll learn in this lesson:

- Customizing the behavior of the keyboard and mouse
- Setting up your computer to conserve electricity
- Customizing the appearance of Snow Leopard
- Leveraging System Preferences to meet your needs

System Preferences

In this lesson, you'll learn how to customize your Mac to meet your needs using the System Preferences available with Snow Leopard.

Starting up

This lesson doesn't utilize any lesson files and therefore doesn't require any files to be copied onto your computer.

See Lesson 9 in action!

Use the accompanying video to gain a better understanding of how to use some of the features shown in this lesson. The video tutorial for this lesson can be found on the included DVD.

System Preferences

System Preferences are a command-center for your Mac. The System Preferences pane provides complete customization of various aspects of Snow Leopard where you can define the behaviors and features of the operating system. This lesson serves as a reference where you can see what features are provided by each individual preference pane within System Preferences. The main System Preferences pane is divided into four primary categories:

- Personal
- Hardware
- Internet & Wireless
- System

The System Preferences pane.

Each of these categories contains various preference panes that allow you to control the different features of Snow Leopard. In addition to these four main categories, some software applications add preference panes when they are installed. These program-specific preference panes are placed into a fifth category called Other. This category is not covered in this lesson, as they are specific to third-party applications, which vary from user to user. Let's take a look at the options available in the System Preferences!

Personal

The Personal category relates to the look-and-feel of your system and pertains to the current user account. This means that each user account on a computer can customize the settings in the Personal category to create a customized working environment.

Appearance

The Appearance preference pane focuses primarily on the behavior and appearance of Finder windows, as well as how text is displayed on your computer's screen.

1   From the Apple menu (), choose System Preferences and press the Appearance button to open the Appearance preference pane.

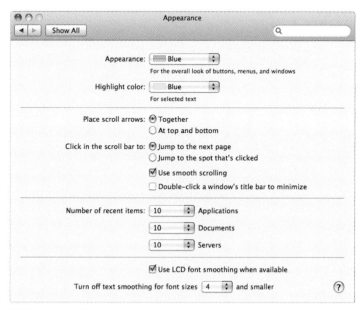

The Appearance preference pane.

- The Appearance drop-down menu controls the color of buttons, menus, and windows. You have two color choices, Graphite and Blue. Choose the one that you prefer. It may help to open a new Finder window so you can see these changes as you make them.

- The Highlight Color drop-down menu controls the color of selected items (files and folders) or selected text in any Finder window. Choose a color from the menu, or choose the Other option to pick a custom color.

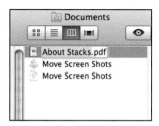

The highlight color after being changed to orange.

- The *Place scroll arrows* option determines whether the scroll arrows will be placed together or at the top and bottom of a Finder window.

- The *Click in the scroll bar to* option determines whether clicking in the scroll bar of a Finder window jumps to the next page in the item list, or to the location that is clicked in the scroll bar.

- The *Use smooth scrolling* option prevents the contents of a Finder window from *jumping* when scrolling through the list. Depending on the hardware configuration of your computer, you may not see much of a difference with this option.

- The *Double-click a window's title bar to minimize* option minimizes a window upon double clicking on the title bar.

- The Number of Recent Items section determines how many items are displayed in each category when you select Recent Items from the Apple menu. Ten is the default, but you can increase or decrease these values to a different value in each drop-down menu.

- The *Use LCD font smoothing* when available option reduces jagged edges for some fonts by smoothing the edges (anti-aliasing) of the font. Small font sizes can be difficult to read when this option is enabled. If you experience this problem, you can choose a value in the Turn off text smoothing for font sizes drop-down menu to minimize this behavior.

Desktop & Screen Saver

The Desktop & Screen Saver preference pane controls the appearance of the desktop and the behavior of screen savers on your computer.

1   From the Apple menu ($\bullet$), choose System preferences and press the Desktop & Screen Saver button to open the Desktop & Screen Saver preference pane.

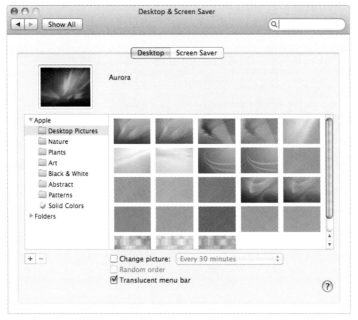

The Desktop section of the Desktop & Screen Saver preference pane.

2 The Desktop & Screen Saver preference pane is divided into two sections: Desktop and Screen Saver. Each section can be activated by clicking on the corresponding button at the top of the preference pane.

3 Press the Desktop button. The active desktop image is displayed at the top of the preference pane with a small preview of the image.

4 The sidebar on the left side of the preference pane contains categories that contain various desktop images from which to choose. Select a category in the sidebar, and then select an image in the window to the right of the sidebar to make that image the active desktop image.

Select a category in the sidebar, and then choose a desktop image to make it the active desktop image.

5 At the bottom of the sidebar are a plus (+) button and a minus (−) button that allow you to add your own folders that contain images to the sidebar to use as desktop images.

6 Click the *Change picture* checkbox at the bottom of the Desktop & Screen Saver preference pane, then choose an option from the drop-down menu to have the desktop image change automatically based on the interval chosen in the drop-down menu. When this option is chosen, you can also click the *Random order* checkbox to instruct Snow Leopard to randomly change the image based on the time interval chosen.

7 Click the *Translucent menu bar* checkbox if you would like the desktop image to slightly show through the menu bar at the top of your screen.

8 Press the Screen Saver button at the top of the Desktop & Screen Saver preference pane. This allows you to control the Screen Saver settings on your computer.

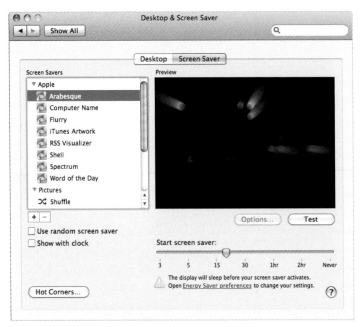

The Screen Saver section of the preference pane.

9 The Screen Savers sidebar on the left side of the preference pane contains categories of screen savers for you to choose from. Select a screen saver in the sidebar, and the Preview window to the right displays what that screen saver looks like. Press the Test button below the preview window to see the screen saver in full screen.

10 Press the + (plus) button below the Screen Savers sidebar to add additional screen savers to the sidebar. There are four choices:

- **Add Folder of Pictures** allows you to select a folder containing images that can be used as screen savers.

- **Add MobileMe Gallery** allows you to select a MobileMe Gallery that was created using the MobileMe service. This option requires that you have a MobileMe account. For more information on MobileMe, see the Internet & Wireless section later in this lesson or go to www.apple.com/mobileme.

- **Add RSS Feed** allows you to add RSS (Really Simple Syndication) feeds that display information from those feeds as the screen saver. An RSS feed is a web link that displays updates to web sites and blogs. Google 'RSS Feed' for more information.

- **Browse Screen Savers** takes you to the Apple web site to download additional screen savers to your computer.

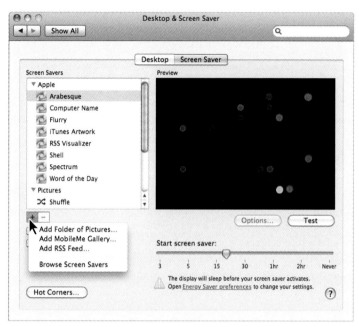

Click the + (plus) button to add additional screen savers.

11 Click the *Use random screen saver* checkbox to have the screen saver chosen at random when the screen saver activates, and click the *Show with clock* checkbox to display a clock when the screen saver activates.

12 The Start screen saver slider at the bottom of the Desktop & Screen saver preference pane controls the period of inactivity required before the screen saver activates. Drag the slider to the left or right to change the setting. If your computer is set to sleep at an interval that is less than the setting for the screen saver, a warning is displayed, indicating that your screen saver will not activate unless you increase the sleep setting in the Energy Saver preference pane or decrease the start screen saver setting.

Dock

The Dock preference pane controls the behavior and appearance of the Dock on your computer.

1 From the Apple menu (), choose System Preferences and press the Dock button to open the Dock preference pane.

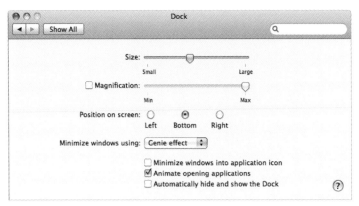

The Dock preference pane controls the behavior and appearance of the Dock on your computer.

2 Drag the Size slider to the left to reduce the size of your Dock, and to the right to increase the size of your Dock. As you add files and folders to the Dock, you may need to adjust the Size slider to compensate for these newly added items.

3 Click the *Magnification* checkbox to enlarge the icons in the Dock when you hover your cursor over them. Drag the slider to the left to reduce the amount of enlargement, and to the right to increase the amount of enlargement.

Clicking the Magnification *check box enlarges the icons in the Dock as you hover your cursor over each icon.*

4 Click each radio button in the *Position on screen* section to position the Dock on the left, bottom, or right side of your screen.

5 Choose either the Genie Effect or the Scale Effect to specify how a window is animated when it is minimized to the Dock.

6   Click the *Minimize windows into application icon* checkbox to minimize a window to the application that it is associated with instead of to the right side of the Dock.

7   Click the *Animate opening applications* checkbox to animate the application icon in the Dock when that application is launched.

8   If you would like the Dock to hide when your cursor is not within the Dock area, click the *Automatically hide and show the Dock* checkbox.

Exposé & Spaces

The Exposé & Spaces preference pane controls the behavior and activation of the Exposé and Spaces feature in Snow Leopard.

1   From the Apple menu (), choose System Preferences, and press the Exposé & Spaces button to open the Exposé & Spaces preference pane.

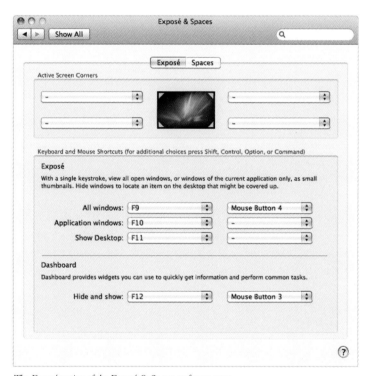

The Exposé section of the Exposé & Spaces preference pane.

2   The Exposé & Spaces preference pane is divided into two sections: Exposé and Spaces. Each section can be activated by clicking on the corresponding button at the top of the preference pane. Press the Exposé button.

3   The Activate Screen Corners section at the top of the preference pane provides four drop-down menus, one for each corner of your screen. In each drop-down menu, you can choose from a list of options that will activate when you move your cursor to that corner of your screen. The options available in each drop-down menu are as follows:

- **All Windows** displays all open windows, regardless of what application each window is associated with.

- **Application Windows** displays all open windows of the active application.

- **Desktop** moves any open window out of view so that the entire desktop is displayed.

- **Dashboard** activates the Dashboard feature in Snow Leopard.

- **Start Screen Saver** activates the screen saver on your computer.

- **Disable Screen Saver** deactivates the screen saver on your computer.

- **Put Display to Sleep** puts the display to sleep, which consumes very little power.

The options available in the drop-down menus for each corner of the screen.

4   The Keyboard and Mouse Shortcuts section allows you to choose a keyboard shortcut for each feature in the drop-down menus, and allows you to specify a mouse button that activates each feature when a specific mouse button is depressed from the drop-down menus on the right.

5   The Dashboard section at the bottom of the preference pane allows you to specify a keyboard shortcut and a mouse button to activate Dashboard on your computer. For more information on Dashboard, refer to Lesson 2, "Customizing the OS X Interface to Suit Your Needs."

6   Press the Spaces button at the top of the Exposé & Spaces preference pane. Spaces allows you to have multiple desktop environments on your computer. For instance, you can have an application open in one space and Finder windows in another space.

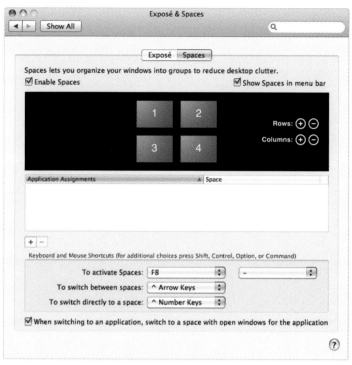

The Spaces section of the Exposé & Spaces preference pane.

7   By default, Spaces is not activated. Click the *Enable Spaces* checkbox to activate the feature.

8   If you'd like quick access to the Spaces feature, click the *Show Spaces in menu bar* checkbox to display an icon for Spaces in the Menu bar of your computer.

9   By default, there are four Spaces configured. Press the plus (+) or minus (–) button to add or remove columns and rows to the Spaces configuration.

10 Press the plus (+) or minus (–) button at the bottom of the Application Assignments section to add an application and assign it to a specific space, or to remove it, respectively. For instance, you can configure Safari to always open in Space 1.

11 The Keyboard and Mouse Shortcuts section, later in this book, allows you to assign keyboard shortcuts to activate and switch between the various spaces. You can also assign a mouse shortcut to activate spaces on your computer.

Language & Text

The Language & Text preference pane controls what language is used to display text in menus and windows, as well as how text is displayed.

1 From the Apple menu (), choose System Preferences and press the Language & Text button to open the Language & Text preference pane.

2 Press the Language button at the top of the Language & Text preference pane to display the Language pane.

The Language pane of the Language & Text preference pane.

3 In the list of languages on the left side of the pane, drag the languages into the preferred order that you'd like the text in application menus and windows to be displayed. If your preferred language is not listed, press the Edit List button in the lower left corner of the pane to add your language to the list. If the application supports the first language listed, it displays using that language; if it can't, it selects the next language listed, and so forth.

4 The Order for sorted lists drop-down menu allows you to influence how items are sorted in Finder windows.

5 Press the Text button at the top of the Language & Text preference pane to display the Text pane.

6   Some applications support the replacement of text when certain characters are typed. The Symbol and Text Substitutions section allows you to define what characters will be replaced. Be sure to enable the checkbox next to each replacement to enable the substitutions.

In order for substitution to work within a given application, you may need to enable text substitution within the preferences of the specific application.

7   The Spelling drop-down menu controls which language is used by other applications when the spell-checking feature is used.

8   The Word Break drop-down menu controls how a word is highlighted when it is double-clicked. Leave this setting at Standard unless you have a specific reason for changing it.

9   The Smart Quotes drop-down menu controls how a single or double quote appears within an application. You may need to enable this feature in the preferences of each specific application for it to work.

10   Press the Formats button at the top of the Language & Text preference pane to display the Formats pane.

The Formats pane of the Language & Text preference pane.

11 In the Region drop-down menu, choose the geographic region that you would like to use for displaying dates, times, and numbers within the Snow Leopard interface. If your geographic region is not listed in the Region drop-down menu, click the *Show all regions* checkbox to display additional options.

12 Select the preferred calendar type from the Calendar drop-down menu and choose which day you'd like to use as the first day of the week from the respective drop-down menu. If you'd like to customize how the calendar appears, press the Customize button.

13 If you'd like to change how the times are displayed on your computer, press the Customize button in the Times section of the pane.

14 If you'd like to change how numbers are displayed on your computer, press the Customize button in the Numbers section of the pane.

15 Choose your preferred unit of currency from the Currency drop-down menu, and choose your preferred unit of measurement from the Measurement units drop-down menu.

16 Press the Input Sources button at the top of the Language & Text preference pane to display the Input Sources pane. The Input Sources pane allows you to specify different languages to use when typing on your keyboard.

17 In the input source list on the left side of the pane, click the checkbox next to each language you'd like to use when typing on your keyboard.

18 The Input source shortcuts section allows you to define keyboard shortcuts to use in order to switch between the various languages that have been enabled in the input source list. This option is grayed out unless you have more than one language enabled in the input source list.

19 The Input source options section allows you to specify whether you'd like to use the same language in all documents or a different language for each document.

20 Click the *Show input menu in menu bar* checkbox to display an icon in the Menu bar that allows you to easily switch the input language.

The input menu in the Menu bar.

Security

The Security preference pane allows you to add security to various aspects of Snow Leopard to help protect the data in each user's account.

1   From the Apple menu (), choose System Preferences and press the Security button to open the Security preference pane.

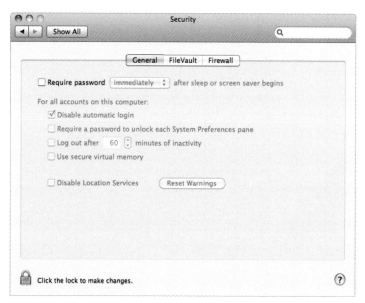

The Security preference pane.

2   Press the General button at the top of the Security preference pane to display the General pane.

3   Click the *Require password* checkbox to require that a password of the active user account be entered upon waking the computer after it has gone to sleep. You can choose a length of time until a password is required after waking the computer from the drop-down menu.

4   To make any further changes, an Administrator's password must be entered to unlock the pane. Click the lock icon () in the lower-left corner of the pane and enter an Administrator's username and password. After you enter the username and password, the remaining options become available.

5   The *Disable automatic login* checkbox prevents Snow Leopard from automatically logging into any account when the computer is started. This prevents unauthorized access to a user's account.

6   The *Require a password to unlock each System Preferences pane* checkbox prevents any user from making adjustments to the System Preferences without having Administrator approval.

7   If you'd like your computer to log out of the active account after a period of inactivity, enable the appropriate checkbox.

8   The *Use secure virtual memory* checkbox encrypts any information written to the hard disk by virtual memory.

9   Click the *Disable Location Services* checkbox if you'd like to stop providing information about the computer's location to applications. Location services provides information to other applications regarding the current physical location of your computer. For instance, an application could determine your current location to provide you with restaurants in your area. If you'd prefer not to allow applications to detect your location, turn this option on.

10   Press the FileVault button at the top of the Security preference pane. FileVault encrypts the contents of your Home folder to prevent anyone from accessing your information.

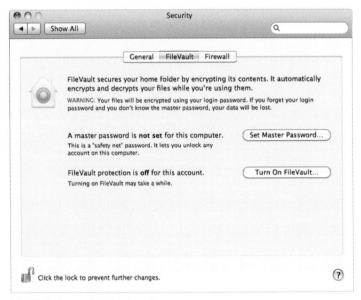

The FileVault pane of the Security preference pane.

FileVault is a very useful tool for protecting your data; however, a user needs to take caution, because if the password is ever forgotten, the data of that user's Home folder will be lost.

11 Press the Set Master Password button to specify one main password that can be used to reset the password of any user account on the computer. Only an Administrator can set the master password.

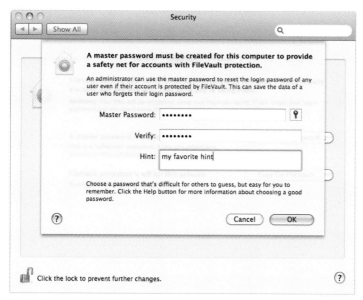

Setting the master password for the computer.

12 To set the FileVault password for the active account, press the Turn On FileVault button and enter a password.

13 A dialog displays, indicating that once FileVault is enabled, you will be logged out of your account and the Home folder will be encrypted. Select the Use secure erase check box to erase the unencrypted version of your Home folder, and click the *Use secure virtual memory* checkbox to encrypt data from memory that is temporarily stored to your hard drive. Press the Turn On FileVault button. You are logged out of your account while your Home folder is encrypted.

14 When the encryption process is complete, log back into your account.

15 From the Apple menu (⬢), choose System Preferences and press the Security button to return to the Security preference pane.

16 Press the Firewall button at the top of the Security preference pane. A firewall controls incoming connections to your computer via the network and the Internet.

17 The Firewall pane requires that an Administrator's username and password be entered to make any changes.

18 Click the lock icon (🔒) in the lower-left corner of the pane and enter an Administrator's username and password.

19 Press the Start button to enable the firewall on your computer.

20 Press the Advanced button. Click the *Block all incoming connections* checkbox to turn off all non-essential services and applications.

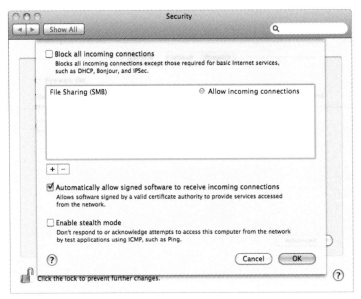

Customizing the firewall settings.

21 To add a specific application, press the + (plus) button and choose an application to add to the list.

22 Click the *Automatically allow signed software to receive incoming connections* checkbox to allow software signed by a certificate authority to provide services accessed from the network.

23 The *Enable stealth mode* checkbox prevents your computer from responding to test applications over the network such as ping. Press OK.

Hardware

The Hardware category controls the behavior of the hardware components of your computer and allows you to customize how each device is utilized.

CDs & DVDs

The CDs & DVDs preference pane controls what happens when a CD or DVD disc is inserted into the CD/DVD drive on your computer.

1 From the Apple menu (🍎), choose System Preferences and click on the CDs & DVDs button to open the CDs & DVDs preference pane.

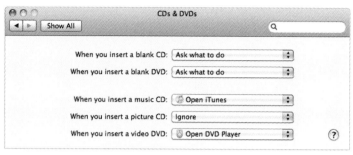

The CDs & DVDs preference pane.

2 In the When you insert a blank CD or DVD drop-down menus, you can control what happens when a blank CD or DVD is inserted into the CD/DVD drive on your computer. You are provided with seven options:

  • **Ask what to do** opens a dialog box, asking you what action you'd like to perform with the blank disc.

  • **Open Finder** opens the blank disc in the Finder, where you can copy files to the disc and then burn those files to the disc.

  • **Open iTunes** launches the iTunes application, where you can burn music to the blank disc.

  • **Open Disk Utility** launches the Disk Utility application, where you can burn data to the disc.

  • **Open other application** allows you to choose a specific application that is launched when the disc is inserted.

  • **Run script** launches an AppleScript that performs a specific action or actions when launched. AppleScript is Apple's scripting language that is used to write scripts to perform specific tasks to save time. For more information on AppleScript, visit *developer.apple.com/applescript/*.

  • **Ignore** does nothing, the disk will be ignored

3 The When you insert a music CD drop-down menu controls what happens when a music CD is inserted into the CD/DVD drive on your computer.

4 The When you insert a picture CD drop-down menu controls what happens when a CD containing images is inserted into the CD/DVD drive on your computer.

5 The When you insert a video DVD drop-down menu controls what happens when a video DVD is inserted into the CD/DVD drive on your computer.

Displays

The Displays preference pane controls all aspects of your monitor, such as resolution and brightness. The options available on your computer may look slightly different than the ones shown in this exercise, depending on the type and model of display you are using.

1 From the Apple menu (⌘), choose System Preferences and press the Displays button to open the Displays preference pane.

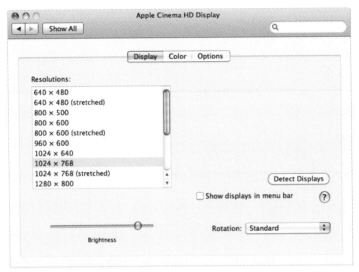

The Displays preference pane.

2 Press the Display button at the top of the preference pane.

3 The Resolutions list displays different combinations of resolutions that can be used on your display. Any resolution that contains the word stretched after the number indicates that the aspect ratio for that resolution doesn't match your display and therefore will be slightly distorted. Select any resolution from the list to change your display resolution.

4 The Brightness slider at the bottom of the preference pane allows you to adjust the brightness of your display.

5 The Detect Displays button highlights each display when more than one display is connected to your computer. If you do have multiple displays connected to your computer, you also see an Arrangement pane that allows you to control how the monitors are arranged relative to one another.

6   The *Show displays in menu bar* checkbox displays an icon in the Menu bar that makes changing resolutions on your computer quick and easy.

7   The Rotation drop-down menu allows you to specify the rotation of your display. Choose between standard, 90 degrees, 180 degrees, and 270 degrees.

8   Press the Color button at the top of the preference pane to display the Color pane.

9   The Display profile section shows ICC profiles that can be used by your current display. Uncheck the *Show profiles for this display only* checkbox to see additional profiles from which to choose.

10 Press the Open Profile button to display detailed information about the currently selected profile in the Display profile section on the left side of the pane. Close this window when you are finished.

11 The Calibrate button guides you step by step through a process to calibrate your monitor for accurate reproduction of color.

12 Press the Options button at the top of the preference pane (if available) to display options for your display. The *Disable power button* and *Disable display preferences button* checkboxes enables or disables the buttons on the currently connected display.

Energy Saver

The Energy Saver preference pane contains settings that enable your computer to conserve energy.

1   From the Apple menu (), choose System Preferences and press the Energy Saver button to open the Energy Saver preference pane.

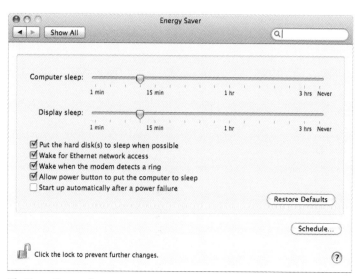

The Energy Saver preference pane.

2 Drag the Computer Sleep slider to the left or right to increase or decrease the length of inactivity required before the computer goes to sleep. This process spins down the hard drive and turns off the monitor to conserve energy.

3 Drag the Display Sleep slider to the left or right to increase or decrease the length of inactivity required before the display goes to sleep. This process only puts the display to sleep, not the computer.

4 Click the *Put the hard disk(s) to sleep when possible* checkbox to force the hard drive to sleep when it is inactive.

5 Click the *Wake for Network access* checkbox to wake the computer if it detects an attempted Ethernet connection.

6 Click the *Wake when modem detects a ring* checkbox to wake the computer when a call comes in on the phone line connected to the modem, if using a MacBook with a modem.

7 Click the *Allow power button to put the computer to sleep* checkbox if you'd like the ability to put your computer to sleep by pressing the power button.

8 Click the *Start up automatically after a power failure* checkbox to force your computer to boot after it loses power to the computer.

9 Press the Restore Defaults button to restore the settings in the Energy Saver preference pane to the factory defaults.

10 Press the Schedule button to open a new dialog that allows you to specify a time for your computer to start or wake from sleep and to go to sleep, restart, or shut down.

If you have Snow Leopard installed on a laptop computer, the Energy Saver preference pane has a category for when your computer is connected to a power source and one for when you are using the battery.

Keyboard

The Keyboard preference pane controls the behavior of the keyboard connected to your computer.

1 From the Apple menu (⌘), choose System Preferences and press the Keyboard button to open the Keyboard preference pane.

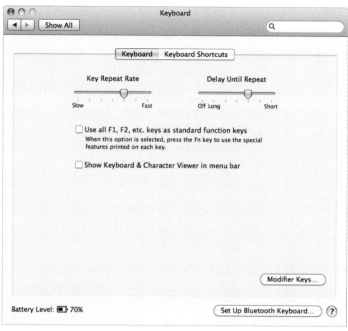

The Keyboard preference pane.

2 Press the Keyboard button at the top of the Keyboard preference pane.

3 Drag the Key Repeat Rate slider to the left or right to decrease or increase the rate at which the key repeats when held down. This option is evident if you are typing text in an application.

4 Drag the Delay Until Repeat slider to the left or right to decrease or increase the amount of time required for a key to be held down until it begins to repeat.

5 Click the *Use all F1, F2, etc. Keys as standard function keys* checkbox to force the function keys to operate without having to hold down the fn key. Newer Apple keyboards combine the function keys with other options. When this checkbox is enabled, you need to hold down the fn key to access the alternate functions on the keyboard.

6 Click the *Show Keyboard & Character Viewer in menu bar* checkbox to display an icon in the Menu bar that gives you quick access to the Keyboard & Character Viewer.

7 Press the Modifier Keys button to change the action performed by each of the modifier keys (Caps Lock, Ctrl, Option, and Command).

8 Press the Keyboard Shortcuts button at the top of the Keyboard preference pane.

9 Select an application from the list on the left, and the currently assigned keyboard shortcuts are displayed. To change an existing keyboard shortcut, select the shortcut in the window on the right, and type the new keyboard shortcut.

10 To add a shortcut for an existing application or for an application that's not listed, press the + (plus) button. Choose an application from the list in the Application drop-down menu and then type the exact name of the menu command as it is listed in one of the menus of that specific application. Type a keyboard shortcut in the Keyboard shortcut field, and press Add.

Adding a keyboard shortcut for the Preview application.

11 In the Full Keyboard Access section, choose the Text boxes and lists only option so that the Tab key moves the focus between only text boxes and lists, or choose the All controls option so that the Tab key moves focus to every possible option. Safari would be a good example for adjusting the Full Keyboard Access Settings.

12 If you are using a Bluetooth wireless keyboard that hasn't been paired with your computer yet, press the Set Up Bluetooth Keyboard button to pair it with your computer.

Mouse

The Mouse preference pane displays options for the mouse that you have connected to your computer. Your available options may be slightly different, depending on the brand and model of mouse you are using.

1   From the Apple menu (), choose System Preferences and press the Mouse button to open the Mouse preference pane.

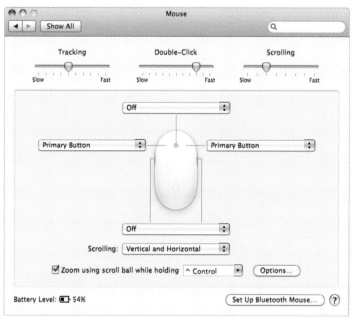

The Mouse preference pane.

2   Adjust the Tracking slider to the left or right to decrease or increase the speed of the cursor as you drag the mouse.

3   Adjust the Double-Click slider to the left or right to decrease or increase how rapidly you must click for the computer to recognize a double-click.

4   Adjust the Scrolling slider to the left or right to decrease or increase how fast a window scrolls when you use the scroll wheel on your mouse (if applicable).

5   The main area of the Mouse preference pane allows you to assign behaviors to all programmable areas of the mouse that you are using. The figure above shows the Apple Mighty Mouse and the areas that can be programmed. Primary Button refers to the normal mouse click, and Secondary Button refers to a right mouse click. Simply click on the drop-down menu for each programmable area to choose the function you'd like each button to perform.

The main area of the mouse window looks different for each brand and model of mouse that is used. Some models have no options at all.

6   The Scrolling drop-down menu at the bottom of the pane allows you to specify the directions by which you can scroll with your mouse. The options available in this drop-down menu depend on the brand and model of mouse you are using.

7   Click the *Zoom using scroll ball when holding* checkbox to enable zooming in on your screen by holding the Ctrl key and scrolling the mouse ball. The modifier key drop-down menu allows you to choose a different modifier key to enable zooming if desired.

8   Press the Options button to control the behavior of the screen when you move your cursor when zoomed in.

9   If you are using a new wireless Bluetooth mouse, press the Set Up Bluetooth Mouse button and follow the onscreen directions.

Print & Fax

The Print & Fax preference pane allows you to add printers and virtual fax machines to your computer to use as output devices. Complete instructions on adding a printer to your computer can be found in Lesson 8, "Printing."

Sound

The Sound preference pane controls the input and output of sound on your computer.

1   From the Apple menu (), choose System Preferences and click on the Sound button to open the Sound preference pane.

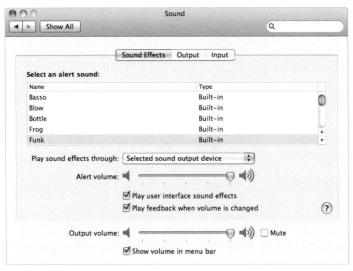

The Sound preference pane.

2   Press the Sound Effects button at the top of the Sound preference pane. The Sound
     Effects pane controls the effects that are played when working in Snow Leopard.

3   In the Select an alert sound section of the pane, choose an alert that you'd like to be
     played when you try to do something in Snow Leopard that isn't allowed. As you click
     on each alert sound, the sound is played so that you can hear the alert.

4   In the Play sound effects through drop-down menu, choose a sound output port on your
     computer where you'd like the alerts to be played. The options available to you in this
     drop-down menu vary, depending on the model of computer you are using. This option
     is useful if you'd like the effects to be played through the internal speakers on your
     computer and not the external speakers connected to your computer.

5   The Alert volume slider allows you to control the volume of the alerts on your computer
     independently of the overall sound output. Drag the slider to the left to reduce the alert
     volume and to the right to increase the alert volume.

6   Click the *Play user interface sound effects* checkbox so that a sound plays for items such as
     emptying the trash.

7   Click the *Play feedback when volume is changed* checkbox to play a sound when you adjust
     the volume on your computer to more easily hear the current volume settings.

8   Drag the Output volume slider to the left to decrease the overall volume and to the right
     to increase the overall volume on your computer. Click the *Mute* checkbox to disable
     sound altogether on your computer.

9   Click the *Show volume in menu bar* checkbox to display an icon in the Menu bar of your
     computer for easy access to your computer's volume.

When the Show volume in menu bar *check box is enabled, an icon appears
in the Menu bar, providing quick access to the volume on your computer.*

10   Press the Output button at the top of the Sound preference pane. This pane controls the
     different output devices available on your computer.

11   In the Select a device for sound output section of the pane, select the output device that
     you would like to use for sound output on your computer.

12   Once a sound output device is selected, the Settings for selected device section displays
     options for that selected device if applicable.

13   Press the Input button at the top of the Sound preference pane. This pane controls the
     different input devices available on your computer. The options available in this pane
     vary, based on the model of computer you are using and the input devices plugged in to
     your computer.

14 In the Select a device for sound input section, choose the device you'd like to use as a sound input device.

15 Once a sound input device is selected, the Settings for the selected device section shows the options available for the selected device. Drag the Input volume slider to the left to decrease the sound input volume and to the right to increase the sound input volume.

16 The Input level indicator displays a real-time volume indicator that shows the current volume of the sound input. Simply speak to see this bar change.

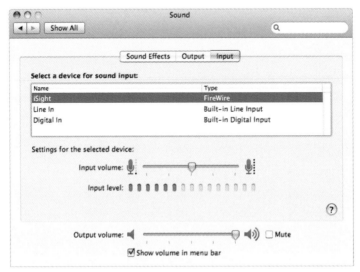

The input level indicator of the Input pane displays the current volume on the selected input device.

Internet & Wireless

The Internet & Wireless category provides preference panes to control how your computer connects to the Internet, networks, and wireless Bluetooth devices such as a mouse, keyboard, or headset, among other options.

MobileMe

MobileMe is a subscription-based service provided by Apple computer. For a yearly fee, MobileMe provides you with an e-mail address and server storage where you can store files and photos, host web sites, and share files with anybody via Internet access. You can also synchronize contacts and information across multiple computers for consistency. For more information on MobileMe, visit to *www.apple.com/mobileme*.

1   From the Apple menu (), choose System Preferences and press the MobileMe button to open the MobileMe preference pane.

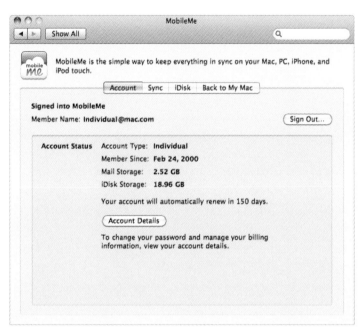

The MobileMe preference pane.

2   Press the Account button at the top of the MobileMe preference pane. This pane provides information about your account. There is a Sign In/Sign Out button that allows you to sign in or sign out of your account. Press the Account Details button to open a Web page where you can log into your account to change settings for your account.

3   Press the Sync button at the top of the preference pane. One advantage of MobileMe is that you can synchronize information between multiple computers to keep your information up to date.

4   Click the *Synchronize with MobileMe* checkbox at the top of the pane to enable synchronization, and then choose whether you'd like the information synchronized automatically, every hour, every day, every week, or manually.

5   Once you have enabled the Synchronize with MobileMe checkbox, simply click the checkbox in the main window next to each component that you'd like to be synchronized between multiple computers.

6 Press the iDisk button at the top of the MobileMe preference pane. The iDisk is a component of the MobileMe service that provides storage on an Internet-based server for safe and convenient access.

7 The iDisk Usage section displays how much storage you are using on your iDisk. Pressing on the Upgrade Storage button redirects you to the Apple web site, where you can purchase additional storage for your account.

8 The iDisk Public Folder is a public area of your iDisk where other users can access and upload files to your Public Folder. Click the *Allow others to write files in your public folder* checkbox to enable other users to put files in your Public Folder. Click the Password-protect your public folder checkbox to allow only users who have a password to write files to your Public Folder. When this checkbox has been checked, the Set Password button is available for you to set the password for your Public Folder.

9 Press the Start button in the iDisk Sync section at the bottom of the pane to synchronize your iDisk to the hard drive on your computer. This allows you to access files from your iDisk quickly and without the need for Internet access. Any changes that are made to the iDisk or to the iDisk files on your hard drive will be synced the next time you have Internet access, based on the Update drop-down menu.

10 The Update drop-down menu allows you to specify whether your iDisk is synchronized manually or automatically. Click the *Always keep the most recent version of a file* checkbox to ensure that the most recent version of a file is always used when there is a sync conflict.

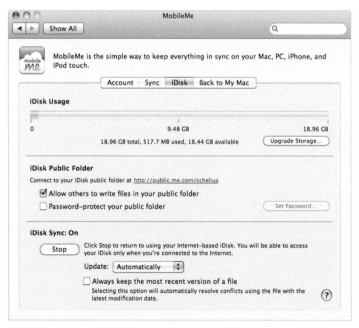

The iDisk pane controls public access to the iDisk Public Folder and iDisk synchronization.

11 Press the Back to My Mac button at the top of the MobileMe preference pane. Back to My Mac is a service that allows you to connect to your Mac remotely via the Internet. Back to My Mac requires advanced setup and configuration and is beyond the scope of this book. For information on setup and configuration of the Back to My Mac service, visit the support page on the Apple web site at *www.apple.com/support*.

Network

The Network preference pane controls all aspects of connecting to a network or the Internet.

1 From the Apple menu (), choose System Preferences and press the Network button to open the Network preference pane. You may need to authenticate as an Administrator to change settings in this pane by clicking the lock icon () in the lower-left corner of the pane and entering your username and password.

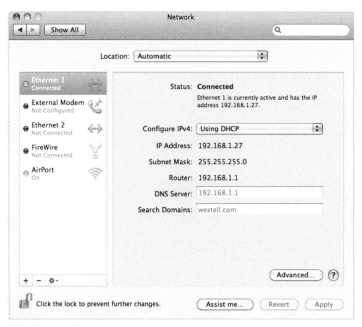

The Network preference pane.

2 The sidebar on the left of the Network preference pane lists all of the network connections on your computer, such as wireless and wired connections. Select one of the connections to display and configure its options.

3 The Status section displays the connection status for the currently selected connection.

4 The Configure IPv4 drop-down menu allows you to choose how this connection will obtain an IP address, which provides connectivity to your computer. Contact your Internet Service Provider (ISP) for instructions on which method to choose here.

5 The IP Address, Subnet Mask, Router, DNS Server, and Search Domains options display the current information for each respective section. A detailed explanation of each of these options is beyond the scope of this book. Contact your ISP or System Administrator for help with these settings.

6 The Advanced button at the bottom of the Network preference pane provides additional options for configuring your network connections.

7 If you are having trouble setting up your network, press the Assist me button to access help in configuring your network connection.

8 If you use a laptop to connect to several different locations, you can choose Edit Locations from the Location drop-down menu and press the + (plus) button to add a new location and configure it independently to make it easier to use your computer at each location.

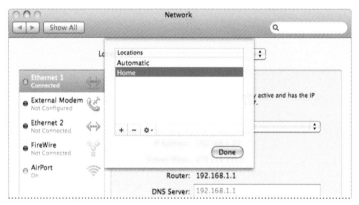

Adding a location makes it easier to connect to different networks when using a mobile computer such as a laptop.

Bluetooth

The Bluetooth preference pane allows you to connect to Bluetooth wireless devices such as a mouse or keyboard, and also allows you to connect to your computer via other Bluetooth devices.

1   From the Apple menu (), choose System Preferences and press the Bluetooth button to open the Bluetooth preference pane.

The Bluetooth preference pane is used to connect to wireless devices such as a mouse or keyboard.

2   Click the *On* checkbox at the top of the Bluetooth preference pane to enable Bluetooth on your computer.

3   Click the *Discoverable* checkbox to make your computer discoverable to other devices on your computer. Bluetooth establishes a connection and allows connections by pairing two devices. This pairing process requires that you enter a unique number provided by the device to which you are connecting to prevent unauthorized connections to your computer or device.

4 The sidebar on the left side of the Bluetooth preference pane lists all of the Bluetooth devices that are connected to your computer. To set up a new Bluetooth device, press the + (plus) button at the bottom of the sidebar. The Bluetooth Setup Assistant is launched, and any discoverable devices are listed in the main window. Select the device that you'd like to connect, press Continue and follow the onscreen instructions.

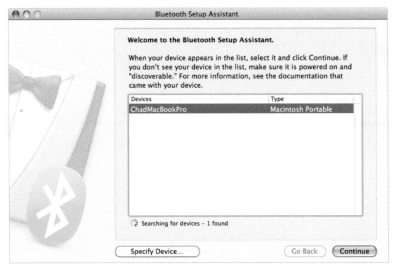

The Bluetooth Setup Assistant helps you connect to other Bluetooth devices.

5 Once a Bluetooth device has been paired with your computer, select it in the sidebar, and the main window displays information about the device, such as the type of device, the services provided by the device, whether it's paired or not, and if it is currently connected.

6 Click the *Show Bluetooth status in the menu bar* checkbox to display a Bluetooth status icon in the Menu bar of your computer.

7 Press the File Sharing Setup button to enable Bluetooth Sharing on your computer so that you can share files between computers using the Bluetooth connection.

8 Press Advanced to configure additional options for the selected Bluetooth device.

Sharing

The Sharing preference pane controls services that can be shared with other computers. Most of these services require that a network be established in order to work.

1   From the Apple menu (), choose System Preferences and press the Sharing button to open the Sharing preference pane.

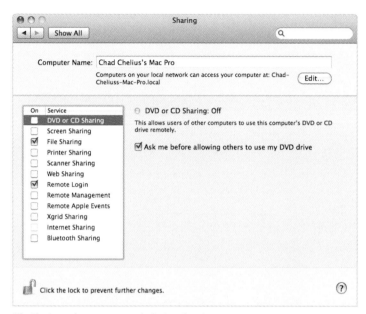

The Sharing preference pane controls sharing of services on your computer.

2   The Computer Name field at the top of the Sharing preference pane is the name that your computer is identified with on the network. To change the name, simply type a new name in the text field. It's generally a recommended practice to keep the name as small as possible.

3 The sidebar on the left side of the preference pane displays the services that can be
enabled for sharing on your computer. Click the service name to display the options to
the right of the sidebar; click the checkbox next to the name of the service to enable
that service. Below is a list of the services offered, and a description of their functionality.

- **DVD or CD Sharing** shares the CD/DVD drive on your computer so that other
  computers can access the drive. This is useful if you need to use a DVD on a computer
  that only contains a CD drive.

- **Screen Sharing** allows other users to share your computer screen and take control of
  the computer. For step-by-step instructions on setting up and using Screen Sharing, refer
  to Lesson 7, "Creating and Using Your Own Network."

- **File Sharing** makes files on your computer available to other users on the same
  network. For step-by-step instructions on setting up and using File Sharing, refer to
  Lesson 7, "Creating and Using Your Own Network."

- **Printer Sharing** allows you to share a printer connected to your computer with other
  users on the same network. For step-by-step instructions on setting up and using Printer
  Sharing, refer to Lesson 7, "Creating and Using Your Own Network."

- **Scanner Sharing** allows you to share a scanner connected to your computer with
  other users on the same network. Simply click the check box next to the scanner listed
  in the area to the right of the sidebar to make the scanner available to other users.

- **Web Sharing** allows users of other computers to view web pages on your computer.
  For step-by-step instructions on setting up and using Web Sharing, refer to Lesson 7,
  "Creating and Using Your Own Network."

- **Remote Login** allows other users to remotely log in to your computer using SSH
  (Secure Shell). This is usually done through the Terminal application, which is covered in
  Lesson 12, "Installing Snow Leopard and Applications."

- **Remote Management** allows other users to access your computer using the Remote
  Desktop application for managing computers.

- **Remote Apple Events** allows applications on other computers to send Apple events to
  this computer. Apple events are used in scripting and by other applications to perform
  specific functions.

- **Xgrid Sharing** allows Xgrid controllers to connect and distribute Xgrid tasks to be
  performed by your computer. Xgrid is used to combine multiple computers into a
  cluster to increase processing power.

- **Internet Sharing** allows you to share your Internet connection with other users. For
  example, let's say you only have one physical Ethernet port that provides Internet access
  but several users that require Internet access. You can share your Ethernet Internet
  connection with other users using your wireless Airport card, providing access to anyone
  who wants to connect.

- **Bluetooth Sharing** allows you to share files on your computer with connected users
  via Bluetooth.

System

The System section of System Preferences controls global settings on your computer and allows you to configure the behavior of each setting.

Accounts

The Accounts preference pane allows you to add and remove user accounts on your computer, as well as configure each account as a standard user, Administrator, managed, or sharing only account.

1   From the Apple menu (), choose System Preferences and press the Accounts button to open the Accounts preference pane.

2   The sidebar on the left side of the preference pane displays existing accounts and allows you to add new accounts to your computer. For step-by-step instructions on adding an account to your computer, refer to Lesson 3, "Using Snow Leopard with a Group."

The Accounts preference pane allows you to add or remove accounts on your computer.

3   To make any changes in the Accounts preference pane, you need to click on the lock icon () in the lower-left corner of the preference pane and enter an Administrator's username and password.

4   Select an account in the sidebar, then press the Password button at the top of the pane.

5   Press the Change Password button to change the password for the selected account.

6   The Full Name text field can be changed at any time by typing a new name. However, the short name that was used when creating the account cannot be changed.

7   Press the Change button in the MobileMe user name section to go to the MobileMe preference pane to make changes.

8   In the Address Book Card section, press the Open button to open the Address Book application with the contact entry for the user of the selected account active. Using the Address Book application, you can make changes to the contact.

9   Click the *Enable Parental Controls* checkbox to impose restrictions on the selected account that are controlled using Parental Controls. Press the Open Parental Controls button to configure the settings for the selected account. For step-by-step instructions on configuring Parental Controls, refer to Lesson 3, "Using Snow Leopard with a Group."

10   Press the Login Items button at the top of the Accounts preference pane. Login Items are applications that launch when the selected account logs in.

11   Press the + (plus) button at the bottom of the main window and then select an application that you'd like to launch when logging in to this account.

Click the + (plus) button to add an application that will launch when the selected user logs in to the computer.

Date & Time

The Date & Time preference pane controls all aspects of how the date and time are set and displayed on your computer.

1 From the Apple menu (), choose System Preferences and press the Date & Time button to open the Date & Time preference pane.

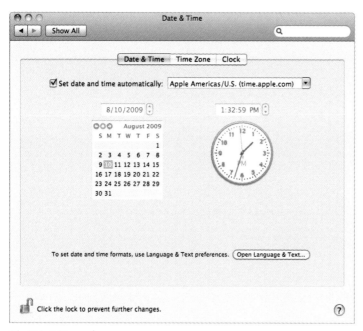

The Date & Time preference pane.

2 Press the Date & Time button at the top of the preference pane.

3 Click the *Set date and time automatically* checkbox to connect to the Apple time servers, using your Internet connection to automatically keep your computer's time current. This option also compensates for daylight savings time changes. If you'd rather not use the Apple time servers, uncheck the *Set date and time automatically* checkbox, then adjust the date and time in the main area of the pane.

4 To change the format in which the date and time are displayed, press the Open Language & Text button. For more information on this option, see the Language & Text section earlier in this lesson.

5   Press the Time Zone button at the top of the preference pane. Click the map in the location that you live to set your current time zone. Click the *Set time zone automatically using current location* checkbox to let Snow Leopard determine your location for you.

6   Press the Clock button at the top of the preference pane.

7   Click the *Show date and time in menu bar* checkbox to display the current date and time in the Menu bar at the top of your screen. Adjust the time and date options as desired.

8   Click the *Announce the time* checkbox to instruct your computer to speak the time. Choose a time period from the drop-down menu to choose how often this occurs. Press the Customize Voice button to choose which voice is used when the time is spoken.

Parental Controls

The Parental Controls preference pane sets limits for each account that controls when a user can log in to the computer, the length of time they can log in for, as well as what content can be accessed using the account. For step-by-step instructions on configuring the Parental Controls for an account, refer to Lesson 3, "Using Snow Leopard with a Group."

Software Update

Software Update is a Snow Leopard feature that checks for updates released by Apple to improve the performance and reliability of your computer. The Software Update preference pane controls how often to check for updates.

1   From the Apple menu (), choose System Preferences and press the Software Update button to open the Software Update preference pane.

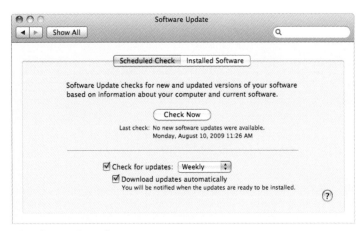

The Software Update preference pane.

2   Press the Scheduled Check button at the top of the Software Update preference pane.

3   To check for software updates immediately, press Check Now.

4   Click the *Check for updates* checkbox to instruct Software Update to automatically check for updates, then choose a frequency from the drop-down menu.

5   Click the *Download updates automatically* checkbox to instruct Software Update to automatically download any updates that are found. A dialog box appears when the updates have been downloaded and are ready to be installed.

6   Press the Installed Software button at the top of the Software Update preference pane. A history of installed software updates is listed as a record of what has been installed on your computer.

Speech

The Speech preference pane controls your ability to speak commands to your computer and allows you to instruct your computer to speak text to you as well.

1   From the Apple menu (), choose System Preferences and press the Speech button to open the Speech preference pane.

2   Press the Speech Recognition button at the top of the preference pane.

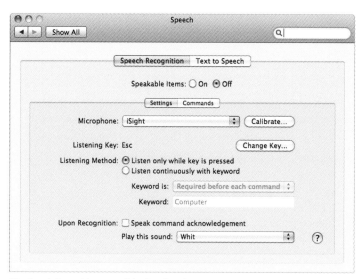

The Speech Recognition pane of the Speech preference pane.

3   In the Speakable Items section, click the *On* option to enable Speech Recognition on your computer.

4   Press the Settings button at the top of the main area of the pane.

5   In the Microphone drop-down menu, choose an input source that you'd like to use for voice recognition. Press the Calibrate button and follow the instructions to calibrate the microphone. This improves the accuracy of speech recognition.

6   The default listening key is the Esc key. To change this key, press the Change Key button and press a new key on your keyboard. The listening key is the key that you hold down to send voice commands to your computer.

7 In the Listening Method section, click the *Listen only while key is pressed* option to require that the listening key be pressed before the computer will listen for instructions. Click the *Listen continuously with keyword* option to instruct the computer to listen for a keyword to activate Speech Recognition. This option requires that you choose when the keyword is required from the Keyword is drop-down menu, and also requires you to specify a keyword in the Keyword text field.

8 In the Upon Recognition section, click the *Speak command acknowledgement* checkbox to instruct the computer to speak an acknowledgement when a command is received, or select an option from the Play this sound drop-down menu when a spoken command is understood.

9 Press the Commands button at the top of the main area of the pane.

10 Click the checkbox next to each command set that you'd like to be able to use when utilizing Speech Recognition. When certain command sets are highlighted, the Configure button becomes active. Press Configure to adjust the settings for the selected command set.

11 Click the Open Speakable Items folder to see a list of speakable commands that can be used.

12 Press the Helpful Tips button to see tips for improving the accuracy of the Speech Recognition feature.

13 Press the Text to Speech button at the top of the Speech preference pane.

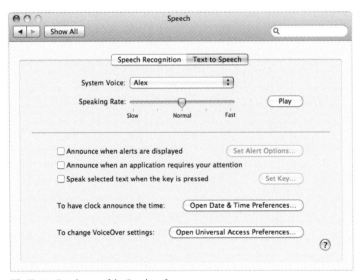

The Text to Speech pane of the Speech preference pane.

14 Choose a voice from the System Voice drop-down menu to select which voice is used when the computer speaks to you. Drag the Speaking Rate slider to the left to make the rate slower and to the right to make it faster. Press Play to hear what the voice sounds like.

15 Click the *Announce when alerts are displayed* checkbox to instruct your computer to speak alerts as they are displayed. Once enabled, press the Set Alert Options button to control attributes of how the alert is spoken.

16 Click the *Announce when an application requires your attention* checkbox to instruct your computer to let you know when an application requires your attention.

17 Click the *Speak selected text when the key is pressed* checkbox to enable the computer to speak a selected range of text when a specific key is pressed. When this check box is enabled, you can press the Set Key button to specify the key to be pressed to speak the selected text.

18 Press the Open Date & Time Preferences button to instruct the computer to announce the current time at specified intervals. See the Date & Time section earlier in this lesson for more information.

19 Press the Open Universal Access Preferences button to change the VoiceOver settings. See the Universal Access section later in this lesson for more information.

Startup Disk

The Startup Disk preference pane allows you to control what disk your computer will boot from when it is started. This preference pane is useful when you have more than one operating system loaded on your computer.

1 From the Apple menu (), choose System Preferences and press the Startup Disk button to open the Startup Disk preference pane.

The Startup Disk preference pane.

2 In the main window of the Startup Disk preference pane, select the disk that contains a valid operating system that you'd like to boot from. Unless you've configured a second system, your computer may only have one disk from which to boot.

3 After selecting a new startup disk, press the Restart button to reboot from that disk.

4 Press the Target Disk Mode button, then the Restart button in the resulting dialog to restart your computer in Target Disk Mode. Target Disk Mode reboots your computer into a state that behaves like an external hard drive. Simply plug a FireWire cable from your computer to another computer, and the computer that you booted into Target Disk Mode displays on the connected computer as an external hard drive.

Time Machine

Time Machine is a feature in Snow Leopard that automatically backs up the data on your computer to protect you from data loss. For step-by-step instructions on setting up and configuring Time Machine, refer to Lesson 5, "Backing Up and Protecting Your Data."

Universal Access

The Universal Access preference pane allows you to set up and configure a computer for users who have difficulty seeing, hearing, or controlling the computer.

1 From the Apple menu (), choose System Preferences and press the Universal Access button to open the Universal Access preference pane.

The Universal Access preference pane controls settings for users who have difficulty seeing, hearing, or controlling the computer.

2   Press the Seeing button at the top of the Universal Access preference pane.

3   Click the *On* option in the VoiceOver section to hear descriptions of items on your computer screen.

4   Click the *On* option in the Zoom section to enable zooming in on areas of your screen to improve readability. Use the shortcut keys Command+Option+plus and Command+Option+minus to zoom in or out on your screen. Press the Options button to refine the behavior of zooming on your screen.

5   Click the *White on black* option to reverse the colors on your screen for easier viewing. Click the *Use grayscale* checkbox to display all content on your screen in grayscale only.

6   Drag the Enhance contrast slider left or right to increase the contrast of colors on your screen.

7   Some applications require that the *Enable access for assistive devices* checkbox be enabled in order to work.

8   Click the *Show Universal Access status in menu bar* checkbox to display an icon in the Menu bar at the top of your screen.

9   Press the Hearing button at the top of the Universal Access preference pane.

10   Click the *Flash the screen when an alert sound occurs* checkbox to cause the screen to flash when an alert sound occurs. Press the Flash Screen button to test this feature.

11   Click the *Play stereo audio as mono* option to instruct any sound to be output as mono instead of stereo.

12   Press the Keyboard button at the top of the Universal Access preference pane.

13   Click the *On* option in the Sticky Keys section to allow treating a sequence of modifier keys, such as the Alt, Shift, or Ctrl keys, as a key combination. Press the Shift key five times to turn Sticky Keys on or off to make it easier to enable and disable Sticky Keys.

14   Click the *Beep when a modifier key is set* checkbox to play an audible sound when a modifier key has been set.

15   Click the *Display pressed keys on screen* checkbox to show the icon of the pressed modifier keys on screen.

16   Click the *On* option in the Slow Keys section to insert a delay between when a key is pressed and when it is accepted.

17 Click the *Use click key sounds* checkbox to play an audible sound after each key is pressed. Drag the Acceptance Delay slider to the left to make the delay longer and to the right to make the delay shorter.

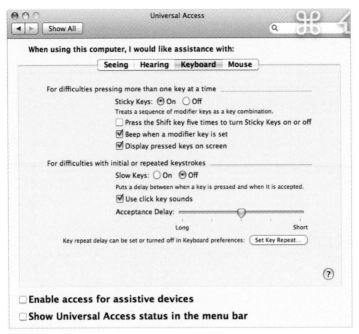

The Keyboard pane of the Universal Access preference pane.

18 Press the Mouse button at the top of the Universal Access preference pane.

19 Click the *On* option next to the Mouse keys section to enable the ability to use the keyboard in place of the mouse.

20 Click the *Press the Option key five times to turn Mouse Keys on or off* checkbox to enable this feature.

21 Drag the Initial Delay slider to the left to shorten the delay or to the right to increase the delay before the pointer starts to move.

22 Drag the Maximum Speed slider to the left to reduce the speed or to the right to increase the speed of the pointer when using the keyboard. To see what keys to use for using the keyboard to control the mouse cursor, press the help icon (⑦) in the Universal Access preference pane.

23 Drag the Cursor Size slider to the right to increase the size of the cursor for easier viewing on screen.

Other

As you install additional software on your computer, some applications may add preference panes to the main System Preferences pane. These are usually added to a category called Other. As they are specific to each individual application, those preference panes are not covered in this book, but you can expect to see them as applications are added to your computer.

Self study

System Preferences provide finite control of your system. There's a good chance that there are several preference panes within System Preferences that you'll never need to use. It is important, however, to become very familiar with the ones that you do use. Spend some time getting familiar with the features inside of each preference pane and remember where the options are located, as it will save you a lot of time later on when you need to make adjustments.

Review

Questions

1 Which preference pane would you use if you wanted to work in a language other than English on your computer?

2 You just purchased a wireless mouse for your computer. Which two preference panes could you use to pair that mouse with your computer?

3 If you work on several different computers at different locations, how can you ensure that all of your contacts, calendars, and mail accounts are synchronized between the computers?

4 Which preference pane allows you to set up and control how data is backed up on your computer?

Answers

1 Language & Text.

2 Both the Mouse preference pane and the Bluetooth preference pane could be used to pair the mouse to the computer.

3 Subscribe to the Apple MobileMe service and set the Sync settings within the MobileMe preference pane.

4 The Time Machine preference pane allows you to designate a drive to use for backup and to set options for the backup.

What you'll learn in this lesson:

- Using Mail to view, send and receive e-mail

- Using Address Book to manage contacts

- Keeping track of events with iCal

- Using iChat to keep in touch via text, audio or video

Using Applications in Snow Leopard

In this lesson, you will explore some of the useful applications found in Snow Leopard. Applications give you the tools to accomplish specific tasks without having to leave the operating system.

Starting up

There are no lesson files with this lesson, so you can get started right away.

See Lesson 10 in action!

Use the accompanying video to gain a better understanding of how to use some of the features shown in this lesson. The video tutorial for this lesson can be found on the included DVD.

Mail

Designed specifically for e-mail, Mail offers you the ability to manage all your e-mail from a single, easy-to-use inbox, even when you're not connected to the Internet, and without being bombarded by advertisements. It's compatible with most e-mail technologies, including IMAP and POP3, as well as most popular e-mail services, such as Yahoo! Mail, Gmail, and AOL Mail. Snow Leopard even makes it easy to access more than one e-mail account. You can simply add all your accounts to the Mail application, and you'll be able to access everything from one central location.

Setting up an e-mail account

Mail walks you through the process of setting up an e-mail account step-by-step.

1   Open the Mail application, either from the Dock or from inside the Applications folder.

2   Type your full name, e-mail address, and password in the Welcome to Mail window, and press Create.

   If you have a .Mac account, Mail checks your account, and then displays an account summary. Verify that your settings are correct, and press Create to finish setting up the account.

   If you have a different type of account, the Incoming Mail Server window appears.

3   Choose the type of account you have (POP, IMAP, or Exchange) from the Account Type drop-down menu. If you're not sure about what type of account you have, consult your ISP (Internet Service Provider).

4   Type a description for your account, such as **My Home Account** or **Work E-mail**.

5   Type your e-mail provider's incoming mail server address in the Incoming Mail Server text field (for example, mail.domain_name.com).

6   Type your account name in the User Name text field. This is usually the text that appears before the @ sign in your e-mail address.

7   Type your password in the Password text field, then press Continue.

8   In the Incoming Mail Security window, follow the instructions from your ISP to select the proper security settings. Press Continue.

9   Type the outgoing server address for your account in the Outgoing Mail Server text field (for example, smtp.domain_name.com).

10 It might take a second or two before Mail verifies your information and displays an Account Summary. If you see an error message stating that Mail could not contact your e-mail server, press the Go Back button and verify that your information is correct before proceeding. Press Create to finish.

Adding an e-mail account

It's a simple process to add an additional e-mail account to Mail.

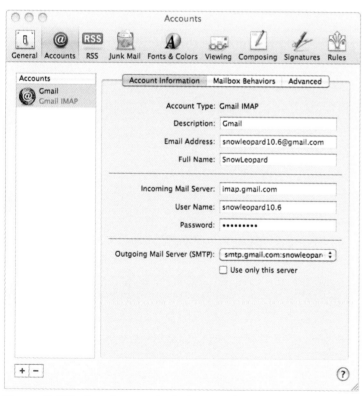

You can add additional e-mail accounts using the Accounts Preferences.

1 From the Mail menu, choose Preferences.

2 Select the Accounts tab to display information about your current accounts.

3 To create a new account, click the plus sign (+) button in the bottom-left corner of the window.

4 Repeat steps 2 to 10 from "Setting up an e-mail account" as required.

Viewing your mail

Mail displays your Mailboxes (Inbox, Drafts, and Sent by default) in a column on the left side of the window, and messages in the Message Viewer pane on the right.

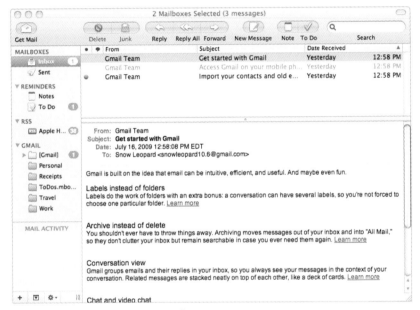

The Mail interface simplifies viewing your mail.

1 To display a list of all messages that have been sent to you, select the Inbox.

2 If you have more than one e-mail account set up, you can also click the triangle next to the Inbox to see (and access) all your accounts.

3 To view a specific message, either double-click an entry to view the message in its own window, or drag the small dot at the bottom center of the window upwards to reveal a message pane and select a message to view it in the pane.

Junk mail

You should use the Junk Mail feature in Mail, especially if you're receiving a lot of junk mail (also called *spam*). Mail filters junk mail by default, but you can also *train* the application if you want to change the way it deals with your unwanted e-mail.

1   When you first use Mail, the Junk Mail feature goes through a training cycle. If Mail thinks a received message is junk, its information appears in brown type in your Inbox.

●	●	From	Subject	Date Received	▲
		Gmail Team	Get started with Gmail	Yesterday	12:58 PM
		Gmail Team	Access Gmail on your mobile ph...	Yesterday	12:58 PM
●		Gmail Team	Import your contacts and old e...	Yesterday	12:58 PM

The message appears in brown type if Mail thinks it is Junk mail.

2   If a message is marked as junk but shouldn't be, press the Not Junk button (▥) to train the Mail application.

3   If a message isn't marked as junk but should be, press the Junk button (▨) to train the Mail application.

4   Choose Mail > Preferences, and click the Junk Mail tab to make changes to the Junk Mail filter. For example, you can make certain types of messages immune to junk mail filtering by selecting the item checkboxes below the line. The following types of messages are exempt from junk mail filtering.

5   If, after a few of weeks of training, you feel that Mail is adequately flagging your junk mail, select the *Move it to the Junk mailbox* radio button in the Junk Mail preferences. This creates a Junk mailbox in the left column, and Mail then automatically moves junk mail to this mailbox. You should check your Junk mailbox periodically to make sure that you aren't missing anything important.

6   If you want to disable junk mail filtering, deselect the *Enable junk mail filtering* check box in Junk Mail Preferences.

Sending e-mail

Simply type a message and send an e-mail, or attach a file by dragging it to the message window.

1. To send someone an e-mail, press the New Message button ( ) to open a New Message window.

2. Type the recipient's e-mail address in the To text field. Mail automatically completes the address as you type it if this person is in your Address Book (or if you've sent or received e-mail from this person before). If you are addressing the message to more than one person, separate the e-mail addresses with a comma. If you want to send a copy of this message to others, type their e-mail addresses in the CC text field.

3. Type a subject for your message in the Subject text field. Type your message in the text box. If you need to send an attachment (such as a photo or other file) with your message, press the Attach button. Then, in the dialog box that appears, navigate to and select the file, and press Choose File. You can also drag the file to the message window to attach it.

4. Press the Send button ( ) to send your message.

Using Stationery

From invitations to birthday greetings, Mail features more than 30 professionally designed stationery templates with coordinated layouts, fonts, and colors. These templates also feature drag-and-drop photo placement from your iPhoto library. You can even create personalized templates. Messages created with Mail Stationery are built with standard HTML that can be read by popular e-mail programs on both Macs and PCs.

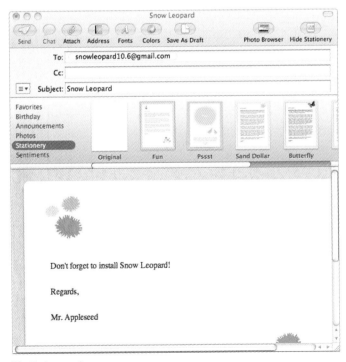

Use Stationery to jazz up your messages.

Searching Mail

The Search field in Mail, which uses Spotlight technology, allows you to search for specific text, in any message, in any mailbox, at any time.

1 Locate the Search text field in the upper right corner of the Mail window. Type the keyword(s) that you want to search for, such as **Vacation** or **Library Hours**.

2 Even before you finish typing, Mail begins to display a list of search results. You can press the Inbox button to display results from your Inbox only, or press the All Mailboxes button to display results from all mailboxes.

Creating Smart Mailboxes

With Mail, you can create a Smart Mailbox that automatically updates its contents whenever you use the application. This allows you, for example, to keep all messages about a specific project in its own folder, and to better track and organize those messages.

Create a Smart Mailbox to better track and organize your messages.

1 From the Mailbox menu, choose New Smart Mailbox.

2 Type a name for your mailbox in the Smart Mailbox Name text field.

3 Use the drop-down menus and text fields to set criteria that match the content of your desired messages (for example, Subject, contains, and so on). If you need to add more criteria, press the plus sign (+) button.

4 Press OK to create the Smart Mailbox when finished. Mail automatically updates this mailbox whenever it finds a message that matches your assigned criteria.

Taking notes

Mail's Note feature lets you write handy notes to yourself that you can access from almost anywhere.

Use Notes inside the Mail application.

1 Press the Note button (⌐) at the top of your Mail window.

2 In the window that opens, type a message to yourself, then press Done.

Notes can include graphics, colored text, and attachments, so it's easy to jot down directions, phone numbers, even shopping lists. And because your Notes folder behaves just like an e-mail inbox, you can access notes from any Mac or PC using an IMAP mail service (such as .Mac or AOL).

Creating to-do lists

Once Mail has been trained, you can make it send all junk mail to its own Junk mailbox automatically.

It's no longer necessary to add a new item to your to-do list every time you receive an e-mail. The To Do feature in Mail automatically creates tasks directly from any e-mail message you choose.

1 Highlight text in an e-mail.

2 Press the To Do button (✓) to create a task from a message.

3 Include a due date, set an alarm, or assign priorities.

Each to-do includes a link to the original e-mail or note, and to-dos appear automatically in iCal, complete with any changes you make. To-dos are also stored with your e-mail, so that if you use an IMAP mail service, you can access them from Mail on any Mac.

Address Book

Regardless of where you've got all your e-mail addresses, phone numbers, addresses, web sites, chat names, and other information stored, the Address Book application simplifies the process of managing the important people in your life.

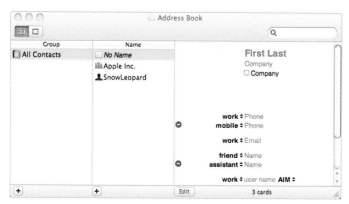

Address Book keeps all your contacts right at your fingertips.

Creating a new contact

Address Book allows you to enter all kinds of information about a person, and then e-mail or chat with that person, or visit their web site directly from an Address Book card.

Enter as much or as little contact information as you want; if you leave a field blank, it won't appear in the final card.

To add someone to your Address Book:

1 Open Address Book from the Dock. You see a Group column on the left (for grouping contacts), a Name column in the center, and a card pane on the right (for viewing contacts' information).

2 Click on the plus sign (+) button below the Name column to create a new contact card.

3 Click in each text field and highlight it to enter the contact's name and information. Each type of contact is grouped by section on the card.

4 Certain fields allow you to choose a label from a drop-down menu to their left. For example, choose mobile from the drop-down menu next to a Phone text field to enter a contact's cell number.

5 To add another field for additional information, press the green plus sign (○) that appears in a category section. Alternatively, you can choose Add Field from the Card menu to add additional fields.

You can also add extra information by typing it into the Note section.

6 To have Address Book display a picture of the contact (or any image), drag the image file onto the square next to the person's name.

7 When finished, choose File > Save (or press Command+S).

Sending an e-mail

As mentioned earlier, you can send e-mail messages directly from within Address Book.

1   Click the person's name in the Name column.

2   From the drop-down menu to the left of the contact's e-mail address, choose Send Email.

Send an e-mail directly from within Address Book.

Creating groups

If you want to be able to address a group of people in an e-mail instead of entering all their e-mail addresses, you can create a group.

1   Press the plus sign (+) button below the Group column, and type a name for your group.

2   Choose All Contacts from the Group column.

3   Drag names from the Name column onto your new group in the Group column to add them.

Create groups to address multiple contacts.

Creating Smart Groups

You can also create Smart Groups, or groups that automatically update themselves if any contacts fit the same search criteria you select.

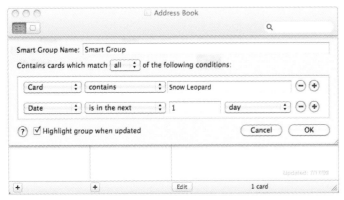

Create a Smart Group, which automatically updates on its own.

1   Choose New Smart Group from the File menu.

2   Type a name in the Smart Group Name text field.

3   Set your search criteria using the drop-down menus and text fields.

4   Press OK. Any contacts that match your search criteria become part of this Smart Group.

Printing an Address Book

If you'd rather have a hands-on list of contacts and their information, you can print out a pocket-sized version of your Address Book.

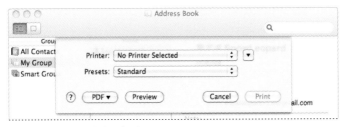

Print your Address Book for a hands-on copy.

1   Select the names that you want to include from the Names column (or select a group).

2   Choose Print from the File menu.

3   In the window that appears, choose Pocket Address Book from the Style drop-down menu, and select any other options you want.

4   Press Print.

iCal

The iCal application helps you manage your time more efficiently by providing tools you can use to keep track of important events.

You can also subscribe to anyone else's iCal calendar, which allows you to see where potential scheduling conflicts may occur.

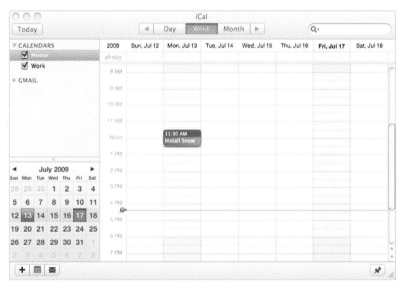

iCal helps you keep track of your time.

Scheduling an event

1   Open iCal from the Dock or the Applications folder.

    The Calendars column on the left lists your calendars (Work and Home by default). iCal also displays a monthly calendar pane below that, a week view in the main pane, and an information pane on the right, which shows a selected item's details.

2   Select a calendar from the Calendars column.

3   Drag across the date and time text field that matches your agenda to add an event. If the date is more than a week away, you can use the calendar pane to advance the view.

4   In the Information pane, double-click the New Event text and type a name for your event.

5   To set the location, click the Location text and type where the event is happening.

6   Click the hour, minute, and time of day text fields next to *from* and *to*, and specify the event's start and end times.

7   If you're scheduling a recurring event, choose how often from the repeat drop-down menu.

8   To list who's attending, click None next to invitees and enter your guest list.

9   To be reminded of an upcoming event, select the type of notification you'd like from the alarm pop-up menu, and set your preferences from the menus that appear.

Choose how you'd like to be notified about an upcoming event.

   To create a to-do list, click the thumbtack button (✹) to open the To Do pane. Choose File > New To Do, and enter your task.

Creating and publishing calendars

You can create separate calendars in iCal. If, for example, you want to create a separate calendar for each family member, and then make those calendars accessible to each family member, iCal lets you do both easily.

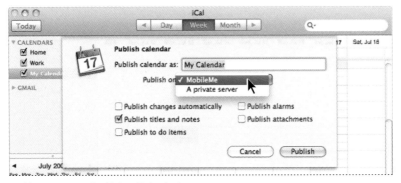

iCal lets you create and publish multiple calendars.

1   Choose File > New Calendar > On My Mac, and type a name for your calendar in the text field.

2   Make your calendar accessible to others by choosing Calendar > Publish.

3   In the dialog box that appears, type a name for your calendar in the top text field.

4   Choose where to publish it (MobileMe or your own server) from the Publish on drop-down menu.

5   Select any of the other options you want, and press Publish.

When iCal finishes publishing your calendar, a dialog opens and displays the URL for the calendar—be sure to record this URL so that others can subscribe to it.

Subscribing to a calendar

If you know the URL of an iCal calendar that someone has published on the Internet, you can add that calendar to your Calendars list by subscribing to it. You can also subscribe by clicking links to published iCal calendars on the Internet or in e-mails you may have received.

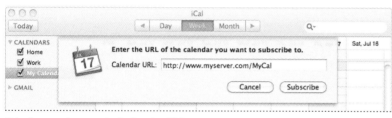

Subscribe to another person's calendar using iCal.

1   Choose Calendar > Subscribe.

2   Type the URL for the calendar you want to subscribe to.

3   If you want iCal to update your copy of this calendar when changes to it are published on the Internet, select the *Refresh* check box.

4   If you want to see any To Do items or hear any alarms associated with the calendar, deselect the *Remove To Do items* or *Remove alarms* checkbox.

5   Press Subscribe.

6   To subscribe to a calendar from a link on the Internet or in an e-mail, simply click the link.

The calendar you've subscribed to appears in your Calendars list with a curved arrow (↩) beside it. You can rename it by double-clicking the name, but you cannot make any other changes to it.

You can subscribe to any of the holiday, sports, or other general calendars in the Calendar Library on the iCal web site. To subscribe to any of these calendars, choose Calendars > Find Shared Calendars, or visit www.apple.com/ical/library.

iChat

iChat enables you to see and hear your friends, family, and coworkers regardless of how far away they are, by allowing you to text chat, audio chat, or video chat over the Internet. Better yet, you won't incur any text messaging, long distance, or video streaming charges.

 You need access to the Internet and a MobileMe, AIM (AOL Instant Messenger), Google Talk, or Jabber account to use iChat.

Setting up iChat

Configuring iChat is easy, as the application guides you through the process.

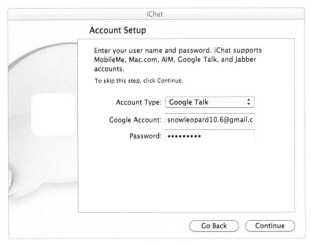

Follow the on-screen instructions to configure iChat.

1 Open iChat from the Dock or from within the Applications folder. A dialog box opens to guide you step-by-step as you set up your account.

2 Follow the on-screen instructions to configure your account, and press Done when finished.

3   When you're finished configuring, iChat displays the Buddy List window. Here you can see who is available to chat from your Buddy List. Other iChat and AIM users who've added you as a buddy can also see your name and status in their window.

4   To change your status, click it and choose a new one from the drop-down menu. You can also choose Custom and type your own customized status message.

5   If your computer has a built-in microphone, or you have an external one connected, you may see a phone icon. This lets your iChat buddies know you're available to audio chat.

6   If you have a FireWire or compatible USB camera connected to your computer (or an iSight or DV camera built-in), a movie camera icon displays to let your iChat buddies know you're available to video chat.

Adding a buddy

To add a buddy, simply choose the type of account he or she has, and type the account name.

Adding a buddy to chat with couldn't be easier.

1   Choose Add Buddy from the Buddies menu.

2   In the resulting window, type the account name.

     iChat helps you by searching through your Address Book. Choose the account type from the menu. You can also enter your buddy's first and last name.

3   Press Add. Your new buddy appears in your Buddy List. If your buddy is online, a status indicator appears next to his or her name. If a buddy isn't currently available to chat, the name appears dimmed.

Text chat with a buddy

Text chat lets you carry on a conversation by typing messages.

1   Simply double-click a name in the Buddy List. A chat window opens.

2   Type your message in the text box at the bottom of the window.

3   Press Return to send the message.

Your buddy receives a chat invitation. If he or she wants to chat with you, you receive a reply back in your chat window.

4   When you get a response, you can carry on a conversation by typing your messages.

To ensure that your words convey the right emotion, you can pick a smiley emoticon to send along with your message.

5   Click the smiley face icon in the bottom right corner and choose an icon from the drop-down menu.

6   To end the chat, close the chat window.

Audio chat with a buddy

If you and your buddy both have built-in or external microphones enabled, you can talk to each other over iChat just as you would on the phone.

 In the Video menu, make sure that Microphone Enabled *is checked.*

1   Choose a buddy from your Buddy List.

2   Click the Phone button at the bottom of the window. An audio chat window opens on your computer. An invitation is sent to your buddy. They hear a ringing phone sound if they are using iChat.

Audio chat lets you carry on a spoken conversation.

3   When your buddy accepts your invitation, your window shows a *connecting* message, and then displays a levels meter when you're connected.

4   Speak into your microphone to converse with your buddy.

5   To end the chat, close the audio chat window.

Video chat with a buddy

If you and your buddy both have FireWire or compatible USB cameras connected (or built in) to your computers, you can video chat with each other.

 Make sure that Camera Enabled *is checked in the Video menu.*

With video chat, you and your buddy can see and hear each other online.

1   Choose your buddy in the Buddy List window.

2   Press the Movie Camera button at the bottom of the window.

     A video chat window opens on your screen and an invitation is sent to your buddy.

3   When your buddy accepts, you see his or her face in the video chat window next to yours.

4   To end the chat, close the video chat window.

You can even get creative in your video chats with Photo Booth effects. Select Video > Show Video Effects to choose an effect, and watch your video change.

Setting up a multiperson chat

iChat offers several options if you want to text, audio, or video chat with more than one buddy.

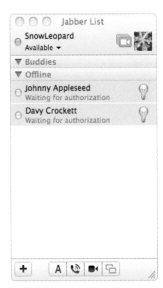

With iChat, you can chat with more than one person, or even share your computer screen.

With multiperson chat, you can:

•   Connect with a lot of people in one text chat;

•   Connect with up to ten people in an audio chat; or

•   Connect with up to four people in a video chat (as long as your system supports it).

The iChat Support page has more information about iChat system requirements.

1   Select the buddies that you want to participate in your multiperson chat. You can press and hold down the Command key to select more than one buddy.

2   To start a text chat, press the A button at the bottom of the Buddy List window. To start an audio chat, press the Phone button. To start a video chat, press the Movie Camera button.

3   When your buddies accept your invitation, they are able to send text, talk, or converse face to face with whomever joins the chat.

4   The chat continues as long as the person who initiated it keeps his or her chat window open. However, anyone can leave the chat at any time by closing their chat window.

Using iChat Theater

iChat Theater lets you present slide shows in an iChat video window. You control the presentation from your desktop, while your buddies view it on theirs. Most files on your computer are available for iChat Theater.

 You don't need a video camera to host an iChat Theater presentation.

Present slide shows in an iChat video window with iChat Theater.

1   Choose File > Share a File With iChat Theater (unless the item you want to present is an iPhoto album).

If you want to present an iPhoto album as a slide show, and you have iPhoto '08 installed, choose File > Share iPhoto With iChat Theater.

2   Choose the items you want to present:

- **Text files, photos, and other files:** Select one or more files. The first file appears in the iChat video window. You control the slide show from a toolbar outside of the video window.

- **QuickTime movies:** The movie opens in the iChat video window. You control the slide show from a toolbar outside of the video window.

- **iPhoto '08 album slide shows:** The iLife Media Browser panel opens. Select the photo album you want to share. The first photo opens in the iChat video window, and iPhoto opens so that you can use its controls for advancing through the photos.

- **Keynote slide shows:** The first slide opens in the iChat video window, and Keynote opens so that you can use its controls for advancing through the slides.

3   When you see a message asking you to start a video chat, highlight a buddy in the Buddy List and choose Buddies > Invite to Video Chat.

If you have a video camera and have already started a video chat, this message is skipped.

4   When the presentation is finished, close the control window.

A quick way to find out if an item can be presented in iChat Theater is to select it in the Finder and choose File > Quick Look. If Quick Look lets you see the item's content, the item can be presented in iChat Theater.

Sharing your screen with a buddy

With iChat, you and a buddy can share a screen, even if you're far away from each other. For example, you could allow a buddy to use your screen so that you could work on a project together. (To share screens, both you and your buddy must have Mac OS X 10.5 [Leopard]).

When you share your screen with a buddy, the buddy has the same access to your computer that you have. Share your screen only with trusted parties, and be particularly careful if you receive a request to share your screen from someone who isn't in your Buddy List.

1 Select a buddy, and then open the Buddies menu and choose one of the screen sharing options.

- To share your own screen, choose *Share My Screen*.

- To share your buddy's screen, choose *Ask to Share*.

2 You can switch between viewing your screen and your buddy's screen. You can also copy files between your computer and your buddy's by dragging them from one desktop to the other.

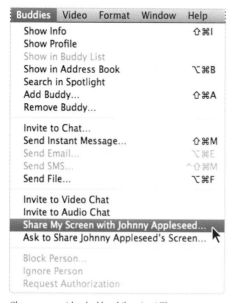

Share screens with a buddy while using iChat.

3 During screen sharing, iChat automatically initiates an audio chat so that you can speak to each other while working.

4 If you need to end a screen sharing session, press Ctrl+Esc.

You can share screens while using any account that iChat supports: .Mac, AIM, Jabber, or Google Talk. You can also share your screen with others on a local network using Bonjour.

Preview

Snow Leopard's Preview application is a built-in file viewer that makes it easy to read PDF files and view images in multiple formats.

Viewing PDF files

Preview allows you to view, work with, and print PDF files.

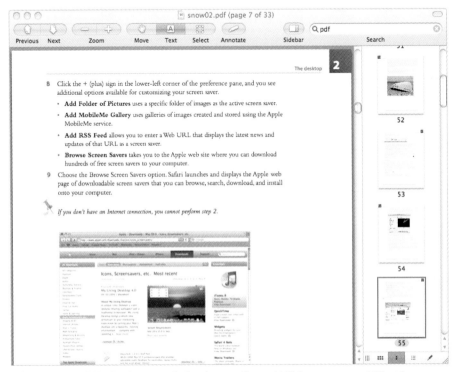

When you open a PDF in Preview, you can bookmark pages, add notes, highlight or copy text, and fill out forms.

1   To view a PDF file, double-click it to open it in Preview.

The first page of the file displays in the main window, while a drawer pane on the side shows its contents. Press the Drawer button at the top of the window if the sidebar pane isn't displayed.

2   Press the TOC button (▦) to view the PDF's table of contents in the drawer pane. You can click the triangle next to any chapter to view a list of its subjects, and choose a title to display the page in the window.

3   To view thumbnail images of each PDF page in the drawer pane, press the Thumbnails button (▦). Click a thumbnail to display the page in the window.

4   You can navigate from page to page by typing a page number in the Page text field, or by pressing the Next or Previous buttons.

5   Press the Zoom In button (☺) to magnify the page.

6   Choose Bookmarks > Add Bookmark to mark a page so that you can come back to it later. In the window that appears, type a name for your bookmark and press Add. When you want to open a bookmarked page, choose the page from the Bookmarks menu.

7   To fill out information in a PDF form, choose Tools > Text Tool, and click a field to type in your information. If the field doesn't highlight in blue, the PDF isn't a fillable form.

8   If you want to copy text from a PDF file, use the Text tool (as shown in step 7), and drag across the text that you want to highlight. Choose Edit > Copy, or press Command+C, then paste the text into your application of choice.

Viewing images

Preview allows you to view and edit JPEG, TIFF, GIF, PICT, and other image file formats.

Use Preview to look at pictures, edit them, convert them, or start a photo slide show.

1   Open Preview from the Dock or from within the Applications folder.

2   Drag the image file to the Preview icon in the Dock to display it.

3   To edit an image, choose Tools > Adjust Color. In the Adjust Color window, use Exposure, Contrast, Saturation, Temperature, Tint, Sharpness, and other controls to perfect your picture.

4   Choose File > Save As to convert your file to another file format. Type a name for your converted file, and click Save.

5   To rotate an image, choose Tools > Rotate Right or Rotate Left.

6   If you'd like to bundle your images into a slide show, drag multiple images to the Preview icon in the Dock. (The Preview window displays one image while the rest are displayed as thumbnails in the drawer pane.) Choose View > Slideshow to start the slide show.

Create a slide show from multiple images in Preview.

Self study

Use the Stationery feature in Mail to create a customized message to send to a friend. Enter contact information for that friend in your Address Book, and use it to send the e-mail. Open iCal and set a reminder for your friend's birthday. Use iChat to confirm with your friend via text chat that they've received your message. Create a slide show in Preview with images of you and your friend to send them for their birthday.

Review

Questions

1 What is a Smart Mailbox?

2 How can you send an e-mail from within the Address Book application?

3 In iCal, can you add someone else's calendar to your Calendars list?

4 What hardware is required to initiate a video chat with a buddy in iChat?

Answers

1 In Mail, a Smart Mailbox uses criteria that you specify to help you track and organize your messages. It automatically updates its contents whenever you use the application.

2 Click on the person's name in the Name column, and from the pop-up menu to the left of the contact's e-mail address, choose Send Email.

3 Yes. If you know the URL of an iCal calendar that someone has published on the Internet, you can add that calendar to your Calendars list by subscribing to it. Simply choose Calendar > Subscribe, and enter the URL for the calendar you want to subscribe to.

4 You and your buddy must both have FireWire or compatible USB cameras connected (or built in) to your computers to use video chat.

What you'll learn in this lesson:

- Why use the Terminal?
- How to run commands using the Terminal
- Valuable UNIX commands
- Navigating your hard drive using the Terminal

Using the Terminal

In this lesson, you'll use the Terminal to unleash hidden features in Snow Leopard and simplify mundane tasks.

Starting up

You will work with several files from the sl11lessons folder in this lesson. This lesson may be easier to follow if you copy the contents of the sl11lessons folder onto your desktop.

See Lesson 11 in action!

Use the accompanying video to gain a better understanding of how to use some of the features shown in this lesson. The video tutorial for this lesson can be found on the included DVD.

The Terminal

As indicated in the very first lesson of this book, Snow Leopard, at its core, is a UNIX-based operating system. Although the primary method of working in Snow Leopard is by using the Finder and its Graphical User Interface (GUI), Snow Leopard includes a program called Terminal that provides you with a direct link to the UNIX underpinnings of Mac OS X. You can perform many of the same tasks that you do in the Finder using Terminal, and you can often do them more efficiently.

Why should you use the Terminal? Well, chances are you could go through your entire computing life without ever having to open the program. That being said, it's an invaluable troubleshooting tool when you do have problems with software on your computer or with the operating system. There may come a time when you contact technical support with a problem that you are experiencing and you'll be asked if you can make some changes to some preferences or configuration files in the Terminal. Being able to do this could mean the difference between a ten-minute phone call and a one-hour phone call. In addition, the Terminal allows you to easily see hidden files on your computer that you otherwise wouldn't be able to see in the Finder. If you're a casual user and have a computer person that you regularly consult with, and who fixes problems with your computer as they arise, you can probably skip this lesson. If, however, you enjoy fixing and troubleshooting problems on your own, read on.

Don't let the word *Terminal* scare you; users often get discouraged at the mere mention of this word. This lesson will show you the basics of using the Terminal and some benefits to doing so. Let's take a look at how the Terminal works.

Launching the Terminal

In order to enter UNIX commands in Snow Leopard, you need to open the Terminal application.

1   In the Finder, choose Utilities from the Go menu to display the contents of the Utilities folder. You can also press Shift+Command+U to open the Utilities folder.

2   Within the Utilities folder, you see an application called Terminal. Because you'll be using the Terminal often in this lesson, drag the Terminal application to the Dock for quick access to the application.

3   Close any open Finder windows.

4 Click the Terminal icon in the Dock to launch the Terminal application. A new shell window appears.

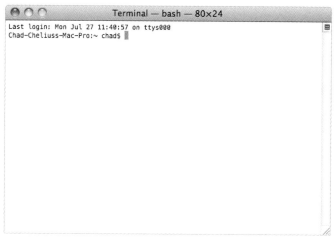

After launching the Terminal application, a new shell window appears.

The shell

When you launch the Terminal, it displays a new shell window. The shell is a program that interprets the commands that you enter within it. There are many shells that can be used to enter commands on a UNIX system, but the shell that is used by Snow Leopard is called the bash shell (Bourne-again shell). This is evident when you look at the title bar of the Terminal window. It displays the name of the application, followed by the shell being used, followed by the current dimensions of the window. It's not important that you know what type of shell you're using at this point; just know that the Terminal opens a new shell window for you.

The title bar of the Terminal window displays the name of the application, followed by the shell being used, followed by the current dimensions of the window.

The shell prompt

When a new shell window has been opened and the shell is ready to receive input, you see two lines of text. The first line lets you know the last time you opened a shell window, and the second line contains the shell prompt or command prompt. The shell prompt, by default, displays the computer name, followed by a tilde (~), followed by your login name, followed by a dollar sign ($). This line indicates that it is ready for you to enter a command.

```
Last login: Mon Jul 27 11:40:57 on ttys000
Chad-Cheliuss-Mac-Pro:~ chad$
```

The shell prompt.

Command lines

A command line is where you tell the UNIX system what to do. There are a lot of commands to choose from, but this lesson will focus on basic commands that you may find useful in your day-to-day work. It's important to remember that UNIX commands are case-sensitive, so pay close attention to this as you're working in the Terminal. Let's enter some commands!

This lesson will indicate the command to be typed in bold lettering, and any options and filenames that follow the command in italics.

Basic Commands

You'll start by entering some basic one-word commands in the shell prompt.

1   With the shell window still open on your screen, type **date** after the shell prompt and press the Return key on your keyboard. This tells the shell window that date is the command, and when you press Return, you are telling the shell that you want to run the command.

    After pressing the Return key, the shell displays the result of the date command, which is the current date, followed by a new shell prompt. The shell is now ready for your next command line.

After entering the command, the shell displays the result of the command, followed by a new shell prompt.

2   Type **cal** and press the Return key on your keyboard. The cal command displays the current month.

```
● ○ ○              Terminal — bash — 80×24
Last login: Mon Jul 27 12:01:31 on ttys002
Chad-Cheliuss-Mac-Pro:~ chad$ date
Mon Jul 27 12:29:20 EDT 2009
Chad-Cheliuss-Mac-Pro:~ chad$ cal
      July 2009
Su Mo Tu We Th Fr Sa
          1  2  3  4
 5  6  7  8  9 10 11
12 13 14 15 16 17 18
19 20 21 22 23 24 25
26 27 28 29 30 31

Chad-Cheliuss-Mac-Pro:~ chad$ ▊
```

The cal command displays the current month.

Adding options to commands

You can obtain a more specific result when you add an argument to a command. An argument tells the command to output a more specific result. An argument can be an option or a filename, and occurs after the command, separated by a space. Let's say you want to see a December calendar for an event that you are planning. In the following steps, you'll use an option to obtain a more specific result for the cal command.

1   Type **cal december 2009** (separated by spaces) and press the Return key on your keyboard. This utilizes two options, december and 2009, which instructs the cal command to display the December 2009 calendar in the shell window.

```
● ○ ○              Terminal — bash — 80×24
Last login: Mon Jul 27 12:01:31 on ttys002
Chad-Cheliuss-Mac-Pro:~ chad$ date
Mon Jul 27 12:29:20 EDT 2009
Chad-Cheliuss-Mac-Pro:~ chad$ cal
      July 2009
Su Mo Tu We Th Fr Sa
          1  2  3  4
 5  6  7  8  9 10 11
12 13 14 15 16 17 18
19 20 21 22 23 24 25
26 27 28 29 30 31

Chad-Cheliuss-Mac-Pro:~ chad$ cal december 2009
   December 2009
Su Mo Tu We Th Fr Sa
       1  2  3  4  5
 6  7  8  9 10 11 12
13 14 15 16 17 18 19
20 21 22 23 24 25 26
27 28 29 30 31

Chad-Cheliuss-Mac-Pro:~ chad$ ▊
```

Adding options to a command returns a more specific result.

2   Type **cal 2010** and press Return on your keyboard. This displays all twelve months for 2010.

Resize the shell window so that all of the months fit. This is an excellent way to see all twelve months at a time—easier and more effective than most GUI applications!

Man

So how do you know what options are available when using the command line? Fortunately there's a feature called *man* (short for manual) that allows you to see what options are available for specific commands. You're not expected to memorize every option, but you can at least look them up. Let's take a look at what options are available for the cal command.

1 In a shell window, type **man cal** and press Return on your keyboard. The manual page for cal is displayed in the shell window, showing additional options that are available for the cal command.

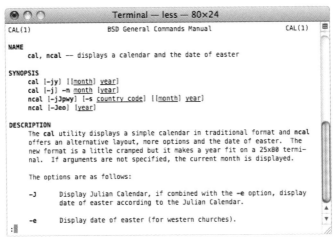

The manual pages for the cal command.

2 Press the spacebar on your keyboard to scroll to the next manual page.

3 Press the spacebar until you see END at the bottom of the shell window, indicating that you've reached the end of the manual pages.

4 Type Q on your keyboard to quit the manual program and return to the shell prompt.

5 Type **cal –j** and press the Return key on your keyboard. The –j option was one of the options listed on the cal man page, and displays the days as they are numbered from the beginning of the year.

There's nothing to it! You see, the shell allows you quick access to useful features within Snow Leopard that would be difficult to access any other way.

Navigating using command lines

Now that you've been introduced to some basic yet useful command lines, you'll learn how to navigate to different folders or directories on your computer just as you would in the Finder. You'll also learn how to make new directories in which to store your files. For this exercise, you'll close out of the current shell window and start fresh with a new one.

1   If the shell window from the previous exercise is still open on your screen, type **exit** at the command prompt and press the Return key on your keyboard. A *Process completed* message appears.

2   Close the shell window. It's a good practice to exit out of your current session before closing the window.

3   Choose Shell > New Window > Basic or press Command+N on your keyboard to open a new shell window.

When you open a new shell window, the default directory is your Home folder. You know this by the ~ that appears before your login name in the shell prompt. If you're ever unsure of what your current directory is, you can find out very easily.

4   Type **pwd** at the shell prompt and press Return on your keyboard. The pwd command shows you the Present Working Directory. The result should be /Users/*Your Username*.

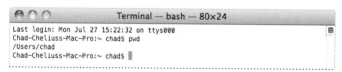

The pwd command shows you the present working directory.

5   Type **ls** and press Return on your keyboard. The ls command is the list command. It lists the contents of your current directory, which is your Home folder.

6   Switch to the Finder and open a new Finder window.

7   Click your Home folder in the Sidebar of the Finder window to display the contents of the Home folder.

8   Position the Finder window next to the shell window, and notice that both windows display the same contents. It's just a different way of viewing the contents of a folder or directory.

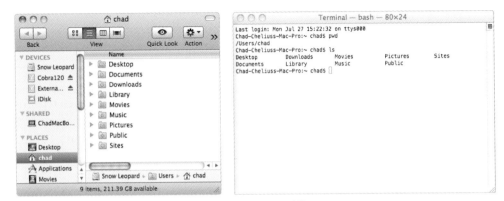

The shell window displays the same contents as a Finder window, just in a different way.

9   Close the Finder window and return to the shell window.

Changing directories

Now you'll start looking into different directories within your Home folder to see the contents of each directory.

1   Type **cd Library** and press the Return key on your keyboard. The cd command means change directory, and the word Library tells the cd command to change the directory to the Library directory. The current directory (Library) is indicated in the shell prompt.

The current directory is indicated in the shell prompt.

2   Type **ls** to list the contents of the Library directory.

3   Type **cd ..** (that's cd followed by a space and two periods). This command goes back one level in the directory structure, making the current directory the Home folder again.

     You don't have to navigate through folders one level at a time. If you know the exact directory that you'd like to navigate to, you can type the absolute path and go directly there. For the following steps, you'll need the sl11lessons folder copied to your desktop, as described in the Starting up section at the beginning of this lesson.

4   Type **cd ~/Desktop/sl11lessons** and press the Return key on your keyboard. This tells the shell to navigate to your Home folder (~), then to the Desktop folder, and then to the sl11lessons folder.

5   Type **ls** and press the Return key on your keyboard.

You've now successfully navigated several folders on your computer. In the next steps, you'll keep working in the sl11lessons folder, but you'll learn some new commands that will help you organize the contents of this folder.

Creating new directories

There are 30 files in the sl11lessons folder, and it would be nice to reorganize these files categorically to make them easier to browse and access.

1   Make sure that your present working directory is the sl11lessons folder, then type **mkdir Text** and press the Return key on your keyboard.

2   Type **ls** and press the Return key on your keyboard. The mkdir command means *make directory*. You'll notice that there's a new directory within the sl11lessons folder called Text. It should appear as the first item in the list.

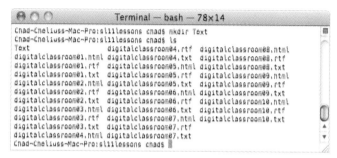

The mkdir command allows you to create new directories in the shell.

3   Type **mkdir HTML** and press the Return key on your keyboard. This creates a new directory called HTML.

4   Finally, type **mkdir Rich\ Text** and press the Return key on your keyboard. That's a backslash after the word *Rich*, followed by a space and then the word *Text*.

The argument for this command is slightly different than the other commands you've been using. You see, to create a directory with a space in it, you have to escape out of the command. In other words, if you simply type *Rich* (space) *Text*, the shell thinks you are separating arguments or separating the argument from the command. Typing a backslash tells the shell to use the literal space instead of the separation of an argument. This also works when you're navigating directories.

5   Type **ls** and press the Return key on your keyboard. You now have three directories listed at the top of the file list.

Moving files

Now that you've created the directories in which to store the files, you'll move them into their appropriate directories. You'll begin by moving a few of the files into their respective directories.

1 Type **mv digitalclassroom01.html HTML** and press the Return key on your keyboard. This command tells the shell to move the digitalclassroom01.html file into the HTML directory.

2 You should see a new shell prompt if the move was successful. To verify that the file was moved, type **cd HTML** and press the Return key on your keyboard.

3 Type **ls** and press the Return key on your keyboard to list the contents of the HTML directory. The digitalclassroom01.html file should be listed.

4 Type **cd ..** and press the Return key on your keyboard to go back to the sl11lessons directory.

5 Type **ls** to list the contents of the sl11lessons directory.

That wasn't very difficult to do; however, you've only moved one file into one of the directories. There are twenty-nine more files to move! Certainly you don't want to repeat the previous five steps twenty-nine more times! After all, the whole point of this lesson is to help work more efficiently using the Terminal. In the next steps, you'll use wildcards to help you streamline the process of moving these files to save a lot of time and energy.

6 Type **mv *.html HTML** and press the Return key on your keyboard. The star (Shift+8) followed by .html indicates that the shell should move any file, no matter what its name, that has an .html extension into the HTML directory.

7 You can list the contents of the HTML directory without having to navigate to that directory first. Type **ls HTML** and press the Return key on your keyboard. Notice that the contents of the HTML directory are listed, but the present working directory is still the sl11lessons directory. Nice!

8 Type **ls** to list the contents of the sl11lessons directory.

9   Type **mv *.rtf Rich** and press the Tab key on your keyboard. This is a great technique
     to save you from having to do more typing than necessary. Start typing the beginning of
     the name of the directory or file, and press the Tab key. As long as there aren't multiple
     files or directories with the same name, the shell automatically types the rest of the name
     for you! Press the Return key on your keyboard to execute the command.

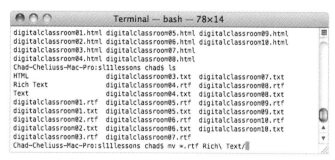

*Start typing the beginning of a directory or filename, then press the Tab key. The shell
automatically finishes the name for you.*

10   Type **ls Rich\ Text** (you can use the Tab key trick again) and press the Return key on
     your keyboard. All of the .rtf files should be listed within the Rich Text directory.

11   Type **ls** and press the Return key on your keyboard.

12   Type **mv *.txt Text** and press the Return key on your keyboard.

13   Type **ls Text** and press the Return key on your keyboard. All of the .txt files should now
     be listed in the Text directory.

14   Type **ls** and press Return on your keyboard. There are now three directories in the
     sl11lessons folder, and all the files are neatly organized within each of those directories.

Copying files and directories

At some point, you may want to make a copy of a file or directory to make an edit or to
create a revision or backup of a file. This can easily be accomplished using the shell and the cp
command.

1   Type **cd ~/Desktop/sl11lessons/Text** to make the Text directory the current
     directory.

2   Type **ls** to display the contents of the Text directory.

3   Type **cp digitalclassroom01.txt digitalclassroom11.txt**. This copies the
     digitalclassroom01.txt file and renames it on the fly as digitalclassroom11.txt. Copying
     is easy enough in the Finder, but you can't rename it as you're copying it using that
     method.

     Next, you'll copy the sl11lessons directory on your desktop so that you have a backup.

4   Type **cd ~/Desktop** and press the Return key on your keyboard. This sets the present working directory to the desktop.

5   Type **cp sl11lessons sl11lessons_copy** and press the Return key on your keyboard. You receive an error that indicates that the sl11lessons directory is a directory and that it hasn't been copied. Directories need more instructions to make a copy.

6   Type **cp –r sl11lessons sl11lessons_copy** and press the Return key on your keyboard. The –r argument tells the cp command to recursively copy the directory, as well as any files or directories within the sl11lessons folder. You can see the results of this copy in the Finder.

```
● ○ ○          Terminal — bash — 78×14
digitalclassroom03.txt  digitalclassroom07.txt
digitalclassroom04.txt  digitalclassroom08.txt
Chad-Cheliuss-Mac-Pro:Text chad$ cp digitalclassroom01.txt digitalclassroom11.
txt
Chad-Cheliuss-Mac-Pro:Text chad$ ls
digitalclassroom01.txt  digitalclassroom05.txt  digitalclassroom09.txt
digitalclassroom02.txt  digitalclassroom06.txt  digitalclassroom10.txt
digitalclassroom03.txt  digitalclassroom07.txt  digitalclassroom11.txt
digitalclassroom04.txt  digitalclassroom08.txt
Chad-Cheliuss-Mac-Pro:Text chad$ cd ~/Desktop
Chad-Cheliuss-Mac-Pro:Desktop chad$ cp sl11lessons sl11lessons_copy
cp: sl11lessons is a directory (not copied).
Chad-Cheliuss-Mac-Pro:Desktop chad$ cp -r sl11lessons/ sl11lessons_copy
Chad-Cheliuss-Mac-Pro:Desktop chad$
```

After copying the directory in the Terminal, you can see the duplicated directory in the Finder.

Deleting files and directories

As you work with the shell, you'll no doubt need to delete a file or directory on your hard drive. This can be easily accomplished using the rm, or remove, command. Use some caution with this command, and verify the file or directory that you are deleting prior to pressing the Return key. There is no undo in the Terminal!

1   Make sure that the present working directory is the desktop, and type **ls** to list the contents of the Desktop directory.

2   Let's remove that copy of the sl11lessons folder that you created previously in step 6. Type **rm –r sl11lessons_copy** and press the Return key on your keyboard. Removing directories also requires the –r argument to recursively delete the directory and all of its contents.

3   Type **ls** and press the Return key on your keyboard. The directory is removed from the desktop.

4   Removing a file is just as easy. Type **cd sl11lessons/Text** and press the Return key on your keyboard.

5   Type **ls** and press the Return key on your keyboard. This directory contains the extra text file digitalclassroom11.txt that you created earlier in this lesson.

6   Type **rm digitalclassroom11.txt** and press the Return key on your keyboard. The file is removed.

7   Type **ls** to confirm that the file was removed.

Editing files using the shell

So far you've created, copied, and deleted files using the shell. Another excellent feature of the shell is that you can also edit files. The shell in Snow Leopard ships with several built-in text editors that can be extremely useful for editing files on your computer. In the following steps, you'll use the pico text editor to edit the contents of a text file.

1   Your present working directory should be Text. If it's not, type **cd ~/Desktop/ sl11lessons/Text** and press Return on your keyboard.

2   Type **pico digitalclassroom01.txt** and press the Return key on your keyboard. The file digitalclassroom01.txt opens in the pico text editor within the shell and displays the name of the document that you are editing at the top of the window.

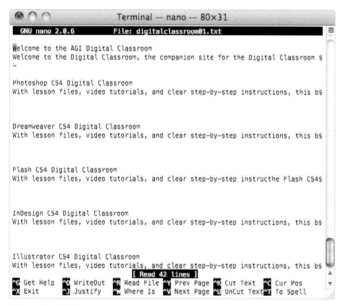

The pico text editor.

The bottom of the pico window displays commands that can be used to perform different tasks within the editor. Press Ctrl+V several times to scroll to the bottom of the digitalclassroom01.txt document.

3   Use the up and down arrow keys on your keyboard to move your cursor so that it's positioned several lines below the last line of text in the document.

4   Type **Snow Leopard Digital Classroom** and press the Return key on your keyboard to go to the next line in the document.

5   Press Ctrl+X on your keyboard. A message at the bottom of the window asks if you want to save the modified buffer (that is, do you want to save the changes?). Press Y on your keyboard.

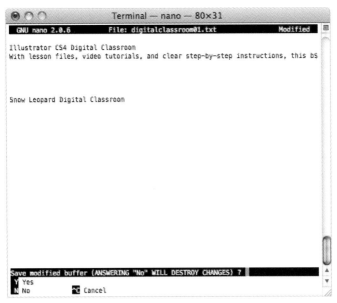

Modifying and saving the file in the pico text editor.

Finally, pico asks if you want to write the same name as the file that you opened (that is, do you want to overwrite the document?). Press the Return key on your keyboard to save the file with the same name as the one you opened. The file is saved.

6   To verify that the change has been made to the file, open the digitalclassroom01.txt file in the Finder using the TextEdit application. The change should appear here as well.

You are now well on your way to impressing your friends by showing them all that you know about the Terminal and the shell.

Change the screen capture format

Snow Leopard provides a feature called screen capture that allows you to take a picture of your screen. This can be useful if you are trying to instruct someone on how to perform a certain action on your computer or to relay a problem that may be happening so that you can show someone the problem that is occurring. In the following steps, you learn how to take a picture of your screen using the screen capture utility and then how to change the default file format that screen capture uses to save the files. Let's get started!

1   Click the Finder icon in your Dock to make the Finder the active application. Close any open Finder windows that appear.

2   Press Command+Shift+3 on your keyboard. This takes a capture of your screen and saves it as a new file on your desktop.

3 Select the file and press Command+I on your keyboard.

4 Open the Name & Extension disclosure triangle, and you see that it has a .png extension. Close the Info window.

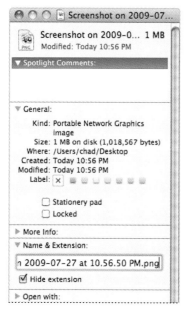

The default screen capture format is a .png file.

5 Go back to the shell window or open a new shell window, type **defaults write com. apple.screencapture type pdf** and press the Return key on your keyboard. This changes the default screen capture format to PDF by changing the preferences for the screen capture program.

6 The format that you type after the word type can be one of the following:

- bmp
- gif
- jpeg 2000
- jpeg
- pdf
- pict
- png
- psd
- sgi
- tga
- tiff

7   Type **exit** and press the Return key on your keyboard to close the shell session.

8   In order for this format change to be applied, you need to log off of your account and log back in. From the Apple menu (), choose Log Out *your username*, then click the Log Out button in the resulting dialog.

9   Log back into your computer.

10 Press Shift+Command+3 on your keyboard to take a new screen capture.

11 Select the new file on your desktop and press Command+I on your keyboard.

12 Click the disclosure triangle next to the Name & Extension section, and look at the file extension for this screen capture file. It should now indicate that it is a PDF file.

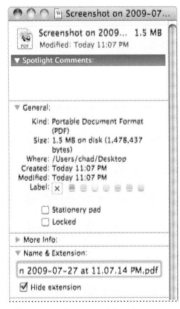

After running the command line, the screen capture format is changed to PDF.

Close the Info window.

You've just successfully changed the default file format for the screen capture files on your computer. Although you could download or purchase a third-party utility to do this for you, the Terminal is an incredibly efficient and controllable way to doing this without any additional software. If you want to change the screen capture format back to the .png file format, simply go back to step 5 and enter the .png format at the end of the command line.

Congratulations! You've just completed Lesson 11, "Using the Terminal."

Self study

The Terminal is an incredibly powerful tool that can be used to execute command lines within a shell to perform tasks quickly and efficiently. You've really just scratched the surface of command lines in this lesson. If you're not one of the two percent of people in the world that have an uncluttered desktop, you can utilize command lines to organize all of the files on your desktop into related folders. Create a folder called Word documents. Using a command line, move all of the word documents on your desktop into that folder. It doesn't get any faster or easier than that! You don't use Word? No problem, pick a different file type and organize your files into specific folders for better organization.

Review

Questions

1   What type of shell is used in Snow Leopard?

2   What command is used in the shell to create a new directory?

3   What is a wildcard?

Answers

1   The bash (Bourne-again) shell.

2   The mkdir command.

3   A wildcard is a character that is used to represent any text in a certain location of a filename.

Lesson 12

What you'll learn in this lesson:

- Installing Snow Leopard
- Upgrading to Snow Leopard from a previous version of Mac OS X
- Installing applications

Installing Snow Leopard and Applications

In this lesson, you'll learn how to install Snow Leopard and what options are available during installation. In addition, you'll learn how to install applications to enhance the capabilities of your computer.

Starting up

This chapter doesn't utilize any lesson files and therefore doesn't require any files to be copied onto your computer.

See Lesson 12 in action!

Use the accompanying video to gain a better understanding of how to use some of the features shown in this lesson. The video tutorial for this lesson can be found on the included DVD.

Installing Snow Leopard

If you've recently purchased a new Mac, Snow Leopard is probably already installed, however, if it's not one of the latest Macs offered by Apple, then it is probably running an older version of Mac OS X, such as Leopard or Tiger. This lesson will guide you through installing Snow Leopard on your computer and show you the options that are available during installation.

System requirements

Before you purchase Snow Leopard, it's important to know the system requirements of the software. System requirements refer to the minimum computer hardware that is required for Snow Leopard to be installed on a particular computer. After all, you don't want to spend your hard-earned money on software that won't run on your computer.

Snow Leopard represents a significant jump in hardware requirements compared to previous versions of Mac OS X, as Snow Leopard only runs on an Intel processor. So if you are running a computer that does not have an Intel processor, you cannot install Snow Leopard on your computer. Additional system requirements include:

- Mac computer with an Intel processor
- 1GB of memory (RAM)
- 5GB of free disk space
- DVD drive for installation

Although these system requirements limit you to computers that are less than a few years old, it's for good reason. Snow Leopard contains numerous advanced features and requires a very fast processor in order for these features to perform at a reasonable speed.

Getting Snow Leopard

Apple offers several upgrade paths for existing users of Mac OS X. If you've purchased a new computer on or after June 8, 2009, then you can upgrade to Snow Leopard for $9.95. Visit the Snow Leopard Up-to-Date web site at *www.apple.com/macosx/uptodate* for more information.

If you purchased a new computer before June 8, 2009 or if you have Leopard installed on your machine, you qualify for the upgrade price of $29. Visit *www.apple.com/macosx* for more information. It seems that with Snow Leopard, Apple is rewarding users who have kept current with their existing copy of Mac OS X.

If you don't qualify for either of the above upgrade options, you have to pay the full price for the product. As you can see from reading the previous lessons, the new features provided in Snow Leopard are well worth the price.

Installation

Once you've received the Snow Leopard installation disc, you're ready to get started. You want to make sure that your computer meets the necessary system requirements as described in the previous section. If you are using a laptop computer, be sure that you are plugged into an electrical outlet and not running on battery. Having your computer lose power during installation is never a good thing.

Upgrading

Chances are that if you have purchased Snow Leopard, you're already running a previous version of Mac OS X on your computer. This version could be Leopard (OS X 10.5), Tiger (OS X 10.4), Panther (OS X 10.3), Jaguar (OS X 10.2), or any other previous version of Mac OS X. When the Snow Leopard installer detects a previous version of Mac OS X, it upgrades your operating system. Upgrading your operating system updates all of the necessary files on your computer, such as system files and printer drivers, with the new files required to run Snow Leopard. All our existing files in each user's Home folder and in the Applications folder, remain intact.

Although the upgrade process doesn't overwrite any of the files in a user's Home folder or any Application files, you need to confirm that any existing applications that are installed on your computer are compatible with Snow Leopard. Applications often require an update to ensure compatibility with newer operating systems such as Snow Leopard.

If you perform a Snow Leopard installation on a disk that already has Snow Leopard installed, the installer automatically performs an Archive and Install. This essentially puts a new copy of Snow Leopard on your computer but retains all user accounts and network settings. In addition, if you've installed any Snow Leopard updates, for instance 10.6.1, the update is retained so you don't have to re-run the update after installation. The installation process is the same, regardless of whether you have a previous Mac OS X version installed or Snow Leopard installed.

1 Insert the Snow Leopard DVD into the DVD drive on your computer. The Mac OS X Install DVD window automatically displays on your screen. Prior to installing Snow Leopard, you may want to read the information in the Instructions folder on the disc in case there are any last-minute changes in the installation process.

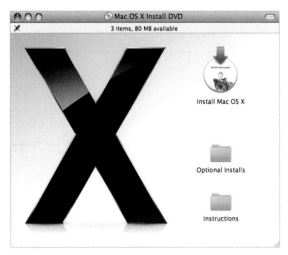

The Mac OS X Install DVD window appears prior to installation.

2 Double-click the Install Mac OS X icon in the Mac OS X Install DVD window. The Install Mac OS X window appears.

The Install Mac OS X window appears.

3 Press Continue to proceed with the installation.

4 A new window appears, displaying the Apple Software License Agreement (SLA). The SLA simply describes the terms and conditions under which you may use Snow Leopard. Once you've read the SLA, press Agree to continue.

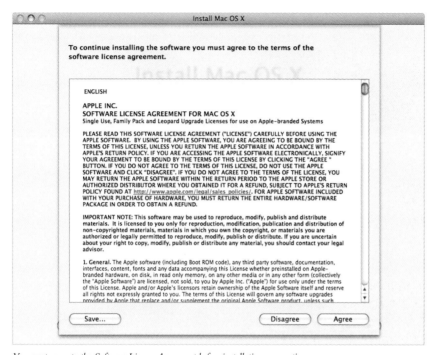

You must agree to the Software License Agreement before installation can continue.

5   A screen appears, asking you to choose the disk where Snow Leopard is to be installed. It is likely that you'll only have one disk to choose from, however, if you have multiple hard disks connected to your computer, you're given a choice. Select the disk where you'd like to install Snow Leopard. If a disk is listed with a warning sign (⚠), then Snow Leopard can't be installed on that disk. A green arrow indicates that Snow Leopard can and will be installed on that disk. Click Install.

A green arrow indicates that Snow Leopard can and will be installed on the disk.

6   A confirmation dialog appears, asking if you are sure you want to install Snow Leopard. Click the Install button.

Confirm that you want to install Snow Leopard on the selected disk.

7   Enter an Administrator's name and password in the resulting dialog. Click OK. The installation process begins.

The beginning of the installation process.

Roughly 15 minutes into the installation process, your computer automatically restarts. During that initial 15 minutes, the installer copies temporary installation files to your hard drive. After your computer restarts, the installer uses the majority of the files that were copied to your hard drive for the remainder of the installation. Snow Leopard uses this installation method to reduce the amount of time required for installation. When installation is complete, the temporary installation files are automatically deleted.

If the computer restarts and you do not see an 'Installation Successful' message, make certain the DVD is inserted and restart your Mac while holding down the C key. This forces your Mac to start-up using the CD/DVD drive. The installation should then continue.

8   When the installation process is complete, a new window appears, asking you to restart. Press Restart. If you don't click the Restart button within 30 seconds, restart occurs automatically.

When installation is complete, you are given 30 seconds to click the Restart button before your computer restarts automatically.

9   When your computer restarts for the second time, Snow Leopard becomes your new operating system! The Mac OS X Setup Assistant launches and plays an introductory movie. Click the Continue button. Congratulations! You've upgraded your computer to Snow Leopard!

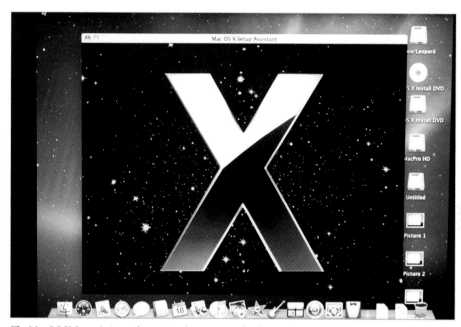

The Mac OS X Setup Assistant plays an introductory movie after the second restart of the installation process.

Erase and Install

Occasionally, due to a variety of circumstances, you may need to completely reinstall Snow Leopard. This could be due to files becoming corrupted, a damaged hard drive, or other issues. Erase and Install provides a method of starting from a "clean slate," and often resolves problems that you may have been experiencing. Erase and Install is a process where you reformat the hard drive, removing all current data and then installing a clean copy of Snow Leopard.

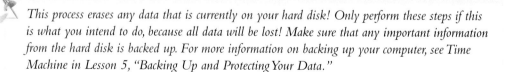

This process erases any data that is currently on your hard disk! Only perform these steps if this is what you intend to do, because all data will be lost! Make sure that any important information from the hard disk is backed up. For more information on backing up your computer, see Time Machine in Lesson 5, "Backing Up and Protecting Your Data."

1   Re-insert the Snow Leopard DVD into the DVD drive on your computer. The Mac OS X Install DVD window automatically displays on your screen. Prior to reinstalling Snow Leopard, you may want to read the information in the Instructions folder on the disc in case there are any last-minute changes in the installation process.

2   Double-click the Install Mac OS X icon in the Mac OS X Install DVD window. The Install Mac OS X window appears.

The Install Mac OS X window appears prior to installation.

3   Press the Utilities button. The Mac OS X Utilities window appears.

4   In order to reinstall Snow Leopard or perform any other tasks in the Utilities window, your computer must be restarted from the Snow Leopard DVD. Press Restart.

5   Enter an Administrator's name and password. Press OK.

6   When your computer restarts, a window displays, asking you to choose a language to
     use for installation. Leave this set to English, or choose another language. Click the right
     arrow button in the lower right corner of the window.

Select a language for installation.

7   After a few moments, the Install Mac OS X screen appears. At this point, you're going to
     bypass the installer.

8   Choose Utilities > Disk Utility from the Menu bar at the top of your screen. The Disk
     Utility application opens. Disk Utility is used to perform advanced operations on the
     hard disk of your computer.

9 The sidebar on the left side of the Disk Utility window displays all the disks and volumes that are available on your computer. Select the partition or volume that you want to erase. This is usually called Macintosh HD, but not always. In this example, it's called Snow Leopard. You can see that Snow Leopard is a partition of a main disk in the following figure.

10 With the partition selected, press the Erase button at the top of the main Disk Utility window.

11 From the Format drop-down menu, choose Mac OS Extended (Journaled) and press the Erase button in the lower-right corner of the Disk Utility window.

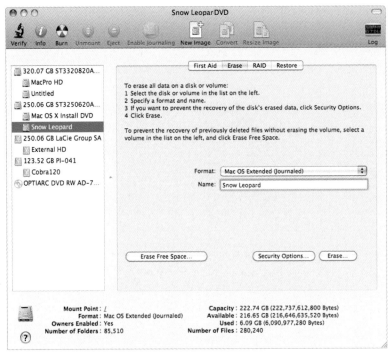

Disk Utility allows you to erase the contents of a disk or partition.

12 You receive one final dialog, informing you that the next step will erase the partition and delete all data. Make sure this is what you want to do! Press Erase. At this point, Disk Utility erases the partition that you selected in step 9.

13 When the Erase operation is complete, choose Disk Utility > Quit to exit the Disk Utility application.

14 After exiting the Disk Utility application, you are returned to the Install Mac OS X window. Press Continue.

15 A new window appears, displaying the Apple Software License Agreement (SLA). The SLA simply describes the terms and conditions under which you may use Snow Leopard. Once you've read the SLA, press Agree.

16 A screen appears, asking you to choose the disk where Snow Leopard will be installed. It is likely that you'll only have one disk to choose from, however, if you have multiple hard disks connected to your computer, you're given a choice. Select the disk where you'd like to install Snow Leopard. If a disk is listed with a warning sign, then Snow Leopard can't be installed on that disk. A green arrow indicates that Snow Leopard can and will be installed on that disk. Press Install. The installation process begins.

17 When installation is complete, your computer restarts, and the introductory movie plays. After that, the Mac OS X setup process begins. Because you did an Erase and Install, there are no existing accounts in which to log into the computer. The Setup Assistant guides you through setting up your computer and creating a new user account. In the Welcome screen, select the country where you live, and press Continue.

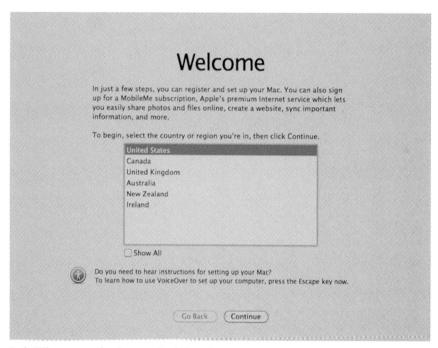

In the Welcome screen, select the country in which you live.

18 Select the language you'd like to use for your keyboard. Press Continue.

19 A screen appears, asking if you already own a Mac. This screen guides you through several choices for migrating any old data to your new Snow Leopard system. You are asked if you would like to transfer your information and you're presented with four choices:

- From another Mac
- From another volume on this Mac
- From a Time Machine backup
- Do not transfer my information now

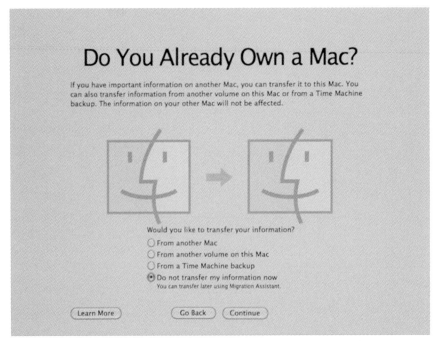

The Do You Already Own a Mac window allows you to transfer existing information from another computer.

From another Mac

If you've installed Snow Leopard on a new computer but your information exists on another computer, this choice allows you to use a FireWire cable to connect the two computers together so that the Setup Assistant can transfer your information from the old computer to the new one.

1 Connect a FireWire cable between the two computers by plugging each end of the cable into the FireWire port on each computer.

2 Turn on the Mac that currently has the information to be transferred. Immediately after pressing the power button, press and hold down the T key on that Mac's keyboard. This boots the computer into Target Disk mode.

3   Follow the instructions on the destination Mac (the Mac on which you've just installed Snow Leopard) to transfer your information to the Snow Leopard installation.

Target Disk Mode

Target Disk mode is used when you need to access files from another computer quickly and easily. Essentially, Target Disk mode turns a computer into an external hard drive. Simply connect a FireWire cable between the two computers. Next, boot the computer whose files you want to access while pressing and holding down the T key on the keyboard and you're done! The computer that is in Target Disk mode shows up as a new hard drive (in the Sidebar of any Finder window as well as on the desktop) on the other computer that is connected to the Target Disk mode computer.

From another volume on this Mac

If you have multiple hard drives or partitions configured on your computer, and have installed Snow Leopard on a different volume than the one that contains your older system, you can choose this option to transfer the information in that manner. Simply follow the instructions to complete the process.

From a Time Machine backup

If you have Leopard (Mac OS X 10.5) installed on your previous system and have been using Time Machine to back up that system, you can restore your files from that Time Machine backup. Simply connect the External drive that contains the backup to your computer using a FireWire or USB cable, and your old information is restored.

Do not transfer my information now

Choose this option if you do not have an older system and simply want to begin working on your new Snow Leopard installation.

Registration

After transferring any data to your new installation, you are guided through the registration process. Internet access is required at some point to submit your registration information to Apple. The Setup Assistant detects whether or not you have an Internet connection, and if it detects any wireless networks, it asks if you'd like to connect to one of them at this point.

1   If the Do You Already Own a Mac? screen is still displayed, and you do not have information to transfer, click the Do not transfer my information now radio button and press Continue.

2   Enter Your Apple ID if you have one. Press Continue.

3 You're asked to enter your registration information, including your name, address, and phone number. Registering your information qualifies you for technical support from Apple should you need it. Press Continue.

Registration Information

Enter your personal information. The information is used to register your Apple product, create your user account, set up your information in Address Book, and set up your Mail account.

First Name
Chad

Last Name
Chelius

Address

Email Address (if you have one)

City

Area Code   Phone Number

State
Select ▾

Zip Code

Company/School

To learn how Apple safeguards your personal information, review the Apple Customer Privacy Policy.

The warranty for your Apple product does not require you to register the product.

(Privacy Policy)   (Go Back)   (Continue)

Entering information in the Registration Information window sends your information to Apple and entitles you to technical support should you need it.

4 The next window asks questions about you and how you use your computer. Choose the appropriate option and press Continue.

5 You now need to set up your account. Enter a username and password for your account and press Continue.

6 The next screen provides the option to take a snapshot using the camera on your computer. Press the Take photo snapshot button to take a picture of yourself to use for your user account, or simply click the *Choose from the picture library* radio button to choose an existing picture provided by Snow Leopard. Press Continue.

7 Finally, a Thank You screen appears, indicating that the setup process is complete. Press the Go button.

Congratulations! You've successfully installed Snow Leopard!

Applications

One of the wonderful things about Mac OS X in general is that there are literally thousands of applications out there that can be installed to add functionality to your computer. Many of them are free or are available at a very low cost.

Installing applications

Applications can be obtained in a number of ways, but the most common methods are on a CD/DVD or via Internet download. Regardless of how you obtain an application, each one has an installer that makes sure that all the files necessary for the application to run properly are placed in the appropriate location on your system. Installers usually come in one of two forms: as a drag-and-drop package, or as an installer package. In the following exercise, you'll download the Firefox web browser and install it on your system to get a better understanding of how installers work. Firefox is an industry-standard web browser.

You need an Internet connection to perform this exercise.

Installing a drag-and-drop application

It doesn't get any easier than this type of application installer. You simply drag the downloaded file to your Applications folder and you're done.

1   Open Safari (or your web browser of choice) and navigate to *www.mozilla.com/en-US/ firefox/firefox.html.* This displays the Firefox home page.

2   Press the Free Download button in the middle of the screen to download the Firefox installer. The version of Firefox that you download may be slightly different than the one in the following figure.

Press the Free Download button to download the installer file.

3   When the application has completed downloading, a window appears with two icons: the application icon and the Applications folder icon, which is actually an alias to your Applications folder. Click and drag the Firefox icon on top of the Applications folder icon and release your mouse button. That's it! Firefox is installed!

Simply click and drag the Firefox icon onto the Applications folder icon to install the application.

4   Open your Applications folder and launch the Firefox application to verify installation.

5   Choose Firefox > Quit Firefox to exit the application.

Installing an application using an installer

Depending on their complexity, some applications utilize a dedicated installer to install the application and all the required components. In the following steps, you'll download the Adobe Reader application that enables you to view PDF files on your computer. Although the Preview application can also read PDF files, the Adobe Reader is a more robust PDF viewer.

You need an Internet connection to perform this exercise. Also, if you want to continue to use Preview to view PDF files, you can skip the actual installation portion of this exercise.

1   Open Safari (or your web browser of choice) and navigate to *www.adobe.com*.

2   Press the Get Adobe Reader button in the located in the middle-right corner of the gray area box of the browser window.

3   Your operating system is detected, and the resulting web page provides a Download button to download the Adobe Reader installer. Press Download.

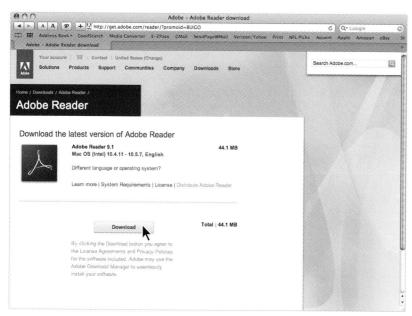

Click the Download button to begin downloading the Adobe Reader installer.

4   When the file is finished downloading, the installer launches, and a dialog is displayed, indicating that an application needs to run to determine if the software can be installed. Press Continue.

An installer analyzes your system and determines if the software can be installed on your machine.

5 The Adobe Reader 9 installer window is displayed. Press Continue.

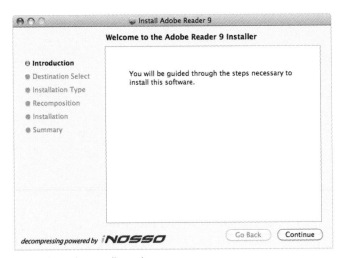

The Adobe Reader 9 installer window.

6 Enter the username and password of an Administrator on your computer. Click OK.

7 A new window with the installation status is displayed. When the process is finished, a confirmation window appears, indicating that the installation was successful. Press the Close button.

A window is displayed, indicating that the installation has completed successfully.

Congratulations! You've completed Lesson 12, "Installing Snow Leopard and Applications."

Self study

Installing Snow Leopard is not something you'll need to do on a regular basis. Especially considering how stable the operating system is, you may not have to reinstall your software for quite a while. When the time comes, this lesson can guide you through the process. However, installing applications is something you'll be doing fairly regularly. As you determine a need for a new application, download and install the application on your computer, using this lesson as a guide. You'll be amazed at how many different applications there are and their different uses. You're sure to find some applications that will make you wonder how you ever lived without them.

Review

Questions

1 Which feature should you choose during installation if you want to transfer information from another computer?

2 Before purchasing Snow Leopard, how can you verify that it can be installed on your computer?

3 What happens if you install Snow Leopard on a computer that already has Snow Leopard installed?

Answers

1 The *From another Mac* option allows you to connect a FireWire cable between two computers to transfer information to your new installation.

2 Consult the system requirements for Snow Leopard.

3 The installer automatically performs an Archive and Install, which retains all user account information but installs a fresh copy of Snow Leopard.

Index

printing
Address Book, 280
to PDF files, 212–214
print dialog
advanced print options, 210
overview, 208–209
presets, 210–211
Print Queue
managing, 206–207
overview, 205–206
viewing completed print jobs, 208
private Internet protocol (IP) addresses, 173
private YouTube videos, 115
privileges, 183
Public folder, 29, 91
public Internet protocol (IP) addresses, 173
Put Display to Sleep option, Activate Screen Corners menus, 230
pwd command, 303

Q

quality options, Movie Recording window, 103
Quality settings, Screen Recording controller, 105
Quick Look, 22–23, 290
QuickTime movies, iChat Theater, 290
QuickTime X Player
controls, 101–102
editing video, 107–108
exporting video
for desktop, 108–111
for Web, 111–112
overview, 100
recordings
capabilities, 102
movie, 102–123
screen, 105–106
sharing movies
for iTunes, 113
for MobileMe, 114
for YouTube, 115

R

–r argument, 308
Radar In Motion Widget, 68
Random option, Desktop & Screen Saver preference pane, 43
Reader, Adobe. *See* Adobe Reader
Record button
Movie Recording window, 104
Screen Recording controller, 106
Recording options menu, Movie Recording window, 103
Region drop-down menu, Formats pane, 234
registering Snow Leopard, 329–330
reinstalling Snow Leopard, 323–324
Remote Apple Events, Sharing preference pane, 256
Remote Login, Sharing preference pane, 256
Remote Management, Sharing preference pane, 256
Remove from Dock option, stack menu, 55
resizing Finder window, 12
Resolutions list, Displays preference pane, 240
resources, 8
Restart button, Startup Disk preference pane, 264

restarting during installation process, 321–323
Restore Defaults button, Energy Saver preference pane, 242
Restore System from Backup feature, 132
restoring backup disk image to internal disk, 139–140
Resume Printer button, Print Queue window, 207
Rewind button, QuickTime X Player, 101–102
rm command, 308
Rotation drop-down menu, Displays preference pane, 241
rotation options, Preview, 294
routers, network, 171–173
Run script option, When you insert a blank CD or DVD drop-down menus, 239

S

Safari browser
Address bar, 155–156
bookmarks, 157–159
Google search, 156–157
overview, 154
Silverlight plug-in, 160–161
tabs, 164
Top Sites feature, 162–163
Satellite access, 146
Save As dialog box, 27, 109
Save for Web dialog box, 111
Save Preset As window, 211
Save the Home folder as a disk image option, Accounts preference pane, 96
Save window, 212–213
Save your movie to iTunes dialog box, 113
Scale effect, 49
Scale field, Print dialog, 209
Scanner Sharing, Sharing preference pane, 256
Schedule button, Energy Saver preference pane, 242
Scheduled Check pane, Software Update preference pane, 260
Scheduler option, Print Options drop-down menu, 210
scheduling events, 281–282
screen capture format, changing, 310–312
Screen Recording controller, 105–106
screen saver, 26–28, 43–47
Screen Saver section, Desktop & Screen Saver preference pane, 44, 225–226
screen sharing
iChat, 290–291
overview, 184–188
Screen Sharing service, 256
Scrolling drop-down menu, Mouse preference pane, 246
Scrolling slider, Mouse preference pane, 245
Search For category, Finder Preferences window, 57
Search For section, Finder window sidebar, 25
Search text field, Mail, 275
Search window, 30–32
security
permissions
changing, 181–183
changing to view DVD lesson files, 3
Drop Box folder, 92–93
overview, 93
Public folder, 91
privileges, 181–183
wireless network, 173

Security Options button, Save window, 213
Security preference pane, 235–238
Seeing pane, Universal Access preference pane, 265
Select a device for sound input section, Input pane, 248
Select a device for sound output section, Output pane, 247
Select an alert sound section, Sound preference pane, 247
Select the applications to allow section, Parental Controls preference pane, 81–82
selecting multiple files, 21
seminars, 8
services, 256
Set Master Password button, FileVault pane, 237
Set Up Bluetooth Keyboard button, Keyboard preference pane, 244
Set Up Bluetooth Mouse button, Mouse preference pane, 246
Settings section, Speech preference pane, 261
Setup Assistant, 328–329
Shared category, 57, 180
Shared section, Finder window sidebar, 24
Sharing & Permissions section, Info window, 181–182
sharing files
    cleanup, 95–96
    Drop Box, 92–93
    in iTunes library, 120
    Public folder, 91
    viewing results, 93–95
Sharing Only accounts, 77
Sharing preference pane, 255–256
shell
    editing files in, 309–310
    overview, 299–300
Shift key, 21
Show activity for drop-down menu, Parental Controls preference pane, 86
Show All Bookmarks button, Safari, 157–159
Show Completed Jobs button, CUPS, 218
Show Completed Jobs option, Print Queue window, 208
Show Desktop mode, Exposé, 71
Show drop-down menu, Customize Toolbar pane, 60
Show Everyone's Jobs option, Print Queue window, 208
Show in Finder option, stack menu, 55
Show Path Bar option, toolbar View menu, 14
Sidebar button, Finder Preferences window, 57–58
sidebar, Finder, 23–25
Silverlight plug-in, installing in Safari, 160–161
Sites folder, 29–30
Size slider, Dock preference pane, 49, 228
SLA (Software License Agreement), 319, 327
slide show
    iChat Theater, 289–290
    Preview, 294
Slow Keys section, Universal Access preference pane, 265
Smart Folders, 30–32
Smart Groups, 280
Smart Mailboxes, 275
Smart Quotes drop-down menu, Text pane, 233
Snow Leopard
    ease of use, 7
    getting, 316–317
    installing
        from another Mac, 328–329

from another volume on Mac, 329
    reinstalling, 323–328
    from Time Machine backup, 329
    registering, 329–330
    running for first time, 7
    system requirements, 316
    upgrading, 317–323
Software License Agreement (SLA), 319, 327
Software Update preference pane
    Apple Support Downloads, 142–143
    overview, 260–261
    running updates immediately, 141
    scheduling updates, 142
    standalone installers, 142–143
Sort by options, stack menu, 55
Sound Effects button, Sound preference pane, 247
Sound preference pane, 246–248
Spaces
    options, 229–231
    overview, 72–73
Spaces section, Exposé & Spaces preference pane, 231
spam, 273
Speakable Items section, Speech preference pane, 261
Speaking Rate slider, Speech preference pane, 263
Speech preference pane, 261–263
Speech Recognition pane, Speech preference pane, 261–262
Spelling drop-down menu, Text pane, 233
Spotlight icon, 34
Spotlight search, Time Machine, 131
Spotlight tool, 34–37
stacks, 53–55
Standard accounts, 77, 78–79
Start Screen Saver option, Activate Screen Corners menus, 230
Start screen saver slider, Desktop & Screen Saver preference pane, 46, 227
Startup Disk preference pane, 263–264
Stationery, Mail, 274
Status section, Network preference pane, 251
Sticky Keys section, Universal Access preference pane, 265
Stop Recording button, Screen Recording controller, 106
Store category, iTunes, 117
Summary option, Print Options drop-down menu, 210
SuperDrive, 126
switches, network, 171
Symbol and Text Substitutions section, Text pane, 233
Sync pane, MobileMe preference pane, 249
System folder, 11
System Preferences pane
    Accounts preference pane, 257–258
    Date & Time preference pane, 259–260
    overview, 257
    Parental Controls preference pane, 260
    Software Update preference pane, 260–261
    Speech preference pane, 261–263
    Startup Disk preference pane, 263–264
    Time Machine preference paneons, 264
    Universal Access preference pane, 264–266
System Profiler window, 174
system requirements, Snow Leopard, 2, 316
System Voice drop-down menu, Speech preference pane, 263

T

tabs, Safari, 164
Target Disk mode, 264, 329
Telephone Number text field, Network preference pane, 149
television, connecting computer to, 123
templates, Mail, 274
Terminal application
    commands, 300–301
    directories
        changing, 304–305
        copying, 307–308
        creating, 305
        deleting, 308
    files
        copying, 307–308
        deleting, 308
        editing in shell, 309–310
        moving, 306–307
    Info window, closing, 312
    launching, 298–299
    man command, 302
    navigation, 303–304
    screen capture format, changing, 310–312
    shell, 299–300
Test button, Desktop & Screen Saver preference pane, 46, 226
text chat, iChat, 286
text editor, Terminal, 309–310
Text pane, Language & Text preference pane, 232–233
Text to Speech pane, Speech preference pane, 262–263
Text tool, Preview, 293
TextEdit application
    creating files, 26–28
    editing Web pages, 196–197
theatrical trailers, 122
thumbnail size, Top Sites screen, 163
Thumbnails button, Preview, 292
tilde (~), 29
Time Capsule, 130
Time Limits section, Parental Control preference pane, 85
Time Machine feature
    deleting old backups, 133
    preferences, 130
    restoring backups, 131–133
    setting up backups, 128–129
    setting up Time Capsule for backups, 130
    Snow Leopard installation from backup, 329
Time Machine preferences window, 129–130
Time Zone pane, Date & Time preference pane, 260
timeline, Time Machine, 131
timeline view, movie, 107–108
Times section, Formats pane, 234
To Do button, Mail, 277
To text field, Mail, 274
TOC button, Preview, 292
to-do lists, creating, 276–277
toolbar, Finder
    changing how files and folders are displayed, 15–16
    customizing, 59–62
    navigating files and folders, 14
    overview, 14
    removing items from, 62
    resetting to defaults, 62

Top Sites feature, Safari, 162–163
Tracking slider, Mouse preference pane, 245
trailers, movie, 122
transmission speeds, Internet, 146–147, 174
Trash icon, 21–22
Trim controls, QuickTime X Player, 107–108
TV, connecting computer to, 123

U

Universal Access preference pane, 264–266
UNIX operating system, 6
Update drop-down menu, MobileMe preference pane, 250
updates, automatic, 261
upgrading to Snow Leopard, 316, 317–323
Upon Recognition section, Speech preference pane, 262
Use LCD font smoothing when available option, Appearance preference pane, 224
Use smooth scrolling option, Appearance preference pane, 224
user accounts
    Administrator, 77
    Automatic Login, disabling, 87–88
    Fast User Switching tool, 89–90
    Guest, 77
    Managed with Parental Controls, 77, 80
    overview, 76
    Sharing Only, 77
    Standard, 77, 78–79
    testing, 88–89
User folder, 11
User Name text field, Incoming Mail Server window, 271
Utilities button, Install Mac OS X window, 324
Utilities folder, 298
Utilities window, 12–13

V

video
    with chat, 285, 287–288
    editing, 107–108
    effects, 288
    exporting
        for desktop, 108–111
        for Web, 111–112
    tutorials, 3, 4
view button, iTunes, 117
View content as options, stack menu, 55
View options dialog, iTunes, 118
Virtual Network Computing (VNC), 188
VoiceOver section, Universal Access preference pane, 265
volume, computer, 4

W

WANs (wide-area networks), 170
WAP (Wireless Access Point), 173
warning icon, Desktop & Screen Saver preference pane, 46
Weather Widget, 66

X

Y

Z

Wiley Publishing, Inc.
End-User License Agreement

READ THIS. You should carefully read these terms and conditions before opening the software packet(s) included with this book "Book". This is a license agreement "Agreement" between you and Wiley Publishing, Inc. "WPI". By opening the accompanying software packet(s), you acknowledge that you have read and accept the following terms and conditions. If you do not agree and do not want to be bound by such terms and conditions, promptly return the Book and the unopened software packet(s) to the place you obtained them for a full refund.

1. **License Grant.** WPI grants to you (either an individual or entity) a nonexclusive license to use one copy of the enclosed software program(s) (collectively, the "Software") solely for your own personal or business purposes on a single computer (whether a standard computer or a workstation component of a multi-user network). The Software is in use on a computer when it is loaded into temporary memory (RAM) or installed into permanent memory (hard disk, CD-ROM, or other storage device). WPI reserves all rights not expressly granted herein.

2. **Ownership.** WPI is the owner of all right, title, and interest, including copyright, in and to the compilation of the Software recorded on the physical packet included with this Book "Software Media". Copyright to the individual programs recorded on the Software Media is owned by the author or other authorized copyright owner of each program. Ownership of the Software and all proprietary rights relating thereto remain with WPI and its licensers.

3. **Restrictions on Use and Transfer.**

    (a) You may only (i) make one copy of the Software for backup or archival purposes, or (ii) transfer the Software to a single hard disk, provided that you keep the original for backup or archival purposes. You may not (i) rent or lease the Software, (ii) copy or reproduce the Software through a LAN or other network system or through any computer subscriber system or bulletin-board system, or (iii) modify, adapt, or create derivative works based on the Software.

    (b) You may not reverse engineer, decompile, or disassemble the Software. You may transfer the Software and user documentation on a permanent basis, provided that the transferee agrees to accept the terms and conditions of this Agreement and you retain no copies. If the Software is an update or has been updated, any transfer must include the most recent update and all prior versions.

4. **Restrictions on Use of Individual Programs.** You must follow the individual requirements and restrictions detailed for each individual program in the "About the CD" appendix of this Book or on the Software Media. These limitations are also contained in the individual license agreements recorded on the Software Media. These limitations may include a requirement that after using the program for a specified period of time, the user must pay a registration fee or discontinue use. By opening the Software packet(s), you agree to abide by the licenses and restrictions for these individual programs that are detailed in the "About the CD" appendix and/or on the Software Media. None of the material on this Software Media or listed in this Book may ever be redistributed, in original or modified form, for commercial purposes.

5. **Limited Warranty.**

    (a) WPI warrants that the Software and Software Media are free from defects in materials and workmanship under normal use for a period of sixty (60) days from the date of purchase of this Book. If WPI receives notification within the warranty period of defects in materials or workmanship, WPI will replace the defective Software Media.

(b) WPI AND THE AUTHOR(S) OF THE BOOK DISCLAIM ALL OTHER WARRANTIES, EXPRESS OR IMPLIED, INCLUDING WITHOUT LIMITATION IMPLIED WARRANTIES OF MERCHANTABILITY AND FITNESS FOR A PARTICULAR PURPOSE, WITH RESPECT TO THE SOFTWARE, THE PROGRAMS, THE SOURCE CODE CONTAINED THEREIN, AND/OR THE TECHNIQUES DESCRIBED IN THIS BOOK. WPI DOES NOT WARRANT THAT THE FUNCTIONS CONTAINED IN THE SOFTWARE WILL MEET YOUR REQUIREMENTS OR THAT THE OPERATION OF THE SOFTWARE WILL BE ERROR FREE.

(c) This limited warranty gives you specific legal rights, and you may have other rights that vary from jurisdiction to jurisdiction.

6. Remedies.

(a) WPI's entire liability and your exclusive remedy for defects in materials and workmanship shall be limited to replacement of the Software Media, which may be returned to WPI with a copy of your receipt at the following address: Software Media Fulfillment Department, Attn.: *Mac OS X Snow Leopard Digital Classroom*, Wiley Publishing, Inc., 10475 Crosspoint Blvd., Indianapolis, IN 46256, or call 1-800-762-2974. Please allow four to six weeks for delivery. This Limited Warranty is void if failure of the Software Media has resulted from accident, abuse, or misapplication. Any replacement Software Media will be warranted for the remainder of the original warranty period or thirty (30) days, whichever is longer.

(b) In no event shall WPI or the author be liable for any damages whatsoever (including without limitation damages for loss of business profits, business interruption, loss of business information, or any other pecuniary loss) arising from the use of or inability to use the Book or the Software, even if WPI has been advised of the possibility of such damages.

(c) Because some jurisdictions do not allow the exclusion or limitation of liability for consequential or incidental damages, the above limitation or exclusion may not apply to you.

7. U.S. Government Restricted Rights. Use, duplication, or disclosure of the Software for or on behalf of the United States of America, its agencies and/or instrumentalities "U.S. Government" is subject to restrictions as stated in paragraph (c)(1)(ii) of the Rights in Technical Data and Computer Software clause of DFARS 252.227-7013, or subparagraphs (c) (1) and (2) of the Commercial Computer Software - Restricted Rights clause at FAR 52.227-19, and in similar clauses in the NASA FAR supplement, as applicable.

8. General. This Agreement constitutes the entire understanding of the parties and revokes and supersedes all prior agreements, oral or written, between them and may not be modified or amended except in a writing signed by both parties hereto that specifically refers to this Agreement. This Agreement shall take precedence over any other documents that may be in conflict herewith. If any one or more provisions contained in this Agreement are held by any court or tribunal to be invalid, illegal, or otherwise unenforceable, each and every other provision shall remain in full force and effect.

The on-line companion to your Digital Classroom book.

DigitalClassroomBooks.com

Visit DigitalClassroomBooks.com for...

 Updated lesson files

 Errata

 Contacting the authors

 Video tutorial samples

 Book samples

DIGITAL CLASSROOM

For information about the Digital Classroom series
visit www.DigitalClassroomBooks.com

You have a personal tutor
in the Digital Classroom

978-0-470-41093-6

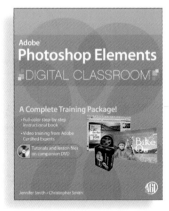

978-0-470-41091-2

978-0-470-41092-9

978-0-470-41090-5

978-0-470-41094-3

978-0-470-43635-6

▉DIGITAL CLASSROOM▉

A Complete Training Package

Each Digital Classroom book features full-color instruction plus video tutorials and lesson files on DVD, all by Adobe Certified Experts. Learn from the best—at your own pace.

For more information about the Digital Classroom series, go to www.digitalclassroombooks.com.

Available wherever books are sold.

WILEY
Now you know
wiley.com

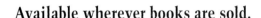
Wiley, the Wiley logo, and Digital Classroom are trademarks or registered trademarks of John Wiley & Sons, Inc. and/or its affiliates.